AFRICA
A SHORT HISTORY

Blacksmiths from the Congo (Seventeenth century Italian print)

A SHORT
HISTORY

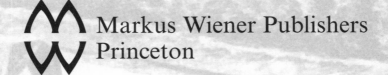

Markus Wiener Publishers
Princeton

Africa

Robert O. Collins

For information contact:
Markus Wiener Publishers
231 Nassau Street, Princeton, NJ 08542
www.markuswiener.com

Library of Congress Cataloging-in-Publication Data

Collins, Robert O., 1933-
   Africa : a short history / Robert O. Collins.
   Includes bibliographical references and index.
   ISBN-13: 978-1-55876-372-2 (hc : alk. paper)
   ISBN-10: 1-55876-372-4 (hc : alk. paper)
   ISBN-13: 978-1-55876-373-9 (pb : alk. paper)
   ISBN-10: 1-55876-373-2 (pb : alk. paper)
   1. Africa--History. I. Title.
   DT20.C56 2005
   960--dc22   2005028450

Contents

Introduction • 1

CHAPTER ONE
Prehistoric Africa • 3

CHAPTER TWO
Ancient and Medieval Africa • 19

CHAPTER THREE
Islam, Trade, and States • 53

CHAPTER FOUR
Europeans, Slavery, and the Slave Trade • 109

CHAPTER FIVE
European Conquest and Colonization
of Sub-Saharan Africa • 151

CHAPTER SIX
Independent Africa • 195

Suggested Readings • 233

Index • 245

About the Author • 249

Maps

Vegetation Regimes of Africa 6

Languages of the African Peoples 13

Diffusion of the Bantu Languages 32

Bantu Classification 34

Ancient and Medieval Northeast Africa 43

Empires of the Plains 64

Islam in West Africa 66

The World of the Swahili 72

Representative States of Pre-colonial Africa 96

Slave Trade 120–121

Missionaries and Explorers in Africa Prior to the Partition 156

African States on the Eve of Partition: 1884 158

1884: Europe in Africa on the Eve of Partition 160

Southern Africa 168

Africa in 1914 178

Introduction

Fifty years ago the Western world knew little of the African past. Ordinary and extraordinary citizens casually accepted the romantic portrait of Africa painted by European and American explorers, missionaries, and soldiers as a "Dark Continent" of exotic fauna, flora, and Africans with no discernable past. How wrong they were, for every people has a past known to them. The task of the outsider is to go and find it from the vast volume of evidence Africans have left behind. In the forty-five years after the "year of African independence" from colonial rule in 1960, an army of African and Western scholars in every discipline has discovered the depth and complexities of the history of Africa. Until the twentieth century, African societies were mostly nonliterate, which aroused the scorn of traditional historians in the West, for without the written word, they maintained, Africans could hardly record the sagas of their past for posterity. How wrong they were. A few historians believed that nonliterate people had a history as legitimate as those who were literate, and in their search for the African past, they soon found stalwart allies in anthropologists, archaeologists, and linguists.

What did this interdisciplinary confederation discover? Certainly not darkness but a rich cultural heritage preserved by ruins and the oral traditions of nonliterate peoples in which the remembrance of things past was a principal dynamic of their education and their cultures. To be sure, the learned traditions of many generations, spanning not decades but centuries, could not match the written record of Western societies, but in a less sterile, more emphatic recollection of

1

the past, they related the vibrant narratives of their peoples—their triumphs and defeats, their states and societies. Challenged by their colleagues in other disciplines and by Western-oriented historians, the pioneers investigating the African past discovered, somewhat to their surprise, a treasure trove of documentation by those who had come to know Africa, or parts of it, from their exploratory, commercial, and missionary efforts. The means to uncover and present the African past to the Western world, and also to Africans themselves, now lay before them.

CHAPTER ONE

Prehistoric Africa

Coastal South Africa, engraving 1746 by a British naturalist

Geography Defines Man and Woman

The history of Africa cannot be understood without knowledge of the continent's geography. Africa's natural features—its deserts, Sahel, savanna, swamps, rainforests, plateaus, mountains, lakes, and rivers—have shaped the evolution of humankind in the geologic past and the historic development of African societies in the last two millennia. The pattern of rainfall has determined the growth and enormous diversity of Africa's fauna and flora, and its diverse geologic, geographic, and natural history has defined the evolution of the African peoples. Africa is an enormous continent, measuring twelve million square miles, larger than North America and four times the size of the United States. It is also the landmass from which Europe, Asia, and the Americas floated away from one another on tectonic plates many millions of years ago. They left behind Africa the ancestral continent, a solid, vast, uplifted flat plateau 2,000 to 4,000 feet above sea level, which slept in its geological continuity.

Africa, however, was not immune to the millions of years of geologic activity that shaped the planet as we know it today. Below the African crust were three stable rock cores that thrust upward when the primal mass of the mobile surface of the earth began to cool. Known as cratons, they are found today in West Africa, the Congo, and Southern Africa. These huge craton masses have remained

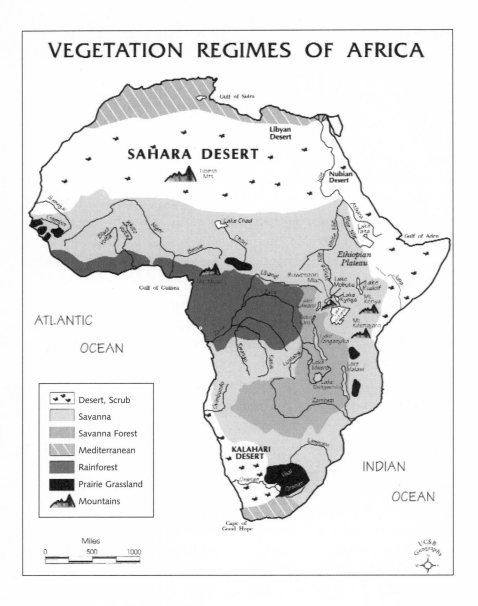

VEGETATION REGIMES OF AFRICA

remarkably stable throughout geologic time while the rest of the continents were in motion. As the earth cooled, its heated core would burst upward in volcanic eruptions, carrying magma and rich minerals through pipes from the oldest rocks of the mantel to the surface of the uplifted African landmass now penetrated by cratons and volcanic intrusions. Thereafter, temperature and rainfall controlled the growth of African vegetation and the evolution of animal life and Homo sapiens.

Africa is the only continent that is equally divided by the equator, and consequently it does not experience the wide fluctuations of temperature of the more temperate zones. Elevation, wind, and the Atlantic and Indian oceans, therefore, have been the decisive elements that have produced the wide variety of environments in Africa. Forty percent of Africa is desert; only 8 percent is tropical rainforest. The rest is a vast expanse of Sahel, savanna, and wooded grasslands punctuated by every geographic and geologic feature, from high mountains and plateaus to the lakes, rivers, Sahel, and savanna in which the natural resources, throughout time, produced the plants and animals that enabled humans to survive in the distant past and to proliferate in the last 2,000 years. Geography shaped the history of the African peoples, who adjusted their way of living and their societies to the demands of the land. Nature determined the way of living, and Africans sought to master it in the diverse regions of their origins or in those into which they had migrated.

Evolution of Man and Woman in Africa

About 160,000 years ago our human ancestors, Homo sapiens, lived in Africa, where they evolved into modern humans, Homo sapiens sapiens (wise, wise men), who migrated in small groups to populate the rest of the world. They passed over the isthmus at Suez to settle in the Middle East about 100,000 years ago. From there, they turned north to become well established in Europe 40,000 years ago. Others wandered eastward to Australia 35,000 years ago and to China 30,000 years ago. Finally, between 30,000 and 15,000 years ago they continued from Asia into North America across the land bridge of the Bering Strait to make their way slowly down the continent into South America about 12,000 years ago. During the three million years of human evolution, there was a great diversity of hominids unconsciously competing in an evolutionary struggle in which Homo sapiens was the lone survivor. The evolution of hominids in Africa to Homo sapiens was largely determined by the ability to be bipedal and by the acquisition of stone tools, water, language, and fire.

Compared to quadrupeds, bipedal humans may be inefficient in moving the body mass over distances, but they are mechanically very efficient in following the herds roaming the East African savanna since 60 percent of their body weight rests on two legs. Some 2.5 million years ago, the ancestral hominid was inspired to pick up a stone to make scavenging more efficient. There is no satisfactory explanation as to when and why the early hominids began to chip stones into razor-sharp edges. Stone tools certainly made meat production more efficient, but they also enabled the digging of tubers, the process of acquiring vegetables, and the crushing of nuts. The first stone tools appeared in East Africa about 2.4 million years ago, and by 2 million years ago their use in processing food had spread throughout the continent wherever the ambulatory hominids wandered.

The human body demands that, each day, at least two and a half quarts of liquid must be lost to maintain consistent water content required to flush out the toxic waste the body produces. People have survived without food for weeks, but they cannot survive without water for more than three days. In the savanna of tropical Africa, our ancestors sweated less but still had to replace six quarts of liquid a day, which limited their mobility in order that they could daily reach water from lakes, streams, rivers, or waterholes. Being erect, they exposed only a small amount of their bodies to the sun. Consequently, they absorbed much less heat than the quadrupeds that revealed their elongated bodies to the sun. By high noon the bipedal hominid could avoid nearly 60 percent of the solar radiation absorbed by the four-footed animals of Africa. Moreover, upright, the hominid was fully exposed to the winds of the savanna that removed by convection the formidable heat from the naked skin on the upper part of the body.

Bipedal and upright Homo sapiens could forage through the African savanna in the heat of the day with a physiology that kept the brain cool and allowed its enlargement and evolution to make decisions as to what was most advantageous to eat. If the cognitive brain could distinguish the nutritious value of nuts and tubers over the leaves of grass, the physiological construction of voice and brain distinguished Homo sapiens from all other mammals. The human vocal tract, with a long larynx and round tongue, makes it impossible for Homo sapiens, unlike other mammals, to drink and breathe at the same time but enables humans to close the nasal passages while speaking. This unique advantage allows the rounded tongue to make nonnasal sounds of articulation by which consonants and vowels can take on a distinctive and understandable meaning. These common and repetitive sounds are the beginning of language.

Equipped with an enlarged brain and language, humans learned how to survive in the different environments of Africa and the continents beyond. They began to manipulate natural resources and to use sources of energy to ensure their survival. Humans were always dependent upon their specialized diet and, of course, on water, but with language and memory families came together in social organizations to satisfy mutual needs and to exploit their environment. These communities consisted of small groups, probably no more than two dozen, that became a clan of perhaps 150 who could never be more than a day's walk from water. The size of the band also appears to have fluctuated through time depending on environmental circumstances, but the use of stone tools stimulated population growth, as did fire.

Fire comes from lightning, volcanoes, and spontaneous combustion from dead vegetation. It can also be created artificially by hands twirling a stick into soft wood. Fire became the instrument for human security in darkness, for all other animals fear its sight and smell. It enabled humans to extend the range in their foraging for food. It produced warmth, fired pots, and cooked meat. Perhaps most important, the flickering flame was a communal offering around which all could come together in their deep psychological fascination with fire.

Peoples of Sub-Saharan Africa

At the beginning of the twenty-first century, the population of the African continent is approximately 750 million, which gives it a density about the same as the United States, roughly 65 people per square mile, compared to Great Britain, with 585 people per square mile. Throughout its history, however, Africa has been underpopulated in terms of its vast landmass. At the beginning of the Christian era, the population of China has been estimated at 57 million people, the Roman Empire at 54 million, and Africa at only 20 million, half of whom resided in North Africa and the Nile Valley, provinces included in the census of the Roman Empire. There were thus only 10 million Africans living south of the Sahara Desert. Fifteen hundred years later, the world population had grown to over 300 million, while the peoples of Africa south of the Sahara had increased only to some 47 million. By 1900 the population of sub-Saharan Africa had soared to 129 million, but during the same centuries the world population had risen from 500 million to over 2 billion. Then in the twentieth century, the population of sub-Saharan Africa, under colonial rule, grew from 142 million in 1920 to 200 million in 1948 and to 300 million at the year of African independence, 1960. Since then, the population of Africa has more than doubled and will double again by the year 2025.

Historically, throughout the millennia the enormous diversity of Africans can only be understood by the common denominator of language. Language remains the ultimate marker whose basic structure endures despite changes in human physical appearance, culture, and society. Although daily spoken language can change very rapidly by slang, street talk, colloquialisms, and regional peculiarities, the core structure of any language changes very slowly. It is one of the most immutable aspects of human existence and consequently the key to understanding the common relationship of peoples speaking mutually unintelligible languages whether in Asia, Europe, the Americas, or Africa. To recognize these African linguistic affiliations is to comprehend the framework, the structure, by which to classify Africans who speak over 800 different languages and innumerable dialects, which makes it possible to understand the relationship of one African to another.

There are four principal linguistic families in Africa—Niger-Congo, Afro-Asiatic, Nilo-Saharan, and Khosian. Niger-Congo, the great language family of Africa, constitutes two-thirds of all the languages spoken in sub-Saharan Africa. The importance of the Niger-Congo classification lies in the close linguistic relationship of a core vocabulary and morphology between the vast numbers of Bantu-speaking Africans from equatorial to southern Africa with those speaking languages in West Africa that linguistically binds Africans from the Senegambia to southern Africa. This great Niger-Congo family has six major branches and hundreds of subbranches. The largest linguistic family of Niger-Congo is the Benue-Congo, the Bantu who from their homelands on the Cameroon-Nigerian frontier expanded to fill the lower half of the African continent.

The other great linguistic family of Africa is Afro-Asiatic, whose speakers originated in Asia and migrated into North Africa, the Sahara, and the Nile Valley from the Middle East and Arabia. Its origins are in Asia, and today those who speak Afro-Asiatic languages are found in North Africa, the Sahara, the Nile Valley, the Middle East, and Arabia. Afro-Asiatic includes the Semitic languages of Arabic and Hebrew but also the languages of the dynastic Egyptians as well as Berber and Tuareg of northern Africa and Africans living today in the Sudan, Ethiopia, Somalia, and northern Nigeria.

The third language family of Africa, Nilo-Saharan, is as distinct as Niger-Congo and Afro-Asiatic and not nearly as numerous. Nilo-Saharan speakers are found today in West Africa, the Sahara, Chad, the Nile basin, and the great funnel of the rift valley in East Africa.

The fourth linguistic family of Africa is the Khosian. Its speakers are found today in south and southwest Africa, though there are remnants of them in East Africa and the Congo rainforest. Their numbers are insignificant compared to the rest of the peoples of Africa. Khosian speakers consist of two culturally different peoples of a single distinctive language family called Khosian. The first are the cattle-raising pastoral people, the Khoi, who historically are known by the colloquial name of Hottentot, which often has a pejorative connotation despite their complex political organization and deep sense of ethnic distinctiveness. The second are the San, who are linguistically related to the Khoi and who are known in the popular literature as bushmen.

The classification of languages can bring clarity to understanding

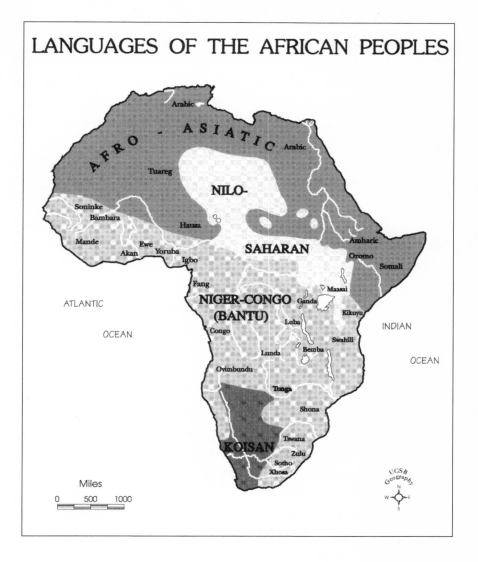

the great diversity of the African peoples and the relationship of one cultural group to another. To the north in a great arc are the Afro-Asiatic speakers, below which are those of the Nilo-Saharan family and, in southern Africa, the Khosian, all of whom lie on the periphery of the vast majority of Africans in the heartland of the continent speaking languages of the Niger-Congo linguistic family and its predominant branch, Benue-Congo, or simply the Bantu. These linguistic families contain many languages that are not mutually intelligible, but they share the same structure and basic vocabulary from a common core.

Crops, Cows, and Iron

Agriculture, the systematic domestication of plants, evolved independently in the Middle East about 8000 B.C.E. and some 3,000 years later in western Africa and along the banks of the Nile and in its delta. The agricultural revolution made possible the evolution of modern humans. Hunting and gathering was an inefficient means of survival, which inhibited any demonstrable increase in population. There are 200,000 species of wild plants, but most are indigestible, poisonous, without nutritional value, hard to gather, or difficult to prepare. Only a very few, no more than a dozen, are edible, but when cultivated by farmers, one acre could support a hundred times the number of people supported by hunting and gathering. In the Sahel and savanna of western Sudanic Africa, indigenous sorghum, millet, and rice had been domesticated as early as 5000 B.C.E. The oldest known cereal grains in the Nile Valley were independently cultivated in the Fayum between 4500 and 4200 B.C.E., and in the tropical rainforests of the West African coast yams were cultivated and palm oil tapped by 3000 B.C.E.

Agricultural food production cannot be disassociated from the pas-

toral revolution. Indeed, the breeding of animals into livestock complemented and paralleled the domestication of plants. Africa has a
large number of animal species, but only six became of any value to
modern humans in Africa, all of Asian origin—camels, cattle, goats,
sheep, pigs, and horses. The great variety, splendor, and awesome
herds of African animals were largely irrelevant to the history of
modern humans on the continent, for the African herdsman was
dependent on domesticated, not wild, mammals for survival and
prosperity. The domestication of sheep, goats, and cattle had preced-
ed the agricultural revolution, becoming common about 6000 B.C.E.
Throughout the vast expanse of a well-watered Sahara from the
Atlantic to the Red Sea, they provided meat, milk, fertilizer, transportation, and hides and pulled the plows in the fields. But they were
few. Only fourteen animal species of many thousands have submitted
to human control, and only those six domesticated animals have supplied the needs of humans in the past and today. Their milk provided
a continuous supply of protein. They increased the yield of crop production by their manure, that ancient reliable fertilizer and dependable source of fuel for the fire. The ox, the horse, but particularly the
camel became the means of transportation far more efficient than the
bipedal hominid. Wool was sheared from the skins of sheep and
goats, and leather was tanned from the hides of cattle.

Farming requires a sedentary lifestyle that in turn creates a more
dense population to live in a permanent place by the fields. It also creates the means and need for families to have more children. A settled
existence enabled the cultivator, unlike the hunter-gatherer, to store
surplus food. The storage of food provided a reliable supply during
the lean months after the harvest and the next planting season, and if
the rains failed and the crops shriveled in the sun, there hopefully
would remain a sufficient stored surplus from the previous year to
forestall famine and have seeds to plant another year. The stockpile
of food was like cash in the bank. The more industrious and success-

ful farmers became members of the social and political elite by gaining control of food production. They became the "Big Men" who no longer had to labor in the fields but used their leisure time for politics, the arts, and war. Indeed, the organization required by cultivation and animal husbandry demanded the cooperation and leadership that produced the village headman, chief, king, and Pharaoh.

The iron revolution transformed agriculture and warfare in Africa by the hoe and the spear, respectively. Although the red earth of Africa, the iron oxides, cover much of the laterite crust of the ancient continent, iron ore also occurs as hematite, the primary ore for iron, sometimes found on the surface but usually dug from shallow deposits. The problem presented by iron ore was not its extraction but its smelting. The conversion of iron ore into a useable metal was complex, and although there is evidence from East and West Africa of independent development of iron working, the process was probably imported from southwest Asia. The earliest known site for smelting iron, dated to 1500 B.C.E., was found in Anatolia in Turkey.

Smelting iron ore required a furnace to hold the heat to produce a chemical reaction. The ore was placed between layers of prepared charcoal into which oxygen (air) was pumped into the base of the fire to produce sufficient heat to melt the ore. Sometimes a flux—lime extracted from seashells, for instance—was added to escalate the smelting process. The first primitive furnace in Africa was a trench or bowl, which was later replaced by a kiln of beehive shape or a more efficient shaft of cylindrical construction whose bellows could raise the heat to 2,200° F. After several hours the smelting was completed, the furnace broken open, and the purified lump of iron extracted and reheated to remove any remaining impurities before being hammered into jewelry, hoes, tools, and weapons.

Although the accepted view is that iron metallurgy came to sub-Saharan Africa across the desert from the Mediterranean, the beehive and cylindrical furnaces of West Africa were quite different from those in North Africa, Mesopotamia, and the Maghrib. Whether imported or independently developed, iron technology was dispersed widely and rapidly throughout western and then eastern Africa. Equipped with iron tools and weapons, Africans could now assault the natural and political obstacles to their expansion. The land could be cleared, the forest penetrated, and large wild animals more easily killed. Iron tools made possible more intensive and productive farming, which required a distinct division of labor in societies where everyone had hitherto been involved in growing a subsistence amount of food. This division of labor not only created a ruling class, who were able to consolidate their authority by supplying their followers with iron weapons, but also artisans, who fashioned the cultural artifacts of society, and merchants engaged in local and long-distance trade, who provided the wealth for both kings and artisans. Those who no longer tilled the soil laid the foundations of civilization.

CHAPTER TWO

Ancient and Medieval Africa

Pyramids of Kush

Dynastic Egypt, 3100–332 B.C.E.

An African desert where rain seldom falls, Egypt would be a land of sand and rock and wind without the Nile bringing water and nutrients that bind Egypt to the equatorial lakes of East Africa and the highlands of Ethiopia. Five thousand years ago, the Pleistocene gradually came to an end, and the relentless desiccation of the Sahara began. Hunters, gatherers, and herdsmen who had roamed its savanna now had to follow the water, without which they could not survive, to congregate by the banks of the Nile. Here they encountered and settled with people who had experimented with agriculture by cultivating the rich Nile loam, living in villages and developing new social and political relationships. Civilization has historically been the product of the town, not the countryside. Coming together in this limited space by the banks of the Nile, hunting camps became villages, and villages became towns dependent upon the surrounding agriculture. Wheat, barley, and millet were cultivated; fish were caught; and domesticated cattle, sheep, and goats foraged on the grasslands by the river. The abundance in the fields and the evolution of political and social organizations enabled the Egyptians to build pyramids, temples, and urban communities whose continuity transcended 3,000 years, longer than any civilization in Asia or the West.

During the rise of the Nile from June to September, the season of inundation, Akhet, the abundant waters loaded with Ethiopian nutrients spilled into the basins beyond the banks of the river. When the flood receded, seeds from grains were planted in the season of growing, Peret, to sprout like magic from the rich moisture and abundant alluvium to produce the crops that were harvested in February and March. The annual cycle was consummated in April and May by the Shemu, the months when the floodplain hardened under an unremitting sun until the Nile waters returned to be celebrated in July by the "Opening of the Year," Wen Renpet. Agriculture provided the economic foundation of dynastic Egypt, but its monumental edifices could not have been achieved without the means to mobilize the powers of the state. The Pharaohs and their officials had to establish a bureaucracy to tax and to move Egypt's grain, stone, and people the 800 miles to the Mediterranean Sea from the first cataract of the Nile and the end of navigation at Aswan.

Dynastic Egypt experienced three millennia of prosperity and depression, but throughout its long history there were certain characteristics that remained remarkably consistent. The extraordinary long-term stability of the state began when King Narmer (known as Menes, the last sovereign of predynasitic and the first king of dynastic Egypt) in 3100 B.C.E. joined upper and lower Egypt into a single kingdom. Thirty dynasties and a hundred generations later, Alexander the Great of Macedonia (356–323 B.C.E.) conquered Egypt in 332 B.C.E. to end dynastic Egypt, but his Greek, Roman, Byzantine, Arab, and Turkish successors maintained the stability of the state created by the first Pharaohs. This stability was made possible by the conservatism of Egyptian society inspired and ensured by the mighty defenses of formidable deserts on either side of the Nile. The Egyptians remained self-contained in the fertile band of soil along the banks of the river. Their rulers, the Pharaohs, followed one another by primogeniture, which ensured continuity, preserved the dynasty, and limited disputes over succession that were so destructive to many African states. This inclusive society enabled the Pharaohs to mobilize the material resources of the kingdom and to organize their sub-jects to erect levees, dig irrigation canals, and build pyramids, tombs, and temples. They used flint, copper, bronze, the wheel, and the *shaduf*, a pole on a fulcrum with a counterweight at one end and a bucket on the other to raise water into the fields. Oxen pulled the plows, and the ubiquitous sheep and goats provided meat and milk and the symbols for ritual sacrifice. The Egyptians lived on cereals, onions, melons, cucumbers, lentils, and their favorite white radish, supplemented by figs and dates washed down with beer.

The population of dynastic Egypt, like its government, was also stable, estimated throughout 3,000 years from two million to no more than four million people. They were ruled by a Pharaoh, the high priest, the god-king on earth, who was protected by the falcon-head-ed god, Horus. The Pharaoh was the link between the gods and humans, the living symbol of the sun-god, Amun-Re, and Osiris, god of the underworld. He gave religious stability by his spiritual author-ity over the priests, who administered to the people from their tem-ples. The Pharaoh was the principal administrator of the kingdom and the center of an administration whose officials were the bureau-crats of his royal court. He was the supreme soldier, the inspiration if not the leader of his armies.

The Pharaohs and their monuments, temples, and tombs are the legacy of ancient Egyptian civilization that the arid deserts have pre-served throughout the millennia. The resources that made possible these structures built throughout the long history of dynastic Egypt came from the farmers. They were peasants but free men who tilled the soil, grew the grain, paid the taxes, supplied the labor and skills to divert the Nile waters, and built the monuments. Slaves from Nubia filled the ranks of the army. Although there were many free Egyptian soldiers, the Pharaohs had no incentive to reduce the number of their prodigious cultivators by drafting them into an unproductive military establishment.

The long history of dynastic Egypt and its conservative, self-contained culture has obscured its relations with Africa south of the Sahara and the Mediterranean world to the north. The earliest written records for precolonial Africa south of Aswan are to be found in Nubia from Egyptian inscriptions in 2900 B.C.E. Known to the Egyptians as Ta-Seti, the land of the bow men, Nubia during the Old Kingdom (3100–2133 B.C.E.) was a peripheral and uncertain place to plunder but in more peaceful times to conduct commerce and trade. Nubia was the land of the Nile, extending from Aswan 1,163 river miles to the confluence of the Blue and White Niles at Khartoum, the modern capital of the Sudan. During the next 2,000 years, relations between dynastic Egypt and Nubia varied from peaceful commerce to warfare and colonization. When imperial Egypt was strong, the Pharaohs sent their military expeditions into Nubia for gold, semi-precious stones, diorite for royal tombs, and slaves for the army, fields, and households. When imperial Egypt was weak from internal strife or confronted by Asian invaders, the Nubians, whose numbers were a few hundred thousand, traded on amicable terms at Aswan, the Gate to the South for dynastic Egypt. This hostile and peaceful interaction over thousands of years led to an ever-increasing influence upon the art, culture, and religion of dynastic Egypt that came out of Africa through Nubia.

During the revival of Egypt under the New Kingdom (ca. 1570–1070 B.C.E.), its Pharaohs secured their southern frontier to exploit the Nubians by incorporating them into imperial Egypt. The New Kingdom Pharaohs established military garrisons, created a bureaucracy to collect taxes, and sent out settlers to consolidate the Egyptian presence in their colonies. They built forts and constructed temples as far south as the fourth cataract, where the great temple of Amun lies below Jabal Barkal. The Nubian elite were deeply influenced by the Egyptians during these five centuries of New Kingdom colonization. The sons of Nubian chieftains were educated in Egypt and adopted Egyptian customs and clothes, but they represented an imperial veneer as official agents for their Egyptian rulers. Most Nubians labored in the fields and the gold mines, served as mercenaries in the Egyptian army, maintained the temples, and were servants of the nobility, but they spoke their own language and maintained their customs and culture.

At the close of the eleventh century B.C.E., the New Kingdom slipped into decline. The unity of upper and lower Egypt established by King Narmer in 3100 B.C.E. disintegrated into banditry, wanton destruction, and civil war, resulting in the end of Egyptian domination of the Nubian Nile about 1000 B.C.E. After the departure of the Egyptians, the indigenous Nubian political, economic, and social structures recovered to dominate the land south of Aswan, that area ruled by local hereditary families who no longer had ethnic or political ties with Egypt. A member of one of these families established himself as the ruler of the Kingdom of Kush between 890 and 840 B.C.E.

Kingdom of Kush: Corridor to Africa, 806 B.C.E.–350 C.E.

Little is known of Kush until 760 B.C.E. when Kashta (ca. 760–747 B.C.E.) and his army crossed the southern frontier of Egypt at Aswan to enter Thebes, where he established himself as the first Nubian Pharaoh to assume the divine mandate to rule from Amun. His successor, Piye (ca. 747–716 B.C.E.), firmly settled Kushite control over upper Egypt, paying scrupulous honor to Amun and Egyptian gods on his march north. His brother, Shabaqo (ca. 716–702 B.C.E.), completed the conquest of Egypt to rule, in alliance with the powerful Amun priesthood, an empire extending more than 2,000 miles along the Nile from the fourth cataract in Nubia to the Mediterranean Sea. He moved the capital of Kush to Thebes and is regarded as the founder of the twenty-fifth Egyptian dynasty (ca. 747–656 B.C.E.).

Unfortunately for the Kushites, their conquest of Egypt coincided with the expansion of a new Asiatic power, the Assyrians. At first the Pharaoh Taharqo (ca. 690–664 B.C.E.) was able to defend his northeastern frontier from his capital at Tanis in the Nile delta, but in 671 B.C.E. the Assyrian king Esarhaddon (681–669 B.C.E.) launched his formidable army from the Euphrates Valley into Egypt. Taharqo and his forces were defeated. The last Nubian Pharaoh, Tanwetamani (664–653 B.C.E.), abandoned Egypt to return to the sanctuary of the Kingdom of Kush in Nubia at his capital, Napata, whose temples and palaces lay at the foot of Jabal Barkal by the fourth cataract. Here the kings of Kush were protected by the desert and the rocks of the Nile cataracts, which enabled them to rule over this corridor to Africa virtually undisturbed for another thousand years. By language and culture they were linked to Africa beyond Aswan more than the dynastic Egyptians, who were drawn increasingly into the Mediterranean world of Mesopotamia, Persia, Greece, and Rome. Nevertheless, the commercial, cultural, and political interaction between Nubia and its Kingdom of Kush, constructed over two millennia, continued to bind two different peoples, their cultures, and Africa and Egypt together.

The rulers of the Kingdom of Kush were mostly male, but the queen was invariably portrayed next to the king and had great influence in the affairs of state. There is evidence that queens occasionally ruled independently. The priesthood usually determined the successor upon the death of the king, but there were instances when the army intervened in the decision presumably to select the queen's most able son. Although the earliest capital was Napata at the fourth cataract, which remained the religious center of the kingdom, Meroe, 156 river miles north of the confluence of the Blue and White Niles at modern-day Khartoum, became the political center after Tanwetamani had abandoned Egypt in the sixth century B.C.E. The kings of Kush were inclined to be peripatetic, the court residing at one of the imperial palaces scattered about the kingdom. The kings and queens were great builders, constructing temples as the guardians of state religion, palaces for their pleasure, and tombs for their souls. The temples at Jabal Barkal, Musawwarat es-Sufra, and Naqa complement the royal palaces at Napata and Meroe to ensure there was no separation of state and religion, and pyramids were constructed for the afterlife of the kings and queens at El Kurru and Nuri at Napata and at Meroe.

The civil service administered the state, but the army secured the state's integrity by defending its frontiers, securing internal peace, and protecting the king, whose legitimacy was derived from the gods but who was dependent on the army for the power of his authority. The Nubians were famous for their courage and fighting abilities as slave troops or as mercenaries in the armies of dynastic Egypt, beginning with the first-century Pharaoh Djer (ca. 2900 B.C.E.). The troops were equipped with shields, axes, pikes, and swords, but they and especially the Nubians, even after the fall of Kush, were most feared as archers, whose skills have been recorded throughout the centuries. Elephants played a central role in the temple cult at Musawwarat es-Sufra and were certainly used by the army. The established religion of Egyptian gods at court and temple enhanced by Egyptian sacred architecture was a veneer that obscured the religious reality of the traditional Nubian gods worshiped by the people of Kush, particularly Apedemak, the Lion of the South, a war god with bows and arrows. There were other local gods, Sebiumeker and Arensnuphis, who were venerated in the countryside and to whom the Nubians appealed in graffiti on temples and rock outcrops. Ariten, Amanete, Harendotes, and Makedeke were all local gods unknown in the Egyptian religious pantheon. There were also many popular religious customs of the ordinary people, funerary banquets on top of hills, for instance, which were of Nubian origin.

Burying the dead was the most important end to life in dynastic Egypt and Nubia, but the graves of each culture are distinct. The Nubian deceased were buried in a fetal position, unlike the extended position in Egypt, and placed underground rather than entombed in pyramids of unique construction. The Egyptian pyramids of the Old Kingdom at Giza outside Cairo are 700 feet high. The numerous pyramids at El Kurru near Napata and those at Meroe are only 100 feet high, but their narrow base gives them a point that belies their height. Unlike in Egypt, there is no internal burial chamber, the mummy being interned in a separate chamber below or, at Meroe, in a mortuary chapel on the eastern face of the pyramid. The construction of temples followed the same diversity as pyramids. The great temple of Amun at Jabal Barkal was Egyptian in design, but those in the south at Meroe, Naqa, Wad Ben Naqa, and Musawwarat es-Sufra, as well as the great temple at Dangeil discovered in 2001, exhibit Egyptian influence but not an architecture found in Egypt.

The kings, the elite, the bureaucracy, and the army depended upon the farmers, herdsmen, and tradesmen of Kush to supply the resources that sustained them. Large herds of cattle, sheep, and goats grazed on the rain-fed pastures. A mixed farming evolved, which has been characteristic of the savanna in sub-Saharan Africa throughout history. There was forage for elephants, and the center of their cult was located at the great temple complex of Musawwarat es-Sufra. Wells and *hafirs* (excavations or walled enclosures to collect water) were common and of local design and construction. The staple foodstuffs consisted of grains—sorghum and barley—and vegetables— beans, lentils, and onions—long cultivated in Egypt. Cotton was grown for cloth, and wine was pressed. The Nile was rich in fish, which was an important part of the Nubian diet.

Kush's wealth also derived from gold and from control of the commercial routes from Egypt to the Red Sea and Asia to the east and Africa to the south. Trade goods came from India and Arabia to

Egypt through Nubia. Nubian gold was mined in the Wadi Allaqi and the Wadi Cabgaba east of the Nile. Diorite to adorn the sarcophagi of the Pharaohs was cut from quarries beyond Tushka west of the Nile. Ivory and slaves came from the upper Nile in the south. The Nubian artisans were skilled goldsmiths and intricate carvers of ivory. Pottery was mostly crafted by hand for domestic use, but the potter's wheel and the designs of the finely decorated Nubian ware have remained unchanged throughout the millennia and always distinctly different from Egyptian pottery then and today.

The difference in language between dynastic Egypt and Kush can be found in Meroitic, the official script of the kingdom. Meroitic (Nubian) is not an Afro-Asiatic language, like ancient Egyptian, in structure and grammar, but a member of the Nilo-Saharan speakers whose linguistic descendants today extend from Nubia through the Sudan and Chad to Uganda, Kenya, and Tanzania speaking mutually unintelligible languages of the same Nilo-Saharan linguistic family. When the capital of Kush was moved from Napata to Meroe about 500 B.C.E., Kush scribes borrowed signs from Egyptian demotic to create a syllabic alphabet in which twenty-three Egyptian symbols are represented in a cursive script to spell the Meroitic language. The first Meroitic inscriptions date from 200 B.C.E. Unfortunately, the language it transcribes has yet to be deciphered and remains unknown except for titles and king lists. This cursive alphabet does not appear to be an evolution from old Egyptian but rather a more practical means to communicate on papyrus and skins, which were widely used during the later centuries of the Kingdom of Kush.

During the thousand years of the Kingdom of Kush, the Butana plain was covered with forests that supplied the fuel to smelt the ample deposits of iron ore, whose locations have yet to be discovered. After the move of the capital from Napata and Jabal Barkal to Meroe, a flourishing iron industry developed that produced axes to cut timber for charcoal to forge iron to make weapons for the army and hoes for the farmers of Kush to clear the land and turn the soil for planting. The slag from the industry's domed furnaces was deposited in huge heaps that today lie like slumbering mounds of the past outside the ruins of the capital, tombstones of the environmental degradation of the Butana.

The Kingdom of Kush at Meroe reached its zenith at the beginning of the Christian era under King Natakamani and Queen Amanitore. By 350 C.E. the authority of the state dwindled into disintegration. Environmental degradation on the Island of Meroe, the collapse of international trade with Asia, the supremacy of Rome in the Mediterranean, and the corrosive disruption by nomadic raiders combined to isolate the kingdom and erode the authority of the kings and queens of Kush. The Kingdom of Kush slowly collapsed into local chiefdoms located between the cataracts of the Nile until Ezana, the Christian Ethiopian king of Aksum (325–350 C.E.), destroyed Meroe and then retired to his highland aerie, leaving behind the Nubians with their historic mission as the cultural bridge over which Africa passed into Egypt. Kush had been closely intertwined with dynastic Egypt for two millennia without abandoning its distinctive Nubian culture and identity, but throughout those twenty centuries Nubia had remained the crucial link—the Kingdom of Kush, the corridor to Africa—between Egypt and sub-Saharan Africa.

Bantu Migrations, ca. 1000 B.C.E. –1600 C.E.

When Europeans began to penetrate into the savanna of central and southern Africa, they encountered peoples speaking languages that were mutually unintelligible but had discernible similarities in structure and vocabulary. The first European to record this phenomenon was Dr. Wilhelm Heinrich Immanuel Bleek (1827–1875) in his *Comparative Grammar of South African Languages*, published in

London between 1862 and 1869. Since then, his observations have proven correct. This vast expanse of the African landmass from Cameroon to South Africa is Bantu Africa, whose 450 closely related languages constitute what linguists classify as the Benue-Congo branch of the larger Niger-Congo language family. The term "Bantu" derives its name from a common root, "*ntu*," meaning "people," which is common to all Benue-Congo languages. The Bantu-speaking Africans are not an organized political unit but African peoples living throughout sub-Saharan Africa who are derived from a common ancestry. They spread throughout the lower half of the continent into separate and distinct peoples who share a common language structure.

Recognizing the cohesiveness of Bantu Africa, scholars began to inquire as to their origins and their subsequent migrations. Where did they come from, and how did they populate the greater whole of sub-Saharan Africa? In order to identify the origins of those Africans who speak Bantu languages and their travels, the historian must return to linguistics, the evidence of language. Languages evolve by fission, constantly changing as a community of people speaking a common tongue separate and develop new words and sounds either under their own initiative or by accommodation with new people and borrowing parts of their language. When people have separated recently, they still share many common words and can understand one another. If, however, populations have been separated for hundreds or a thousand or more years, the understanding diminishes, despite common words and morphology. By assembling the basic vocabulary shared by related societies, the linguist can determine those cognates that are derived from the ancestral language. The higher the percentage of cognates, the more closely related are languages. Those Africans speaking languages with a very low percentage of cognates are obviously peoples who have retained the core of the original language but drifted apart long ago.

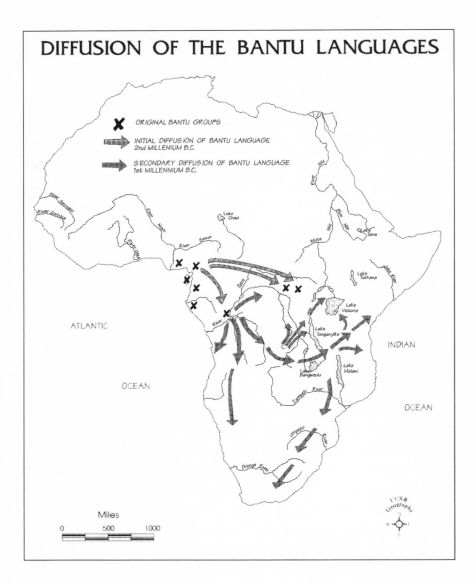

DIFFUSION OF THE BANTU LANGUAGES

By comparing these cognitive relationships, the Bantu homeland can be located with uncommon accuracy to an area some 25,000 square miles on the borderlands between the Republics of Cameroon and Nigeria. In this upland region, the original eight subgroups of the original Bantu are to be found. Some decided to leave, migrating east along the northern edge of the equatorial rainforest to the interlacustrine regions of the great lakes of equatorial East Africa, the Congo, Uganda, Kenya, and Tanzania. Other groups of Bantu wanderers went south through the rainforest to swing northeast to the East African coast and south to occupy the savanna of central and southern Africa. As a result, most of the Bantu languages of sub-Saharan Africa are very closely related since they derived from the one primary subgroup that came up the rivers of the Congo, the paths through the rainforest.

The initial dispersion of the Bantu probably took place during the first millennium before Christ. We do not know what precipitated three small bands of Bantu to leave the homeland. Nor do we know why the other subgroups of Benue-Congo stayed home in the borderlands of Cameroon and Nigeria. The migration, however, took place over centuries rather than decades, for the Bantu did not arrive in southern Africa until the sixteenth century, which can be substantiated by archaeological evidence as well as the more ephemeral calculations as to the rate of linguistic diffusion.

The migration of the Bantu was not an organized emigration or conquest by a central authority. Comprised of small groups of kin or households or with related individuals and their families moving together, it was a slow, steady diffusion of a few people who, for whatever reasons, were inspired to leave their homeland for new territories. They came up the rivers through the rainforest, where they settled for generations on the cultivatable enclaves that are to be found along all the rivers in the Congo basin. They had canoes, the word for which today is one of the most common in Bantu languages and spoken by

BANTU CLASSIFICATION

Lake Chad

River Niger

River Benue

White Nile

Blue Nile

Lake Tana

Pibor

Juba River

Tiv
Ekoi

Bube

Ewondo

Fang

Ngombe

Kusu

Mbete

Boma   Yanzi

Songe   Ena

Toro
Nkore
Rwanda
Rundi

Ganda

Kikuyu

Swahili

Duma

Kongo

Chokwe

Luba

Fipa

Gogo

Hehe

Zigula

ATLANTIC

OCEAN

Mbongala

Luchazi   Lunda

Bemba

Yao

INDIAN

OCEAN

Mbundu

Yeye   Luyana

Lenje

Tonga

Makua

Subia

Rue

Herero

Ndebele

Shona

Tonga

KHUI-SAN

(non-Bantu)

Tswana

Venda   Tsonga

Copi

UCSB
Geography

N
W   E
S

Swazi

Sotho

Zulu

Xhosa

Miles

0   500   1000

Primary groups

Secondary Sub-groups

Tertiary Sub-groups

(NOTE: The names of Bantu groups
are only representative of the
many Bantu peoples in each
region.)

those who have never lived by a river. They ate fish. At its slowest rate, the passage of the Bantu through the rainforest has been calculated statistically at an average of one mile per year. Rather than move a little distance each year, the Bantu in the rainforest appear to have remained in one place for long periods of time, even generations, and then moved on a few or many miles to a new and more fertile site. The Bantu migration was thus a discontinuous movement of small groups passing through the rainforest in centuries rather than decades.

Once beyond the rivers of the rainforest, the great savanna of eastern, central, and southern Africa spread before them. In the rainforest the Bantu had grown tubers, particularly yams, which provide an important source of nutrition. As with the word "canoe," many Bantu languages today have derivatives of words for root crops, even in regions where those who have lived on the savanna for a thousand years have never known such crops. Conversely, the Bantu languages in the homeland areas of Cameroon and Nigeria lack any words for the indigenous grain sorghum, which became the dominant food crop for the Bantu of the savanna. Similarly, the Bantu languages spoken by those who had reached the equatorial lakes contain words for grain crops that they acquired from the Cushitic (Nilo-Saharan) speakers after arriving in East Africa. Here on the savanna grassland, sorghum became the staple grain crop that revolutionized the Bantu migration.

The Bantu flourished and proliferated on the high veld of Africa and moved on with their grain crops by shifting cultivation and iron. A homestead or a community would cultivate the land, growing sorghum and raising chickens, goats, sheep, and cattle until the land was exhausted. African soils, even on the savanna, do not have long fertility, and during the millennia of the Bantu odyssey they were exhausted within two or three years. When the land could no longer produce a sufficient crop, it was abandoned. It was then time to move on a short distance to clear the land and begin anew for another two or three years. Shifting cultivation became the dynamic of Bantu migration. It could not have been accomplished without the iron tools to break the sod of the savanna.

The Bantu almost certainly began their migrations through the paths of the rainforest with iron tools, particularly the hoe. The technology to smelt iron and forge tools most likely arrived in the western Sudan about 1000 B.C.E. from the north across the trans-Saharan routes, but there is also evidence that iron smelting had local, independent origins in West Africa. Iron tools are superior to stone tools, but the early forges did not sufficiently harden tools to slash through the rainforest. The amount of iron available to the Bantu would have been very limited and forged in furnaces that could produce the ubiquitous hoe rather than the sword. Nevertheless, the iron hoe can be mightier than the sword, and it enabled the Bantu to cultivate the enclaves in the rainforest and to turn the turf of the savanna beyond. The greatest contribution of iron was not for conquest but the tools that enabled the Bantu to migrate into new and unfamiliar lands and to increase their agricultural production on the more fertile savanna.

Although Africa before the coming of the Bantu had a very low population density, it was not empty. During the millennia of their migrations, the Bantu encountered peoples who had roamed the continent for centuries. They were small groups of hunters and gatherers belonging to the Khoi and San, Khosian-speaking families, the "aboriginal" Africans. The Bantu did not come as conquerors but as farmers with a superior technology, iron, and with cattle, sheep, and goats. They interacted with the Khosian peoples, intermarried, and adopted many characteristics of their speech, but the relentless advance of the farmer and the herder pushed the hunters and gatherers ever southward from the extensive lands they required for their way of life.

Aksum, 200–700 C.E.

The great eastern African Rift Valley slices through East Africa and Ethiopia to become the trench for the Red Sea, Gulf of Aqaba, Dead Sea, and the River Jordan to end its declivity at Mount Hermon rising 9,230 feet in southern Lebanon. In Ethiopia, the western escarpment of the rift rises dramatically as the buttress to its highlands only forty miles from the shores of the Red Sea and the ruins of the ancient port of Adulis not far from modern Massawa. Above the torrid Danakil desert at the bottom of the rift, the Ethiopian highlands tower between 6,000 and 10,000 feet above ground, overlooking the surrounding arid plains of the Horn of Africa. They are transformed into green pastures and cultivated fields by some forty-five inches of rainfall per year. Located just north of the equator, the altitude creates a mild temperature, averaging 60° F, which inhibits the spread of the deadly diseases from the lowlands below—malaria, bilharzia, sleeping sickness in humans, and the fatal nagana in cattle. This huge volcanic uplift, measuring half a million square miles, dramatically demonstrates the power of geography in shaping the African past. These towering highlands trap the rain clouds rolling across Africa from the South Atlantic and the moist winds from the Red Sea that rise above the escarpment. As a result, the clouds drop their rainfall, often in violent thunderstorms.

The rugged escarpments that force the rain clouds to rise were also the battlements of a great natural fortress. They defied invaders from the plains below, while deserts and arid grasslands discouraged invasion from the south. These natural barriers produced a dramatic landscape of gorges, ravines, and canyons, that of the Blue Nile as deep as the Grand Canyon of the Colorado in the United States. They also enabled the evolution of an ecosystem unique in Africa and a people who developed their own distinctive culture from it. Ethiopia has mammals, birds, and plants found nowhere else in Africa. Coffee was first domesticated in Ethiopia as were the ensete (*Ensete edulis*), a banana that was long the staple foodstuff in the southern regions of the Ethiopian plateau, and noog, an oil plant. Finger millet (*Eleusine coracana*) originated in Ethiopia, and there were Ethiopian varieties of wheat, barley, and sorghum, but the cereal unique to Ethiopia was teff.

Teff (*Eragrostis tef*) was first cultivated in northern Ethiopia as early as the eighth century B.C.E. to become the staple cereal of the Kingdom of Aksum before the Christian era. Wheat and barley were brought from South Arabia by Sabaean immigrants but could not compete with the indigenous teff, which flourished from long adaptation to the distinctive environment of northern Ethiopia. A prolific plant, it produces in abundance very small grains that contain more carbohydrates, protein, and amino acid to sustain life than the seeds of larger cereals. Teff may yield less per acre than barley, wheat, or sorghum, but it will ripen with little rain when other grains wither, the reason that it remains today the most valued crop of subsistence farmers in Ethiopia.

Adulis was the ancient gateway to the Ethiopian highlands, an African port in the commercial and cultural world of the Red Sea that embraced modern Eritrea, Saudi Arabia, and Yemen divided only by the narrow seventeen-mile strait of the Bab el-Mandeb that separates Africa from Asia. Sometime between the eighth and third centuries B.C.E., Sabaean colonists from Arabia crossed the straits to Adulis and Africa. They did not linger in the heat of the coastal plain but made their way up the escarpment to the cool fertile highlands, where they were assimilated into the pastoral culture of the indigenous Cushitic peoples of Ethiopia to become the Kingdom of Aksum. The Sabaeans brought with them the plow for the Cushite ox and the skills for irrigation and terracing. They also brought the Sabaean alphabet. The highlands, however, were connected to Adulis and the Red Sea trading complex only by narrow trails twisting down the escarpment, which reinforced the ecological isolation of the Cushitic inhabitants, who transformed the imported Sabaean script and its vocabulary for their own use. A new vocabulary was adopted to describe the conditions and culture of the highlands. The calligraphy distinctive to the Kingdom of Aksum developed into Ge'ez, the ancestral writing of modern Ethiopia. With the plow and the pen, Aksum emerged as an indigenous state supported by its rich resources on a fertile plateau and the vital though often tenuous link through Adulis with the larger commercial networks of the Red Sea, the Gulf of Arabia, and the Indian Ocean. In their highland fortress, the people and rulers of Aksum were able to select the most advantageous foreign innovations without eroding their indigenous culture, establishing the beginnings of literate, agricultural, and commercial states in northeast Africa over 2,000 years ago and unknown at that time in sub-Sahara Africa.

Despite the difficulties of travel up and down the escarpment, the kingdom took advantage of its protective location in the highlands to exploit the trading complex of the Red Sea that prospered from the growth of Greek and later Roman mercantile technology and trade. The combination of its agriculture—irrigated, terraced, and tilled by the plow—literacy for the social elite, and commerce through the port of Adulis enabled the chiefs and then kings of Aksum to build a powerful state in northeast Africa. By the third century B.C.E., the kings of Aksum ruled from urban centers. Limestone temples were constructed at Yeha, Haoulti, and Mantara for the pantheon of gods that came with the colonists from the Kingdom of Saba along with their bronze and iron axes, swords, sickles, rings, and jewelry. There was at first racial stratification between "red" people from Arabia and the indigenous "black" Cushitic pastoralists, but by the first century of the Christian era this distinction had disappeared in the evolution of the social, commercial, and cultural life of Aksum, whose inhabitants had become the ancestors of the modern Ethiopians.

The kingdom exported ivory, the horn of the rhinoceros worth a fortune in Asia as an aphrodisiac, hippopotamus hides, gold dust, frankincense, spices, and even live elephants. They were exchanged for cattle and salt from the Danakil desert, the most precious commodity in sub-Saharan Africa. Equally desired by the elite of Aksum was the merchandise—cloth, beads, porcelain, and ironware—brought to Adulis by merchants from the Mediterranean, the Black Sea, India, and China to be carried up the escarpment for eight days to Aksum. In the fifth century, Aksum reached the height of its development and prosperity. The capital, Aksum, was well known throughout the Roman and Persian empires and as far as China in the east. Over 20,000 Aksumites inhabited the city, whose elite spent their wealth from agriculture and commerce on pretentious houses and conspicuous consummation—fabrics from India and China; glassware and ceramics from Persia; and spices, wine, and hardware from the eastern Mediterranean. Upon their death, the rulers and the elite were buried in stone tombs. They also erected tall obelisks of finely cut granite carved with decorative relief to represent a multistoried building, each taller than its predecessor. More than 140 stelae have been found in Aksum, but only a few remain upright. One still standing is 69 feet tall, but the largest stelae, exceeding 108 feet and weighing over 700 tons, cut from a granite quarry two and a half miles west of Aksum, has fallen. The chiseling of these monuments with stone and iron tools most certainly required artistic and technological skill, political stability, social organization, and leadership. The era of the obelisks coincided with the arrival of Christianity, which demanded the worship of Christ in a church rather than using the resources of the state to commemorate kings by their stelae.

In the fourth century, King Ezana of Aksum was converted to Christianity by two brothers, Frumentius and Aedesius, Christian traders returning from India who were shipwrecked on the Red Sea coast. Taken from Adulis to the court of Aksum, they converted

King Ezana and his court to Christianity and assisted in the administration of the kingdom. Aedesius returned to Syria, but Frumentius
traveled to Alexandria, where he was installed by the patriarch
Athanasius (297–373 C.E.) as a bishop of the Egyptian Coptic Church
and sent back to Ethiopia as the *abuna*, "our father," about 333.

Armenia had become Christian in 301, Rome in 312. Twenty years
later in Aksum, the Abuna Salama Frumentius established the beginnings of Ethiopian Christianity. He was the first of 111 Egyptian
monks who followed him to be appointed by the patriarchs of
Alexandria as the *abuna*, or head, of the Ethiopian Church for the
next sixteen centuries, until 1951. This theological link was to remain
vital to the Ethiopian Church and the monarchy for nearly two millennia. After the rise of Islam, it was their intellectual, religious, and
psychological channel to the outside world. The authority of the
patriarch in Alexandria gave the Ethiopia Church its legitimacy and a
confirmation of the apostolic succession and hence the link with the
oriental Christianity of the Eastern Church.

At the Council of Chalcedon in Syria in 451, the clerical leaders of
Christianity were deeply divided over the nature of Jesus Christ. The
majority, who claimed orthodoxy, argued that Christ's manhood and
godhood constituted two separate natures, human and divine. Those
who adhered to the minority Monophysite doctrine believed that
these two separate natures were fused into one, in which his divinity
superseded his humanity. The Orthodox-Monophysite struggle has
been long and bitter and remains today one of the principal schisms
in the Christian church, but at the end of the Council of Calcedon
priests supporting the Monophysite doctrine fled from persecution,
nine of whom reached Ethiopia. Here they laid the foundations for
the Ethiopian Orthodox Church, translated the scriptures into Ge'ez,
and established monasticism, which became the historic institution
for the continuity of Ethiopian Christianity. The Nine Saints are
deeply revered today. They not only established the Ethiopian

Orthodox Church in the fifth century but also preserved that vital connection with the Mediterranean world through the Monophysite Coptic patriarch in Alexandria and in Jerusalem, where Ethiopian monks established their hospice after the collapse of the Roman Empire. The institution of the Egyptian *abuna* survived until the twentieth century because of its mutual advantages. When Christian Copts were persecuted by Muslims in Egypt, the patriarch threatened to appeal to his Christian brethren in Ethiopia to obstruct the waters of the Nile. The Ethiopian Orthodox Church provided the critical institutional support for the monarchy and whose king was crowned by the *abuna* that conferred upon him God's legitimacy. When Islam sought to isolate Christian Ethiopia, the close ties between the Ethiopian Orthodox Church and the Egyptian Coptic Church were the only remaining link between Ethiopia and Christendom. The solidification of church and state in Ethiopia has been the principal reason for Ethiopia's longevity as an independent kingdom and state to the present day.

After reaching the zenith of its prosperity and power in the fourth and fifth centuries, Aksum slipped into decline because of environmental degradation, the collapse of the Roman Empire and its Mediterranean and Red Sea commercial network, and changes in global climate. Rain from the South Atlantic would normally reach Aksum in northern Ethiopia in April and May and continue until September, which enabled farmers to plant twice and harvest two crops each year in soils of marginal nutrients. Terracing, irrigation, the plow, and manure made possible food for the Aksumites. Its deciduous forests provided the energy for smelting iron and manufacturing glass, brick, and pottery for the marketplace; charcoal for the kitchen stove; and timber for the house. Like the Kingdom of Kush, where the Island of Meroe was denuded of its woodlands for charcoal and iron smelting, northern Ethiopia was stripped of its trees from the fourth to the seventh centuries. There was the need for more inten-

ANCIENT AND MEDIEVAL NORTHEAST AFRICA

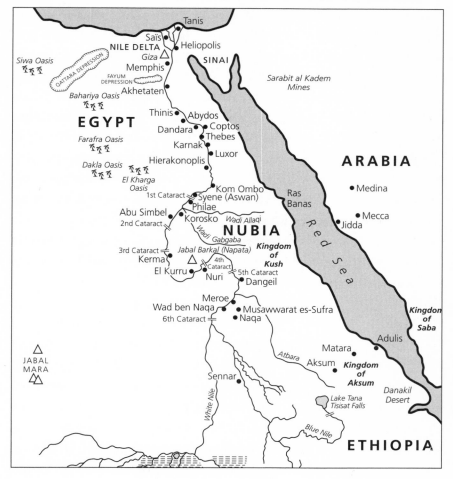

sified cultivation to supply a growing population who consumed ever-larger amounts of timber for charcoal and an industry that exposed the land to fatal erosion as the rains now washed the hillsides bare.

Aksum grew from its agricultural resources but prospered from the Mediterranean, Red Sea, and Indian Ocean trade. This came to an end with the dissolution of the Roman Empire in the Mediterranean and the conquest of southern Arabia by the Persians, who now controlled the trade routes to the Persian Gulf and India. No longer able to barter the wealth of Africa through Adulis, which was destroyed in the eighth century by the Arabs, Aksum was confined to its degraded highlands at a time of global climatic change. Beginning in the eighth century, the annual rainfall became limited to just the spring rains, which meant that farmers could plant only one crop, not two. Most farmers raised teff, for it could pollinate without regular rainfall. By the ninth century, the Kingdom of Aksum had been reduced to a few monasteries and villages, the Aksumites having followed the rains into central Ethiopia, where they laid the foundations for the Solomonic dynasty of the modern Ethiopian state. Aksum left behind its stelae, both erect and fallen, a place of pilgrimage, and the symbiotic relationship between church and state in Ethiopia.

Christian States of Nubia

Just as geography conditioned the highland history of Aksum, so, too, did it determine life in the Nile Valley, a thin sliver of fertile soil sharply confined by desert sands that has shaped the history of its Christian states. The disintegration of the Kingdom of Kush and its symbolic end by Ezana, the Christian king of Aksum, in 350 C.E. was followed by the arrival of the Ballana, who came out of Africa from the southwest to settle and rule in Lower Nubia for 200 years. They established three kingdoms—Nobatia, Makouria, and Alwa—in the fifth century from the first cataract at Aswan to the confluence of the Blue and White Niles. Nobatia was soon absorbed by Makouria to dominate Lower Nubia as far as the fifth cataract, while south of it the smaller Kingdom of Alwa ruled the Nile from Meroe to its capital at Soba across the Blue Nile from modern Khartoum. Little is known of the history of Nubia during the reigns of the Ballana kings.

Between 543 and 580, the Nubians discarded their old gods and the idols of pharaonic Egypt to embrace with religious enthusiasm the new Monophysite Christian faith that became the state religion of the Christian kingdoms of the Sudan. The evangelization of Nubia had been undertaken by missionaries perhaps sent by the great Byzantine emperor Justinian (527–565 C.E.) but more likely sent by his empress Theodora, who was an outspoken advocate of the Monophysite persuasion. Justinian had the great temple of Isis at Philae near Aswan converted into the Church of St. Stephen, and at the request of the empress the missionary Julian traveled up the Nile in 543 to convert the Nubians of the Kingdom of Nobatia. His success was assured by the king accepting the faith, which was followed by a spate of building churches on the remains of old temples. Julian was succeeded by Longinus (569–575 C.E.), who continued the conversion of Nubian rulers and their subjects by expanding the Christianity of the Monophysite doctrine into the Kingdoms of Makouria and Alwa. The new religion was adopted with a spiritual passion that produced an astonishing ideological transformation. The great symbols of dynastic Egypt and Kush—tombs, temples, statuary, and the divine kingship—soon disappeared to be replaced by the strict observance of one god, the faith in whom inspired Nubian Christian churches, art, and literature.

Although the Monophysite Christianity of medieval Nubia was regarded as heretical by both the Western Church in Rome and the Eastern Church at Constantinople, the arrival of Christianity restored the historical ties of Nubia with the Mediterranean world and renewed its cultural relationship with Egypt. It gave an identity to the peoples of the Nubian Nile by preserving their past culture in a Christian context that enabled them to resist for another 500 years the later challenge from Islam. Christianity was a new message easily understood in the oneness of God, and it fulfilled a spiritual need that the Egyptian and Kushitic gods of the past could no longer satisfy. Even if regarded by other Christians as heretics, the Christian Nubian kings and their subjects became part of the larger world that embraced the new dynamic ideology and faith of Christianity.

We do not know the details of this rapid and remarkable conversion. Was it the charisma and rhetoric of a wandering mendicant, a fiery missionary, perhaps Julian, who could captivate the populace? Or were these early missionaries more ambassadors than evangelists, who began at the court of an absolute Ballana monarch whose baptism would be quickly imitated by his courtiers and soon followed by that of his subjects? The rapid and complete acceptance of Christianity in Nubia by the end of the sixth century was probably a bit of both. The acceptance of one omnipotent king in heaven no longer permitted divine kings on earth. The Christian kings of Makouria and Alwa, mere mortals, acknowledged the spiritual supremacy of the Coptic patriarch of Alexandria and his appointed bishops in Nubia and in return received support for their secular rule. The Nubian kings embraced the new religion with the same fervor as their subjects, but their interests were as much political as spiritual. A religious alliance with the Coptic patriarch of Egypt and the Byzantine emperor would strengthen their isolated rule in Nubia. The appeal for a new ideology coincided with royal decrees to adopt the new faith. The bricks and stones from palaces and temples scattered along the Nubian Nile were now used to build the naves of Christian churches. The average Nubian church was the size of a modern-day chapel, but there were large churches, cathedrals, at Old Dongola, Faras, and Qasr Ibrim.

Unlike Aksum, however, the institution of monasticism never developed in Makouria and Alwa. The monasteries of Ethiopia were the repositories of its history, literature, and language (Ge'ez) and were the bastions against Muslim invasion. The reasons for the failure to establish a monastic tradition in Nubia perhaps lie more in geography than ideology. Unlike the highland plateau of Ethiopia, the Nubian Nile is a thin band of green by the river, where there was only room for the church and not the expansive Ethiopian estates required to support a monastery. Moreover, the Monophysite missionaries in Nubia were concerned with conversion, which required their presence at court and preaching in the village rather than retiring into the Nubian desert to contemplate the nature of Christ in a wasteland that could barely support the most ascetic monks.

Moreover, the Nubian church never established the ecclesiastical unity of the Ethiopian Orthodox Church. The primate of the Ethiopia church was the *abuna* appointed by the patriarch of the Egyptian Coptic Church. Although an Egyptian monk, the *abuna* was accepted by every Ethiopian emperor, noble, and peasant as the symbol of the centrality and continuity of the church. The organization to establish this unity in the Nubian church could never be achieved when each of its thirteen bishops was consecrated separately by the patriarch of Alexandria and answered separately to him. There was no *abuna* and consequently no single individual in Nubia to unify the church under the control of rival bishops who were one in doctrine and spirit but who were determined to defend their bishoprics against all rivals by appeals to their spiritual authority and as patrons of art and literature.

After the death of the prophet Muhammad in 632, Muslim Arabs erupted from the desert steppes of Arabia to conquer the lands to the east and west. By 641 they had occupied Egypt, where the Egyptian Coptic Church had to accept its position as a minority religion. But Arab control of upper Egypt on the borders of Christian Nubia was precarious and characterized by frontier raiding between Arab invaders and Nubian defenders. In 651–652 the Arab governor of Egypt, Abdallah ibn Sa'd Abi Sarh, led a well-equipped expedition to subdue the Nubians of Makouria. The Arabs marched as far as Dongola and laid siege to the town, but they suffered heavy casualties from the skilled Nubian archers and were satisfied to make peace, the Baqt. One of the most famous documents of medieval times, the Baqt defined the terms of peace on the frontier between Christian Nubia and the Islamic world for another 600 years (652–1257), a record in the history of international relations. It was originally regarded as a truce, not a treaty, whose longevity was more the result of reality and the benefits both sides derived from it than any immutable covenant of ambiguous jurisprudence. An agreement of accommodation that regularized trade, the Baqt was unique in the Muslim world, for it recognized that Christian Nubia was sovereign and exempt not only from the Dar al-Islam (land of the faithful) but also from the Darb al-Harb (land of the enemy). This anomalous distinction reflected the invincibility of the Nubian army and the accuracy of its famous archers more than the erudition of Islamic jurists. The Baqt brought peace and stability to the Christian kingdoms of Nubia during the centuries of Islamic expansion at the expense of Christians throughout the Mediterranean world. It certainly encouraged the Nubians to rely increasingly on slave raiding to meet the terms of the Baqt: "Each year you [Nubians] are to deliver 360 slaves, whom you will pay to the Imam of the Muslims from the finest slaves of your country, in whom there is no defect. [They are to be] both male and female. Among them [is to be] no decrepit old man or any child who has not reached puberty. You are to deliver them to the Wali of Aswan."[1]

The slave raiding precipitated by the Baqt, however, also increased Nubian dependency on African slave labor, which created a leisure class of Nubian nobility whose petty rivalries and intrigues substantially contributed to the isolation and decline of the Christian kingdoms of Nubia. Moreover, the coming of Islam to Egypt and the Nile limited and ultimately ended the contact of both Ethiopia and Nubia with the Mediterranean world. This isolation forged by the anvil of Islam disrupted the commercial relationships facilitated by the Christian Egyptian Coptic Church, but the Muslim rulers were never sufficiently strong to conquer either of these two Christian states of northeast Africa. The Ethiopians were protected by their highlands, the Nubians by the rocks of the Nile cataracts and the burning sands of their deserts.

When Muslim Turkish mercenaries, the Tulunids, took control of lower Egypt in the ninth century, they sought to rid themselves of their unruly Bedouin Arabs in upper Egypt by encouraging them to roam into Nubia. The desert, which the Nubians avoided for the banks of the Nile, was the home of the nominal Muslim Bedouin Arabs who rode out of the desert to raid the Christian settlements by the Nile. Once again, the Christian Nubians of Makouria defended their kingdom against Islam for another 300 years, until the Mamluk sultans established their rule over Egypt in the second half of the thirteenth century. The Mamluks perceived that their principal duty was to protect the Dar al-Islam from infidels—Mongols, Crusaders, and Christian Nubians. Sultan Baybars (1260–1277) and his successor, Qalawun (1279–1290), sent military expeditions south of Aswan to pillage the Nubian Nile, but they made no effort to occupy or colonize Makouria.

By the thirteenth century, the collapse of the Christian kingdoms of the Sudan did not need the Mamluk incursions. During the centuries of the Baqt, the authority of the monarchy had gradually been eroded by the hierarchy of the church. Bishops had increasingly allied with the feudal nobility to undermine the Crown, which was besieged by the incipient intrusions of Bedouin Arabs from upper Egypt. These Bedouins were, by far, more corrosive to the Christian kingdoms than the challenge from Mamluk sultans. When the last Mamluk expedition was sent to Nubia in 1366, the Kingdom of Makouria had disintegrated into petty chiefdoms into which the Bedouins had settled. During these undocumented times, trade disappeared, as did the Baqt, the church, and the nobility who imploded upon their own impotence. Christianity was no longer a threat on the frontier of Islam at Aswan. The vacuum was filled by the arrival of the Muslim *fuqura* (holy men, *faqir*, sing.). The *fuqura* practiced Sufism, Islamic mysticism, in fraternal brotherhoods, the *turuq* (*tariqa*, sing.), and brought Islam to the Sudan. They were neither warriors nor traders but religious teachers who spread Islam among the rustic Arab nomads and Nubian farmers, just as Julian and Longinus had converted the Nubians to Christianity 600 years earlier.

By the fifteenth century, Nubia was open to Arab immigration, particularly after the Juhayna of upper Egypt learned that the grasslands beyond the hostile Aswan Reach could support their herds and there was no longer any political authority with the power to obstruct their advance. They occupied Lower Nubia, where they intermarried and introduced Arabic and Islam to Nubian Christians. Inheritance among the Arabs is through the male. Among the Nubians, it was passed through the female. Intermarriage consequently resulted in Nubian economic and political inheritance passing from Christian Nubian women to Muslim Arab sons and thereafter through descent of the male member of the family. The Juhayna and other Arab nomads wandered east and west from the Nile with their cattle, camels, sheep, and goats. Some settled in Nubian villages by the Nile to become farmers. In Upper Nubia, the Kingdom of Alwa remained the last indigenous Christian barrier to Arab infiltration of the Sudan.

Medieval Arabic writers called the northern frontier of Alwa, al-Abwab, the Gates, a term that still applies to the regions from al-Kabushiyya south of the confluence of the Atbara River with the Nile to Sennar on the Blue Nile. Alwa appears to have been more prosperous than Makouria. It preserved the iron-working techniques of Kush, and its capital at Soba near Khartoum on the north bank of the Nile impressed Arab visitors with its buildings, churches, and gardens. Alwa was able to maintain its integrity as long as the Arab nomads failed to combine against it, but the collapse of the Kingdom of Makouria resulted in a steady infiltration of Arab herdsmen. Alwa disappeared into unrecorded history. By the sixteenth century, an Arab confederation led by the Islamic folk-hero Abdallah Jamma, the Gatherer, destroyed Soba, leaving the Christian remains of the Kingdom of Alwa to the mysterious Funj.

Note

1. W. Y. Adams, *Nubia: Corridor to Africa* (Princeton, N.J.: Princeton University Press, 1977), pp. 450–453.

CHAPTER THREE

Islam, Trade, and States

Mosque of Sankore

Arabs and Islam

Arabia had always been on the margin of the Roman Empire, but it was a geographic link between Roman commercial intercourse with the ports on the Red Sea, Aksum, and the Sabaean Lane, the oceanic arch from the coast of East Africa to the Persian Gulf and India. The trading cities of Arabia had long-standing commercial connections with the Persian Sassanian Empire to the northeast, which controlled much of Mesopotamia and in the sixth century extended its control over southern Arabia and Yemen. The prophet Muhammad was a merchant involved in this trade. By 620 his inspired message had mobilized hitherto rival nomadic clans throughout western Arabia to believing in the concept of one god. Despite opposition in Mecca, which drove Muhammad to Medina on his hejira in 622, the beginning of the Muslim era, his followers were ultimately victorious. By 630 Mecca had accepted Islam, and at the time of Muhammad's death in 632 both the nomadic and sedentary peoples of Arabia were united under the banner of Islam.

The religious enthusiasm inspired by Muhammad's message spilled east and west out of Arabia to establish the faith throughout the coasts of North and East Africa. In 639 the Arabs invaded Egypt, and in 642 the Byzantines surrendered Alexandria to them. The Arab armies swept westward to defeat the Byzantine army in modern Tunisia in 647. Kayrawan (Kairouan) was founded in 670 to govern the new Muslim Arab province of Ifraqiya (Tunisia), from which Africa derived its name. The Arabs continued their advance all the way to the Atlantic Ocean, but during the next four centuries Arab Muslim authority became subordinate to Berber Muslim power.

Although enthusiastically accepting Islam, the Berbers were deeply resolved to retain their language and culture, which was characterized by its egalitarianism and individuality. Arab authority extended along the Mediterranean littoral only as far as Ifraqiya, while the Maghrib al-Aqsa, the Far West (Morocco), was Muslim in religion but Berber-Arab and politically independent, from which evolved throughout the subsequent centuries a series of Arab-Berber states—the Fatimids, who ruled North Africa from Egypt to Morocco (959–1171), and the Almoravids (1062–1145) and the Almohads (1145–1269), whose Berber empires included the Maghrib al-Aqsa and southern Spain. The Almoravids were succeeded by the Marinids (1269–1415), who ruled Morocco for another 200 years. Meanwhile, in the Egyptian Nile Valley the Mamluks seized power from the Kurdish Ayyubid dynasty (1169–1250) in 1250 to rule Egypt until its conquest by Napoleon in 1798.

During these thousands of years, two events had a lasting impact on Arab and Berber society in North Africa—the arrival of the Banu Hilal in the eleventh century and the Black Death, the bubonic plague, in the late fourteenth century. Faced with rebellion in the west and unrest in upper Egypt among the Banu Hilal, the Fatimid caliph, Abu Tamim al-Mustansir (r. 1036–1094), made a fateful decision. He unleashed these nomadic and unruly Arabs westward along the Mediterranean littoral to leave Egypt in peace. The Banu Hilal were illiterate Bedouin warrior nomads who descended upon the Arab states of North Africa like "locusts." The Berber herdsmen retired to the far west, and the Berber cultivators sought refuge in the moun-tains. This left the coastal plain to the Banu Hilal, whose plundering was more by infiltration and occupation of the land than a planned, methodical conquest. Their colloquial Arabic became the local dialect, and there is no doubt their voracious wanderings westward destroyed the long-established economy of North Africa. Ifraqiya never fully recovered from the depredations of the Banu Hilal.

The destruction by the Banu Hilal was followed by the ravages of the Black Death, which first erupted in the Gobi Desert of Mongolia during the early decades of the fourteenth century to sweep westward into Europe and across the Mediterranean to North Africa. The Black Death derived its name from the black splotches that discolored the skin caused by the bacterium *Yersina pestis*, which was transmitted in three forms—bubonic plague by fleas with a mortality of 30-70 percent, pneumonic plague spread by the breath of one human to another with a fatality rate of 90 percent, and the rare septicemica, which attacks the blood and from which there is no recovery. By the mid-fourteenth century, it had killed 40 percent of the inhabitants of Europe. From Spain, the Black Death reached the Maghrib and, from Sicily, Ifraqiya, to sweep eastward to the Sinai Peninsula. More than the dynastic squabbles, racial tensions, and conflict between herdsmen and cultivators, the loss of the greatest resource of any state, its people, by the Black Death plunged North Africa into decline unknown to the prosperity of past empires—Carthage, Rome, Byzantium, and the Islamic dynasties. There was no cure for the Black Death, only prayer and appeals to God to relieve the people from its insidious power. In the latter half of the fourteenth century, Egypt lost nearly a third of its population. The demographic destruction in Egypt coincided with the overthrow of the Ayyubid dynasty and the rise of the Mamluks.

Trans-Saharan Trade

The Arab conquest of the Maghrib, the spread of Islam, and the rise and fall of subsequent Berber and Arab dynasties appear to have been confined to the Mediterranean littoral and the Nile Valley. This is an illusion. During the centuries, each of these Muslim states of the Maghrib became linked economically and by religion with Africa south of the Sahara. The coming of the Arabs, the spread of Islam, and the emergence of Muslim states increased the demand for African goods in return for those of the Mediterranean world, which could only be satisfied by the trans-Saharan trade.

Humans have always crossed the Sahara, even after it became a desert some 5,000 years ago. Why? The way was long, about 1,500 miles. The dangers from predators, animal and human, were real. The terrain of gravel, rock, and sand was treacherous. There was a dearth of water and food found only in widely spaced oases. The needs and desires of both Arabs and Africans for goods the other could provide were, however, insatiable and sufficient for them to confront the dangers of the trans-Saharan crossing. When the merchandise of Europe, the Mediterranean world, and the Middle East could be exchanged for that of Africa, merchants, mendicants, and travelers mounted their camels in great caravans to venture south into the sands of the Sahara along well-established routes.

The camel revolutionized trans-Saharan travel and trade. The single-humped camel, the dromedary, could travel at two and a half miles an hour, the same as humans, or thirty miles a day. Depending on the conditions of the terrain, a smooth-flowing sea of sand in contrast to the vast fields of rocks and stones that characterize much of the Sahara, the camel could even make as many as sixty miles a day. A well-fed camel could carry the same load as an ox, 350 pounds, but the dramatic difference was its freedom of movement. With fat from its hump and a water tank in its belly, a camel could move methodically for ten days without a drink, three times that of an ox or horse. It could sustain the extreme desert heat of the day and the extreme desert cold of the night. Its splayed feet were cushions on sand and gravel.

By the fourth century, the Berbers had made the camel the principal beast of burden throughout the Mahgrib. By the fifth century, they had trained the camel to be the principal vehicle for desert travel. The camel gave the nomadic Sanhaja Berbers of the west and the Tuareg Berbers of the central Sahara astonishing mobility and transport. It enabled the Berbers to organize the long-distance trans-Saharan trade. Hitherto, the passage through the Sahara was in stages and periodic. With the camel, the trans-Saharan trade evolved through the centuries into organized and regular caravans to cross the whole of the Sahara with Sanhaja Berber and Tuareg cameleers and led by Toubou guides. By the twelfth century, caravans of 12,000 camels have been recorded, and although not always an annual passage, the trade was consistent through the centuries. Following tracks used since 500 B.C.E., the caravans traversed the most favorable terrain along an archipelago of well-watered oases, but with heavy losses in camels and men and the payment of tolls to the Sanhaja, Taureg, and Toubou who controlled these oases. Sometimes a caravan would be totally annihilated by the great sandstorms that swept across the desert, but the prospect of huge profits always brought men back to cross the Sahara. The importance of these routes from the African Sahel to the Mediterranean shore varied during the centuries, depending on the demand for the commodities carried out of Africa—gold, slaves, ivory, and kola nuts.

The historic, constant, and common commodity crossing the Sahara were slaves, but gold brought the highest price. Until the exploitation of the New World in the sixteenth century, the gold for European kings, queens, and merchants came from West Africa. It was mined from thousands of holes, shafts no more than forty feet deep; some had lateral galleries. The gold-bearing alluvium was brought to the surface in calabashes, washed by women to separate gold from gravel in the same manner as California miners panned gold dust in 1849. The mining required the organization of labor around a chief of the mine. He collected the gold dust and nuggets and negotiated the sale. The gold, which was mostly dust and the occasional nugget, became a royal monopoly of the rulers of the western Sudanic kingdoms from which they derived great wealth, but they never minted their own gold coins.

The West Africans were not about to part from their gold without an equally valuable commodity in exchange, salt. Men and women can live without gold, but they cannot live without salt. Salt, sodium chloride, is essential to most bodily functions and can become addictive. The individual African of the western Sudan in the past and present has consumed about ten pounds of salt per year. Salt was also used as a preservative and for medicinal purposes. The demand for salt in sub-Saharan Africa was insatiable, for there are few sources of salt in Africa south of the Sahara, and the desert remains its greatest repository. Salt was mined by slaves and cut into pure white blocks weighing sixty-six pounds to fit on either side of a camel's hump. The volume of the trade throughout two millennia was enormous. The salt deposits at Bilma alone sent annually 6,000 tons to Niger, Chad, Nigeria, and the forest regions of sub-Saharan Africa. The value of salt can best be understood by its very high price in the marketplace. Salt from the Sahara was carried south by camel caravans to the Sahel and savanna. There it was passed on in stages by donkey to the edge of the tsetse-fly belt, where it was then carried by human portage through the rainforest. From Timbuktu on the Niger, it was transported up and down the river by canoe.

Empires of the Plains

South of the Sahara on the great plains of the Sahel and savanna
that stretch across Africa from the Atlantic to the Red Sea, empires
rose and fell during the second millennia of the Christian era. Each of
these states had a definable heartland and flexible boundaries on the
periphery, and each was ruled by a central authority, a monarch, who
was responsible for the commercial, ethnic, political, and religious
preservation and prosperity of its people. The emergence and evolution of these states after 1000 C.E., and their ability to last for 1,000
years, were made possible by agriculture, iron, trade, religion, and ethnicity. The agricultural revolution begun by the cultivation of
sorghum, indigenous to the western Sudan, was facilitated by the
introduction of iron tools to produce the surplus food necessary for
settlement and state building.

The trans-Saharan trade, now long distance after the appearance of
the camel in the fourth century, created wealth for the merchants and
the indigenous elite upon whom they were dependent for the success
of their commercial operations. The conduct of trade at both the
northern and southern markets required security, without which commerce could not continue, let alone flourish. Trade required regulation, which in turn created the opportunity for the leaders in the communities of the western Sudan to acquire economic resources and
political power without relying solely on surplus foodstuffs produced
by cultivators and herdsmen. They were the rulers who could provide
protection for the merchants, but their entourage of noble retainers
also possessed the resources to purchase luxury goods—salt, cloth,
hardware, horses, and books—unknown in the western Sudan. Many
Sudanese rulers and their elites adopted Islam and employed Arabic
in their commercial and political transactions, but the kings fiercely
retained their control of the sale of gold, slaves, and ivory.

After a hazardous journey of two months, the Muslim Arab and

Berber merchants arrived exhausted in the commercial emporiums of the western Sudan. There in the great market towns the authorities encouraged them to complete their transactions and return across the desert, leaving the distribution of their goods throughout West Africa to local traders, the Dyula. The Dyula are a class, or caste, of African merchants from the Sahel, savanna, and forests of the West African coast. They were not Arabs or Berbers and were not involved in the trans-Saharan trade, but they controlled the commerce across the savanna plains, east and west, and south through the rainforest to the coast of West Africa. They were nominally Muslim, having dealt with Berber and Arab merchants from North Africa, but their primary objective was trade, which was best accomplished for generations by intermarriage and observance of local customs, the traditional religions, and cultivating the goodwill of the non-Muslim chiefs in order to do business. During the centuries, the Dyula established elaborate commercial networks based on shared ethnicity—Malinke, Bambara, or Soninke. They brought the gold from the mines on the upper Niger to the commercial centers downstream, where it was exchanged for goods from the Mediterranean world. They also brought the kola nut, which grows on the Cola Nitida tree in the forests of West Africa. It contains caffeine and is widely used and accepted by Muslims as a mild stimulant that invariably accompanies social occasions throughout West Africa, the Sahara, and the Maghrib. The Dyula were the merchants who had the local resources and transport to invest in the commodities of the trans-Saharan trade, which they distributed throughout West Africa in alliance with the political authorities.

Historically—in Asia, Europe, and Africa—religion has been inextricably intertwined with kingship. Every traditional African religion required ritual specialists to perform the revered ceremonies for ancestors and to interpret the wishes of the gods according to custom. They gave legitimacy to economic and political power. The Dyula exploited these traditional religions, particularly at the local level, to advance their commercial interests. The Muslim merchants from the north, however, carried the Quran to proselytize Islam among those practicing the traditional religions whom they regarded as infidels, unbelieving *kafirin*. The African political authorities, however, sought the wealth from the goods of the Maghrib to enhance their power and legitimacy by embracing a religion that would transcend their parochial traditional rituals and bind them to peoples far beyond the western Sudan. In the empires of the plains, Islam thus became a court religion, the result of the relationship between Muslim merchants of the trans-Saharan trade and the ruling African elite with whom they had to negotiate their commercial transactions. Not surprisingly, the monarch and his nobles became by custom, wealth, and religion increasingly isolated from the countryside and villages, where the cultivators and herdsmen of the western Sudan were quite content to worship with all the African religious ritual and ceremony, to demonstrate respect for the ancestors, and to placate the African gods to ensure individual and social prosperity that created a pervasive tension between Islam and the traditional African religions—each competing for the allegiance of the respective followers. Moreover, each of these Sudanic empires was plagued by the problem of succession so common in Islamic societies, for there was no tradition of primogeniture, and the practice of multiple wives and concubines produced large numbers of contenders for the throne who were supported by ambitious mothers and by rival factions of the nobility. Each of these empires of the plains also had to cope with the perennial and piratical *razzias*, raids, by the Tuareg of the Sahara from the beginning of the trans-Saharan trade to the present day.

Although there were numerous lesser Sudan states during the thousand of years before the French conquest of the western Sudan, there were only a few that are remembered as "empires"—Ghana (700-1240), Mali (1235–1599), Songhai (1464–1591), and Kanem-Bornu (1075–1846). Ghana, the oldest Sudanic empire, was named after its

EMPIRES OF THE PLAINS

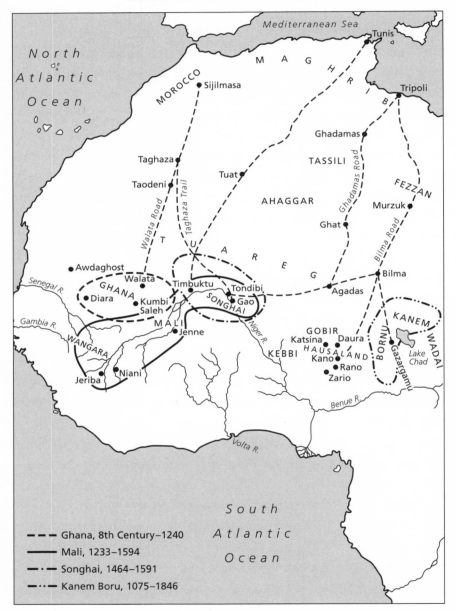

ruler, the Ghana, and his "land of gold" of the Soninke people who were farmers, fishermen, and herdsmen. They provided the basic agricultural and pastoral resources of the state but had little contact with the mercantile community who paid the taxes on the gold and salt trade that provided the wealth for the imperial court. In 1076 the Berber Almoravids sacked the Soninke capital, Kumbi Saleh. Although the Ghana recovered his independence, the empire dissolved into rival chieftaincies, political instability, and economic depression until Sundiata, the Mansa of Mali, destroyed the capital in 1240. As the Mansa, Sundiata, the "Lord Lion," forged the religious and secular ideology of the Malinke people to become master of the land and the traditional religions, as well as the guardian of the ancestors. Sundiata and the Mansas who succeeded him understood how to exploit the agricultural resources of the Malinke and their subject peoples, manipulate the gold and salt trade, and by conversion to Islam employ the new religion to expand the empire of Mali throughout the middle Niger Valley by the fourteenth century. The very symbol of the power, wealth, and greatness of Mali was the famous pilgrimage, the hajj, of Mansa Musa (1312–1337) to Mecca in 1324–1325 accompanied by a hundred camels laded with gold, which created consternation, envy, and respect in both the European and Islamic worlds. He established cultural and economic relationships with the Arabs, whose scholars returned to Mali with him. One of them, Ishal al-Tuedjin (al-Sahili), became the principal architect for the famous mosques at Gao, Timbuktu, and the capital of Mali, Niani. Overextended, raided by predatory Tuaregs, and torn by internecine strife at court, usually over succession, by the middle of the sixteenth century the disintegration of the empire was confirmed when the Songhai sacked Niani in 1545–1546.

The Songhai are unique in the long history of the empires of the plains. They are descended from the Sorko fishermen, whose mastery of the Niger controlled the trade across and along the 1,200 miles of

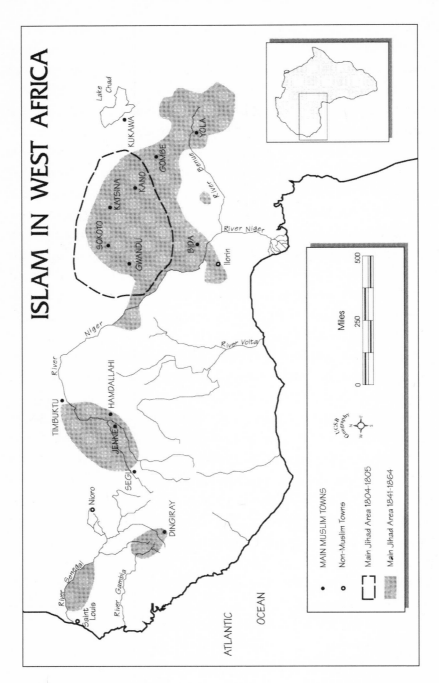

ISLAM IN WEST AFRICA

Lake Chad

KUKAWA

YOLA

GOMBE

KATSINA   KANO

River Benue

SOKOTO

GWANDU   BIDA

Ilorin

River Niger

Niger

River Niger

River Voltar

TIMBUKTU   HAMDALLAHI

River

JENNE

SEGU

Nioro

DINGIRAY

River Senegal

River Gambia

Saint Louis

ATLANTIC

OCEAN

USSR
Geography

N
W   E
S

Miles

0   250   500

• MAIN MUSLIM TOWNS

○ Non-Muslim Towns

⌐⌐⌐ Main Jihad Area 1804–1805

▓ Main Jihad Area 1841–1864

the great bend in the river from its middle delta to the rapids at Bussa. The riverine world of the Songhai distinguished them from the farmers and herdsmen on its banks, as did their speech. Both the Soninke of Ghana and the Malinke of Mali, not to mention the Fulbe, Mossi, Serer, Wolof, and other West African peoples, spoke languages of the Niger-Congo linguistic family. Songhai, however, was a language related not to the peoples who surrounded them but to those speaking Nilo-Saharan languages living far away in the Sahara, the Upper Nile basin, and East Africa. Under a warrior king, Sunni Ali Ber (1464–1492), the Songhai replaced Mali with an empire extending along the whole of the middle Niger from the Songhai capital, Gao, in the east to the great commercial emporium of Jenne in the west. Upon the death of Sunni Ali in 1492, one of his generals, Muhammad Ture (r. 1493–1528), seized control of the state, taking the title of Askiya and founding a new dynasty that lasted until 1592. Like Mansa Musa, he made the hajj to Mecca in 1496–1497, but his rule and subsequent Askiyas were compromised by the historic problem of succession that produced internal strife, Tuareg raiders. His rule ended when the sultan of Morocco, Mawlay Ahmad al-Mansur (1578–1603), invaded Songhai with an army of some 4,000 musketeers with cannons who crossed the Sahara Desert and routed 20,000 spear-carrying swordsmen of the Songhai army at Tondibi thirty miles north of Gao on March 12, 1591. The western Sudan had to await an Islamic revival in the nineteenth century to rebuild its states, at a time when the trans-Saharan trade and political stability had moved eastward to the central Sudan and the empire of Kanem-Bornu.

The empire of Kanem-Bornu was farther east, older, and more enduring than the empires of the Niger. At the end of the eleventh century, the Zaghawa, who live northeast of Lake Chad and speak a Nilo-Saharan language, were united under Humai ibn Salamna (ca. 1075–1086), who founded the Kingdom of Kanem at his capital,

Njimi, with an Islamic court. He took the title of Mai as head of the Saifawa dynasty, which lasted for 771 years, the longest continuous dynasty in recorded history. During the reign of Mai Dunama Dabalemi ibn Salma (r. 1221–1259), Kanem reached the apogee of its power throughout the central Sudan, after which the kingdom slipped into decay from internecine struggles over succession and debilitating raids by the Tuareg and the Bulala, Nilo-Saharan speakers from the eastern savanna of the Nile basin. In 1370 the Bulala captured Njimi, driving the rulers of the Saifawa dynasty to seek refuge west of Lake Chad in Bornu. Here in the fifteenth century, Mai Ali Gaji ibn Dunama (ca. 1476–1503) reasserted his authority over Bornu, built a fortified capital at Birni Gazargamu, and defeated the Bulala in Kanem. Thereafter, Bornu expanded during the sixteenth century under a succession of able Mai, the greatest of whom was Idris Alawma (ca. 1571–1603), who consolidated the internal administration of the state, expanded the empire and particularly its trans-Saharan trade, stabilized the turbulent Bulala frontier in the east, and encouraged the spread of Islam. Faced with pervasive Fulbe immigrants from the western Sudan, drought, famine, and the importation of firearms across the Sahara, which accelerated the ferocity of warfare, the Saifawa dynasty slowly disintegrated, but the Mai managed to rule their diminishing domain until incorporated into the emerging Kingdom of Wadai and the death of the last Mai in 1846.

East Africa Coast and the Indian Ocean World

On the East Africa coast, long-distance trade over the waters of the Indian Ocean made possible the exchange of commodities between the city-states of the East African coast and southern Arabia, the Persian Gulf, and the Indian subcontinent by dhows that plied the Sabaean Lane, named after the Kingdom of Saba in southern Arabia.

The merchandise for trade in the great market towns were much the same—gold, ivory, perfumes, exotic woods, and slaves from East Africa in return for cloth, porcelain, salt, and hardware from Asia. This ancient long-distance trade was made possible by wind and sea. From November until March, the monsoon winds of the Indian Ocean blow dry and steady from the northeast out of central Asia, assisted by the central Indian Ocean current (the Equatorial Current) that strikes Somalia and turns south to provide a well-defined seaway down the East African coast. During the winter months, the merchants brought goods out of Asia to exchange them for those of Africa and to enjoy the hospitality and intercourse with the Azanians, the inhabitants of the coast in the first millennium C.E. who were eager to sell their African merchandise. In May the monsoon reverses its direction. Until October the winds blow moist and steady from the southwest to fill the lateen sails of the dhows and to add to the powerful flow of the central Indian Ocean current, which enabled them to reach Asia from East African ports in thirty days. These commercial transactions were facilitated by a symbiotic and complex network of intercoastal petty African traders in their catamarans bringing goods and supplies from the hundreds of lagoons, creeks, and reefs for the ocean-going dhows beached or anchored in the harbors of major market towns.

Who were these incomers from Asia? There were the Indonesians who settled in Madagascar between the second and fourth centuries, bringing with them the banana. Some came from China as early as the seventh century, and between 1405 and 1433 Chinese merchant fleets were conspicuous in the trade across the Indian Ocean. Official relations were established between the Ming court in Beijing and officials on the East African ports of call at Mogadishu, Malindi, Mombasa, and Kilwa. In 1415 a delegation from Malindi arrived in the Chinese capital with a magnificent giraffe for the Ming emperor, which created a sensation in the capital. Later, however, the internal

isolation of the Ming dynasty (1368–1644) ended the Chinese connection with East Africa. The most frequent visitors were Arabs from
southern Arabia and Persians from their gulf. Arabs from the Yemen,
Hadhramaut, and Oman had come to the East African coast centuries before Christ and Muhammad, but they did not establish permanent settlements until the eighteenth century. The Persian influence originated, according to the mythology of the coast, in Shiraz in
southwestern Persia, but most Arab and Persian settlers arrived in
East Africa in the seventeenth century.

City-States of the African Coast

The many small states scattered on the long coasts of Africa facing
the Indian and Atlantic Ocean worlds evolved by the nature of oceanic trade into city-states rather than empires of the plains or the large
kingdoms that developed on the savanna grasslands of the interior.
Most of them had common characteristics that differentiated them
from those states beyond the coast. Each was fiercely independent,
partly to protect its share of the transoceanic trade, partly because its
citizens proudly enjoyed managing their own affairs. Each looked to
the ocean and had no territorial ambitions in the interior, whose environment and people they regarded as hostile. Moreover, there was no
need to blaze a trail into the interior when its inhabitants were only
too eager to carry the material and march the human wealth of
Africa to the coast. It was much safer and satisfying for the men and
women of these city-states to play the role of intermediaries, buying
and selling and facilitating the transshipment of goods and slaves at
a considerable profit. Commerce, of course, dominated life in the
African city-state, whose inhabitants, however, had to be fed from the
farms and plantations, mostly worked by slaves, that surrounded the
city walls. Nonetheless, the import of foodstuffs did not make them

completely dependent upon local agriculture, as were the kingdoms of the interior. Society in each city-state was highly stratified, from the slaves at the bottom to the middle-class freemen, merchants, and artisans, culminating in the notables at the top. Most of these coastal city-states had councils that governed the terms of trade and public policy. These councils were usually dominated by the heads of one of more of the dynastic families that arose to political and social prominence through their commercial acumen. Unlike the empires and kingdoms of the interior, the city-states did not require a large army, for they were not interested in territorial expansion and depended for defense upon their landward walls and the open sea rather than on a large, unproductive, and all-consuming military force that would be an unnecessary burden on the success of trade and commerce.

SWAHILI

In the seventh century these same traders from southern Arabia, who had been coming to the East African coast for centuries, now brought with them Islam, which had a powerful influence on the Africans of the coast, who sometime before the eighteenth century became known as Swahili, the People of the Coast, from the Arabic *sahil* (shore). Before the emergence of the Swahili, Islam had forged among the maritime coastal people a common identity through intermingling, intermarriage, and interbreeding of a multicultural society. Islam gave literacy to their language, KiSwahili, an African language of the Benue-Congo branch of the larger Niger-Congo family. The term "Swahili" and Swahili culture both became a reality when KiSwahili evolved as the commercial and cultural language. The monotheism of Islam instilled in the Swahili the belief they were a special chosen people, which their wealth appeared to confirm, and immune from the spiritual chaos of traditional religions with many gods. Moreover, the Swahili looked east across the calm waters of the Indian Ocean to prosper from their historic commercial relations with Asia rather than

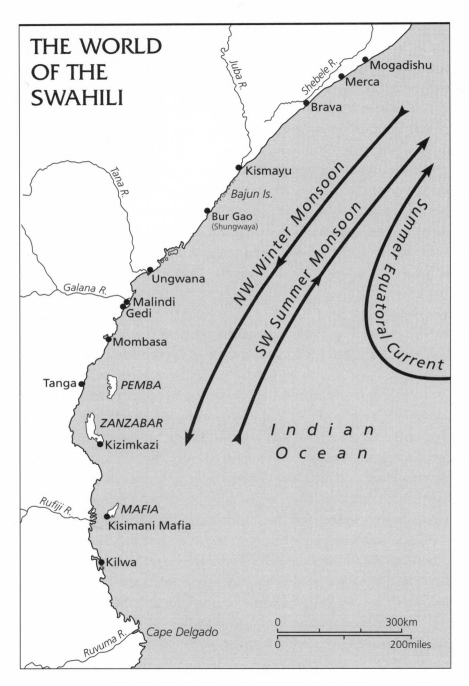

THE WORLD
OF THE
SWAHILI

Juba R.

Shebele R.

● Mogadishu

● Merca

● Brava

● Kismayu

Bajun Is.

● Bur Gao
(Shungwaya)

Tana R.

Galana R.

● Ungwana

● Malindi
Gedi

● Mombasa

Tanga ●

⟩ *PEMBA*

ZANZABAR

● Kizimkazi

Rufiji R.

● *MAFIA*
Kisimani Mafia

● Kilwa

Cape Delgado

Ruvuma R.

NW Winter Monsoon

SW Summer Monsoon

Summer Equatoral Current

I n d i a n
O c e a n

0 ⊢―――――⊣ 300km

0 ⊢―――――⊣ 200miles

west to the little-known interior of the African continent, which they scrupulously avoided if possible. Islam linked them to this international world of Arabs, Persians, Somalis, and the Muslims of India, Indonesia, and the Orient, with whom they carried on extensive trade. Such trade led to personal prosperity, enabling them to support the development of their distinctive culture.

The principal Swahili trading towns were Shanga, Pate, and Lamu in the north; Malindi and Mombasa on the central coast; and Kilwa in the south. Local Swahili artisans fashioned pottery for their kitchens, but the trading elite used porcelain from China for dinner and decoration in their houses, in mosques, and on tombs. Glassware from the Netherlands, the Levant, and southern Arabia was in great demand for the household, as was iron from India and copper from Persia for hardware, weapons, and jewelry. These precious imports were exchanged for elaborate furniture and handsome doors of inlaid ebony and ivory and the more standard African commodities—ivory, slaves, ambergris, copal, spices, leopard skins, tortoise shell, pearls, and particularly gold. The gold came from the shallow mines of Great Zimbabwe in central Africa and was carried to the coast at Sofala and then north by sea to Kilwa.

Swahili society was highly stratified into those who controlled the wealth from the Indian Ocean trade and those who supplied the goods for export. The ruling class, patricians, were the wealthy merchants. They were African Muslims who claimed Arab or Persian ancestry for religious and social legitimacy and convenience in commerce. They built ornate, multiroomed stone houses with baths and internal pit-toilets and clad their women in silk and cotton robes bedecked with elaborate gold jewelry. They ate Swahili cuisine on porcelain dishes from China and Persia and were patrons of the arts, particularly Swahili poetry written in Arabic script, regarded as the epitome of aesthetic expression. The literacy of the Swahili elite was an essential instrument in commerce that to them also confirmed their superiority over slaves brought from the African interior and their nonliterate, non-Muslim neighbors, the Mijikenda, with whom they met in the market and upon whom they relied for mutual defense but seldom married. The affairs of the community—internal order, Indian Ocean traders, and religious and legal matters—were the responsibility of the leading patrician families, whose officials were hereditary but from which the most talented were selected to preserve the influence and position of the family.

Some Swahili settlements—Kilwa ca. 800, Pate ca. 900, Mombasa ca. 1000—began as mud, wood, and thatch huts as early as the end of the first millennium of the Christian era. These had evolved into stone buildings by the twelfth century, whose construction continued for the next 700 years. The great era of stonework at Kilwa—mosques, palaces, harbors, and public baths—was in the fifteenth and sixteenth centuries. These stone structures may have found their inspiration from wealthy Muslim merchants familiar with Arabia or Persia, but the architectural plans were indigenous to the coast, and those who came with the resources to build adopted local designs suitable to the environment of the East African shore.

The patricians may have supplied the wealth, but the less prosperous Swahili built the towns. These Swahili came from families that cultivated the fields outside the walls and supplied the artisans and sailors for oceangoing dhows. They were illiterate Muslims with no claim to Arab or Persian ancestry, but they comprised the overwhelming number of inhabitants of the Swahili commercial city living in mud, wood, and thatch huts or occasionally single-room stone houses surrounding the more pretentious stone structures of the patricians or spread out among the fields beyond the city walls.

Scattered along the length of the East African coast between the stone-walled cities were the more humble Swahili towns of the countryside. They varied in size and were separated by several miles of fertile land tilled by shifting cultivation. Their inhabitants lived in mud-

and-wattle homes clustered together, divided by streets and alleyways of sand and by gardens (*shamba*) with coconut palms, mango, and citrus that produced fruit, oil, and wood. In the center of the town was the market square, with mosque, small shops, coffeehouses, and places for washing.

Slaves have been exported from East Africa for 2,000 years, but many remained on the coast. Every member of the patrician class had slaves, the wealthier having large numbers. The Swahili, however, made a distinction between slaves for export and slaves for domestic and local use. Those shipped overseas were regarded as chattels to be used as animals, but those who were kept on the coast were divided into recognized categories of servitude from the lowest laborer to the trusted retainer. Female slaves were used as domestics, field hands, and concubines for the owner. Even if freed, which was frequent, particularly upon the death of the owner, former slaves could never become a full member of Swahili society. Upon the death of the slave, the slave's corpse had the same status as an animal carcass thrown into a pit.

The long-distance and ancient trade spanning the Indian Ocean over two millennia enabled the Bantu African societies of the East African coast to exchange the goods from the deepest interior for those from Asia. This transfer of commodities required technological and navigational skills to sail the seas and commercial acumen to barter in the marketplace. Not all were successful, but those who possessed the nautical and commercial skills prospered. Their wealth enabled them to pursue arts and letters, build public works, and construct the mosques for Islam, all of which defined their cultural unity in the competitive commercial world of the East African city-states.

NIGER DELTA AND THE IGBO

The great delta of the Niger River is a vast labyrinth of creeks, rivers, swamps, and islands extending 300 miles from the Benin River in the east to the Cross River in the west. Its inhabitants in the past were fisherfolk, the Ijo, who lived in relative isolation disrupted only by those who came by canoe to visit, settle, or trade. In the sixteenth century, life in the delta began to change with the arrival of the European sea-merchants, who found in the maze of estuaries facing the ocean ample anchorage denied them on the surf-swept beaches of the African coast to the west. Trade transformed the delta. Newcomers paddled into its rivers from the north—Igbo, Edo, Jekri, Ibibio, Efik—to position themselves in strategic settlements on the navigable estuaries as middlemen between the sea-merchants and the states of the interior. They were known as the People of the Salt Water, Ndu Mili Nnu, protected by the waterways and dense vegetation of the delta from any political or commercial ambitions by their neighbors on the surrounding high ground. In this unique environment, they developed in the seventeenth century institutions to govern themselves to achieve the best advantage in the competitive commerce with the sea-merchants.

In order to exploit the rapidly expanding trade and now having the resources to do so, the delta peoples living in single settlements on the rivers and islands surrounded by protective intricate waterways developed systems of governance for their own city-states. In East Africa, there were the coastal Swahili city-states of Mombasa, Malindi, and Kilwa, among others. On the coast of West Africa, there were the city-states of the Niger Delta and those of the Igbo in the estuaries to the east, whose citizens devised the means to administer law and order and make war and peace in order to promote their prosperity.

Each delta city-state had its own distinct methods of governing. Some had kings elected by the heads of wealthy and prominent families in Bonny, New Calabar, and Warri. Others were republics ruled by the members of political organizations, such as a senate. There was Brass, located at the mouth of the delta river of the same name, and on the Cross River in Old Calabar there were Creek Town, Henshaw

Town, Duke Town, and Obutong. In the city-states of Old Calabar, the Ekpe, or Leopard Association of wealthy men, mostly merchants, ruled the town principally to ensure the flow of peaceful and thereby profitable trade. Anyone was free to join the Ekpe if he or she could afford the exorbitant entry fee that ensured that only those in power represented the interests of the wealthy merchants. The Ekpe regulated the terms of trade with the Europeans and made the rules by which the community was governed by its constituent organizations, known as the House System.

Traditional African societies were based on the clans and lineages of large families, which were not always the most effective organizations to manage a business. Rather than the family firm, the House was a cooperative commercial trading company run not by kinship but by the ability of the head of the House, his immediate family, and a host of assistants, servants, and even slaves, whose status in the company depended on their success to promote its trade rather than on kinship ties or social privilege. The House System evolved throughout the latter half of the eighteenth century as a commercial response to the dramatic increase in the slave trade and was firmly established throughout the delta by the nineteenth century. Some of the Houses, the Pepples of Bonny, for example, became powerful commercial firms well known in Europe and the Americas.

East of the lower Niger River and its delta, the forest continues between the ocean and the savanna grasslands densely populated by the Igbo (Ibo) people since beyond memory. The fertility of its soil and a long tradition of iron working enabled the Igbo to develop their own distinctive culture and way of life during the millennia. The Igbo have been content to govern themselves without powerful chiefs. Spread over a large and fertile land, the Igbo developed differences in language, customs, and ways of living, but these differences could not disrupt the basic unity of the Igbo people, who encompassed a much larger population than several forest states of West Africa. All the

Igbo regulate their community affairs through age-sets to which all men and women belong, and many have political associations whose leaders would take responsibility for the governance of the community. These communities, however, were composed of many individual villages, each of which had its separate local government that decided the affairs of everyday life.

It was popular government in which all the male and occasionally the female members of the village had a say in the local assembly, where matters of common interest were decided. Many Igbo societies had women's associations to represent the interests of women. Among the Nnobi, Igbo patrilineal daughters were organized into the *umu okpu*, the oldest being the leader, to settle disputes in the lineage. All women—wives and daughters—were subject to the decisions of the women's council, the *inyom nnobi*, responsible for the welfare of women and possessing the authority to levy fines against those violating their customary rights. There was an infinite variation in the actual form of these local governments, yet in these freewheeling Igbo societies there were ample opportunities for those with ability and through hard work to produce a rich harvest or demonstrate commercial acumen in their enclaves on the coast uninhibited by the restraints of clans or kings.

Kingdoms of the Forest and Savanna

Like the city-states of the coast, those kingdoms of the interior had many common characteristics, but each in its own way established distinctive institutions. Unlike the coastal city-states, all of the forest and savanna kingdoms of the African interior were more dependent upon the revolution in agriculture and pastoralism, whose success was governed by the geographical environment that determined rainfall, quality of the soil, and the cultivation of edible crops.

Trade, particularly long-distance trade between states and the coast, played an important role in the social stratification of the kingdom, but it was the agricultural produce of its subjects that provided the economic foundations of the state. Many of the kingdoms of the savanna attributed their origins to some mythical or historical figure as the founder that defined the hierarchy of his descendants. As rulers, they sought support from an aristocratic class of notables who owed their wealth to the distribution of land and labor by the monarch, which ensured a more rigid social stratification than in the freewheeling commercial world of the coastal city-states. Traditional religions played a significant role in the political and social life of these kingdoms, for in many instances the ruler was regarded as "divine," whose godlike authority as the chief priest made no distinction between church and state. Each supported the other in the perpetual pursuit of temporal power. Finally, unlike the coastal city-states, the kingdoms of the West African forest states required a large army for expansion and then to preserve what had been conquered while defending the kingdom from rival rulers. The rulers of the central and southern savanna were more disposed to employ their religious and political prestige, rather than armed force, to expand their influence. At first, rulers relied on the nobility and their freemen to fill the ranks of their armies, but when these groups proved to be unreliable or often rebellious, the monarchs increasingly relied on slave troops, whose undivided loyalty would protect the king from nobility scheming to enhance their independence at the expense of the monarchy.

There was also disease that spared neither farmer, herdsman, noble, nor king. Malaria was endemic in the well-watered areas around the lakes. Ulcers, yaws, and intestinal parasites were common. Leprosy and sleeping sickness were prevalent in regions of heavy rainfall. Rodents carried the plague, and a mild strain of smallpox was widespread on the Lake Plateau of East Africa in the fifteenth century. The ravages of disease, however, did not have the same devastating depopulation as the Black Death in North Africa, for its germs failed to cross the interior of East Africa, for the savanna, woodlands, and highlands in the interior were spread over a vast region, the inhabitants of which were relatively few and widely dispersed into villages of cultivators or pastoral herdsmen. There were no urban enclaves, where endemic disease is most destructive. Specialists of traditional healing in East African societies used indigenous medicines from herbs and incantations to cure some of the sick, and the more salubrious climate of the interior of East Africa and polygyny helped to offset the loss of children from disease to produce a modest but steady increase in the population.

State Building in the Interior of East Africa

During the past 2,000 years, the history of the interior of East Africa has been one of migrations from the west and north onto the fertile Lake Plateau surrounding the great lakes of equatorial Africa. The first to arrive were the Bantu-speaking peoples from the plateau on the border between the modern Republics of Cameroon and Nigeria during five centuries (945–525 B.C.E.). They were farmers whose social and political organizations were limited to the homestead and the village. Their numbers were not great, and they settled in a newfound fertile land with abundant rainfall and adopted the banana, which had appeared in eastern Africa in the first centuries of the Christian era from Southeast Asia. This enabled them, with their iron implements, to settle permanently rather than practice shifting cultivation.

During the next 2,000 years, the Bantu settlements restricted the wanderings of the Khosian hunter-gatherers, who drifted south, but the Bantu farmers exchanged crops for the meat and hides of Cushitic herdsmen from Ethiopia. Despite common dependence on agriculture and herding, each of the states of East Africa evolved its own unique characteristics and institutions—the complex ruins of the Cwezi, the stratified hierarchy of the Tutsi, and the Bito clans of the Luo. Sometime in the fifteenth century, the first immigrants from the north, the Cwezi, arrived with their cattle on the Lake Plateau. The Cwezi came and vanished, leaving behind ruins and legends. Their extensive concentric earthworks at Bigo symbolized the evolution of a more centralized political organization, without which their eroded monuments could not have been constructed. They are remembered as real and spiritual intermediaries between the Bantu past and their impending confrontation in the sixteenth century with the two latest waves of pastoral immigrants from the north, the Hima and the Luo.

The Hima, known as Tutsi, also came from the north with their long-horned cattle to establish control of the summits of a thousand hills in modern Rwanda and Burundi, a political and social symbol of their domination of the Bantu Hutu farmers in the valleys below who supported and intermarried with the Tutsi aristocracy. When the Tutsi began state building during the sixteenth century, the Luo left their homeland in the southern Sudan to settle among the Bantu of the northern Lake Plateau, modern Uganda. The Luo were primarily interested in grazing land for their herds among the Bantu farmers of the Lake Plateau, whose crops were complementary and exchanged for milk, meat, and manure from Luo cattle. Such exchanges could best be achieved by political rather than religious control, for which they possessed institutions the Bantu did not. During the next 200 years, their relationships with the Bantu evolved by acceptance and assimilation. The Bantu acknowledged the authority of Luo Bito clan leaders. In return, the Luo accepted their assimilation by the Bantu in speech and customs, which was facilitated by the mutually advantageous economic exchange and intermarriage by which the minority immigrants provided positions of political leadership for an enlarged state while becoming culturally Bantu as they were absorbed by the indigenous majority.

States of the West African Forest

From the Senegambia in the west to Cameroon in the east lies a belt of dense tropical rainforest over 200 miles wide broken by short but deep rivers flowing to the sea. Several of these rivers, collectively known as the oil rivers, make up the maze of the Niger Delta and in the past were famous for their prolific oil palms. Other rivers, such as the Bandama, Volta, Ouémé, and Benin, reach the beaches that extend, with few exceptions, in an unbroken line of coast pounded by heavy surf and laced by an intricate series of lagoons behind and parallel to the long stretches of sand. Behind the lagoons looms the West African forest, which appears from the shore as an impenetrable wall except for the funnel of savanna, the Dahomey Gap, a north-south corridor from the grasslands of the Bilad al-Sudan to the coast of the Bight of Benin that facilitated the flow of people and trade from the interior to the coast. This rainforest has been created by the heavy annual rainfall (50–80 inches) in two seasons, April to July and September to November, when the southwest monsoons sweep out of the south Atlantic Ocean.

Settlement in the rainforest was laborious and slow, for it required heavy work to clear the forest and time to adapt to new crops, the yam, a tuber that flourishes in the rainforest but is unknown in the savanna. Despite the initial difficulties, the penetration of the rainforest by peoples from the north continued gradually but inexorably. By 1000 C.E. villages defined by earthen boundaries had been constructed, while the fields beyond were cleared from the bush with iron implements. The rivers and lagoons provided abundant and high-protein fish supplements to the carbohydrates of the yam. Equatorial agriculture required a collaborative effort, which could only be accomplished by a greater cohesion of community organization than in the open grasslands of the western Sudan. Enclosed residential compounds surrounded the marketplace, beyond which lay belts of farmland and then the wasteland, wild bush, inhabited by evil spirits and heroic hunters. The common core of the village gradually expanded into ministates requiring political and social institutions. During the second millennium of the Christian era, these clusters grew in size as they adapted to equatorial agriculture and resistance to tropical diseases, but the forest inhibited the creation of expansive empires found on the savanna plains to the north. Although these states shared a similar environment, agriculture, culture, myths of origin, and authoritarian rulers, each developed, like the states of eastern Africa, its own distinctive characteristics—the commercial urban centers of the Yoruba; the famous cavalry of Oyo and its powerful council, the Oyo Mesi; the bronze sculptures and cosmopolitan rulers of Benin; and the efficient army and civil service of the Asante.

YORUBA

The Yoruba were a forest farming people with villages, hamlets, and small market towns scattered throughout the bush, but the innovative contribution of the Yoruba to West African civilization was the big town, an urban center for iron smelting, terracotta figures, brass work, cloth weaving, and the capital of the ruler, the Ilú Aládé. These capital towns sustained large populations with similar configurations of the palace, *afin*, at the center from which radiated wards that included temples, shops, and the compounds that comprised the homes of the extended families. They were surrounded by extensive walls; that of Old Oyo was twenty-four-feet high and twenty-four miles in circumference.

The Yoruba attributed their origins to the legendary Oduduwa, who arrived in Ile-Ife as a heroic leader. Oduduwa's sons became kings, and his daughters were the mothers of rulers in collateral states: the Alafin of Oyo's son became the first Oba of Benin; another son was the first Onisabe of Sabe; a daughter bore the first Alaketu of Ketu (in Dahomey); and another daughter gave birth to the first Olowu of Owu. The Yoruba states were bound together into a confederation of the rulers from the big towns under the spiritual and political leadership of the senior Yoruba ruler, the Oni of Ife. Each ruler was autonomous in his state, but he was bound in his relations with neighboring states by elaborate arrangements between the ruling families under the watchful eye of the Oni. Thus the Yoruba towns were ruled by a king, the Oba, whose agents carried out the important decisions of the kingdom made in a council of aristocrats. The self-interest of each, however, undermined the revered tradition that the Yoruba were one large family, and, as in most families, there were intense rivalries that produced intense competition among the Yoruba towns. One of these towns was Oyo.

OYO

Unlike other Yoruba, the inhabitants of Oyo had not migrated from the savanna into the rainforest but had remained in the woods and grasslands on its northern edge. In order to sustain its independence, Oyo depended upon an army of horsemen trained in cavalry warfare whose horses were purchased from the savanna states to the north. Moreover, Oyo was ideally situated at the center of the long-distance north-south trade routes for goods from the rainforest to the large markets in Hausa land to the north and for those goods going east and west to the bustling commercial centers of the trans-Saharan trade at Gao, Timbuktu, and Jenne. By the seventeenth century, the wealth of Oyo was more than sufficient to build a formidable cavalry to defend its independence and expand its political power. By the eighteenth century, Oyo dominated kingdoms from the Volta River in the west to the Niger in the east. Dahomey was incorporated into the empire by the Oyo cavalry, which could ride to the coast through the relatively tsetse-free grasslands of the Dahomey Gap and the Egbado region to secure a firm control of the coastal trade with the Europeans, first at Whydah and later at Ajase (Porto Novo). Alafin Abiodun (1770–1789) reaped the economic resources of rapid growth and profits from the trade in slaves in the latter half of the eighteenth century to control, directly or indirectly, some 7,000 towns that constituted his empire.

The Alafin of Oyo, however, had to listen not only to his council, the Oyo Mesi, but also to his wives and particularly the queen mother, surrounded and supported by titled women of high rank. The queen mother held a powerful position at the court, and her approval was needed to seek an audience with the Alafin. She undoubtedly advised him on matters of state in the cauldron of court intrigue. In the towns of Oyo and Yoruba land, the Iyalade represented the women. She was elected, probably for her personality and ability, with her own insignia of office and a court to adjudicate commercial disputes among the women and their quarrels over the governance of the town. With the expansion of the slave trade in the eighteenth century, these women acquired great wealth in the trade, which made them influential members in their own right in the governance of the Yoruba.

In the latter half of the eighteenth century, local rebellions against the authority of the Alafin erupted, particularly in the rainforest, where the cavalry could not intimidate the insurgents and the Alafin's illiterate representatives at the courts of the subject states could not contain the spread of the rebellion. Without the presence of the military, these agents of the Alafin were reduced to govern an outpost of empire when they could neither read nor write, and no extensive empire in a tropical rainforest could be governed by word of mouth alone. These internal and imperial troubles were exacerbated by the rapid growth of the coastal slave trade, the profits from which the local leaders used to purchase firearms that enabled them to ignore the central authority, which hastened its dissolution. When the trade routes to the coast could no longer be controlled by the Oyo army, the tributary states began to assert themselves by intervening in the internal disputes at the capital between the Oyo Mesi and the Alafin while carrying on their commercial transactions, particularly involving slaves, without interference from his officials. If there was dissent at the capital of the empire, the vassals of the Alafin were only too happy to advance their own independence at the expense of their suzerain. By the second decade of the nineteenth century, the once proud empire of Oyo had been reduced to a minor state of little importance in the northern region of the Yoruba-speaking peoples.

BENIN

The Edo live southeast of the Yoruba on the western fringe of the Niger Delta. They speak Edo (Benin), a language of the Kwa subfamily of Niger-Congo. Like the Yoruba, their beginnings were to be found in the obscure settlements in the rainforest whose inhabitants cleared bush with iron tools as early as the fifth century and supplemented their diet by hunting and fishing. The settlements grew into villages and cultivated areas protected by earthworks. They were governed by institutions of authority and social groups that were connected by trade routes through the rainforest to the markets of other towns, one of which was called Benin. The traditions of Benin recount that sometime in the past, the Edo inhabitants became dissatisfied with their own kings and asked the legendary Yoruba ruler of Ife, Oduduwa, for one of his sons to rule them. He sent Prince Oranmiyan, who inaugurated the political development of Benin sometime before the fourteenth century.

The Edo may have borrowed Yoruba political town organization, but they retained and developed their own distinctive culture, preserved by their skilled artisans using the lost-wax technique in the famous sculptures that celebrate the authority and power of the ruler, the Oba. The Benin bronzes—as they are erroneously called, for they were brass—were not limited to royal sculpture, for there were many brass plaques and metal pictures of warriors and acrobats to adorn the palace of the Oba. Among Western aficionados of African art, these brass sculptures of kings and queens have often regrettably eclipsed the equally artistic styles of figures that were popular with the ordinary folk. This extraordinary flowering of artistic achievement could not have succeeded without the extensive trading network of the Edo- and Yoruba-speaking peoples. Brass cannot be produced without copper, and there is no copper in southern Nigeria. It had to be imported from the western Sudan in exchange for the goods of the rainforest that provided revenue to support the state and its expansion and the surplus to support artists.

In the mid-fifteenth century, Benin accelerated its policy of expansion under the famous warrior Oba, Ewuare (ca. 1450–1480), who organized the state for imperial conquest. He symbolized his rule by a sumptuous palace within whose spacious compound, enclosed by a mighty wall and ditch, were housed the artisans and courtiers. He relied for advice on a state council composed of the palace chiefs, the Uzama, who represented the heads of the powerful families, and the town chiefs, who were the leaders of the craft guilds. Having centralized and secured his authority, he launched thirty years of war upon his neighbors that had achieved, by the time of his death, a West African forest empire extending from the Niger Delta in the east to Dahomey in the west and even incorporating Yoruba towns on its northern frontier.

The golden age of the empire was enjoyed by the successors of Ewuare. In 1504 his grandson, Esigie (1504–1550), succeeded to the throne. Esigie realized that the arrival of the Europeans would dramatically change West African societies and made every effort to maintain good relations with the Portuguese envoys, traders, and missionaries, who responded with glowing accounts of Benin and its ruler. Esigie could speak and read Portuguese, practiced astrology, and presided over an empire of high culture and great wealth. As in Oyo, the queen mother, who produced the first son and heir of the ruling Oba, wielded enormous power, for she presided over a competitive court of the Oba's wives, concubines, and eunuchs who owned and managed their own village estates.

During the latter half of the seventeenth century, frustrated Obas appeared increasingly impotent to reverse the decline of the king's authority and the power of the state. Firearms offered by the European sea-merchants for slaves introduced new opportunities for local leaders to rebel against the Oba's rule. Warfare, local or widespread, produced prisoners readily sold as slaves in return for an ever-increasing number of firearms now in the hands of the Oba's rivals and rebels. The erosion of central authority was not accompanied, however, by economic depression. Benin continued to remain prosperous until the middle of the eighteenth century, relying on the demand for its crafts—weaving and metalwork—agriculture, and slaves. The centuries of social, political, and cultural growth in Benin did not immediately disappear with its imperial decline. Benin just gradually fell apart when the center could no longer hold, symbolized by the styles of artistic sculpture in brass that became crude and belligerent.

ASANTE

The original Asante were Akan farmers who spoke Twi, a language of the Kwa subfamily of Niger-Congo. They lived along the West African coast of the modern Republic of Ghana. Sometime during the seventeenth century, they gradually moved into the interior to settle north of Lake Bosomtwi to farm and trade in gold and kola nuts. Using slaves acquired from the coast, they cut clearings in the rainforest for villages and fields for the cultivation of yams. They built towns between the Pra and the Ofin rivers. Although they called themselves the Asante, they were, in fact, only a loose alliance of Akan settlements in the rainforest that, when threatened, would band together for defense under a common leader.

At the end of the seventeenth century, Osei Tutu (ca. 1695–1717) transformed Asante society and became their legendary hero. With his friend and religious adviser Okomfo (priest) Anokye, Osei Tutu combined spiritual divination with temporal power to forge the Asante Akan into a single strong union symbolized by a golden stool "brought down from the sky" by Okomfo Anokye, which contained the soul of the Asante people. They swore allegiance to it and to their new Asantehene, Osei Tutu, at his capital, Kumasi. Using the sanctity of the stool, Osei Tutu united the Asante by laws defining a common citizenship and responsibilities to serve the state, particularly in the Asante national army. He introduced into the army new methods of organization and fighting, which transformed what had been little more than a militia into an efficient and proficient fighting force. By 1701 the Asante army had conquered the neighboring state of Denkyira, acquiring much booty, but more important, the Asante "window to the sea" was opened. They now had unrestricted contact with the sea-merchants on the coast and particularly with the Dutch at Elmina, whose trade in firearms for gold and slaves enabled the expansion of the Asante empire. Osei Tutu died in 1717, to be succeeded by a line of extraordinary able Asantehenes who built the Asante kingdom into a far-flung empire encompassing all of modern Ghana and much of the Ivory Coast and Togo.

Asantehenes inherited their position by virtue of descent through their mothers, but the men appointed to offices of political power were chosen by patrilineal descent. Although office earned by descent, either through the mother or father within the clan or lineage, was traditional in many African societies, this system of ascription was ill-suited to govern an empire with distant provinces inhabited by non-Asante tributaries, a complex commercial network, and a military machine to defend the empire and collect the revenues on which the central government depended. The strong Asantehenes of the latter half of the eighteenth and early nineteenth centuries relied increasingly on ability and less on birth in the selection of their officials. They wanted men personally devoted above all to the Asantehene and who had demonstrated their achievements in battle, commerce, administration, or diplomacy, whose advancement and promotion in the civil service depended upon merit rather than birth.

The same principle applied to the internal security and administration of the Asante heartland, both of which were designed to guarantee the power of the king. The Ankobia, a special police force, was permanently stationed in the capital, Kumasi, and in major towns under an officer specially appointed by the Asantehene. Its long-serving members consisted of the king's bodyguard, his intelligence agency, and those equipped to prevent or crush rebellion by troublesome tributaries or hereditary Asante chiefs. The Ankobia were complemented by the civil service of able and reliable officials within Asanteland and the outlying conquered territories. Men of humble origins rose to positions of political power as provincial governors or in the central administration at Kumasi. This imperial administration would never have worked successfully without a swift and reliable system of communication through the rainforest and northern savanna. The empire had an extensive road network by which large quantities of trade flowed back and forth from the major commercial cities of the middle Niger to the great European trading forts on the coast. For over a hundred years the Asante dominated government and trade in the center of the West African forest on a scale comparable to the earlier kingdoms of the western Sudan—Mali, Songhai, Kanem-Bornu—and to the east in Benin and Oyo until challenged by the power of Great Britain in the nineteenth century.

States of East-Central Africa

The early history of the east-central African savanna emerges with greater clarity after the immigration into the region of the Bantu-speaking farmers from West Africa; their dispersal into small, isolated communities; and the integration of these communities after 1400. New institutions of government were created by the Luba people of the upper Kasai River valley that were adopted and reformulated by the neighboring Lunda, and the Lunda disseminated these institutions throughout the savanna. The widespread expansion of the Luba-Lunda influence has been corroborated by the many savanna states that have claimed descent from Lunda origins. Regardless of the historical validity of such claims, the prevalence of Lunda cultural and political characteristics throughout the savanna confirms the prestige and influence of the Luba-Lunda systems, despite the fact that each of these savanna states acquired its own defining character-istics—the political system of the Luba, the unique succession of the Lunda monarchy, and the complex containment of the Zambezi floodplain by the Lozi.

LUBA

The first archaeological evidence of the Luba state is located at Sanga on the shores of Lake Kisale near the upper Kasai River, a tributary of the Congo, and near the fertile floodplain of the Upemba depression, which offered opportunities for riparian agriculture. The marshes and streams of the depression teemed with fish, and the rivers offered easy transportation for commerce. This diverse economy of fishing, farming, mining, and hunting enabled the population to increase steadily. The fertility of the soils in the valleys and surrounding the lakes encouraged migrant farmers to settle in this region, and from their communities they engaged in trade. An enlarged population soon produced social stratification that created a hierarchy of chiefs in a unitary state sometime before the fourteenth century. During this early era, Luba kings combined existing social institutions with new political concepts to create a dynamic royal institution. The first mythical Luba king was the tyrannical Nkongolo, meaning "rainbow," who was overthrown by his legendary son, Kalal Ilunga, the heroic hunter and founder of the ruling dynasty. Rulers over a relatively large population and wealthy in salt and iron, the Luba kings established a confederation of tributaries who recognized the authority and legitimacy of the dynasty over a wide swath of the eastern savanna. The Luba kings believed that the founding myth endowed a member of the royal clan as the paramount chief, Bulopwe, who was blessed with divine right. All male members of the royal family were expected to assist in the administration of the kingdom as subordinate chiefs loyal to their monarch. His divinity defined his supreme religious role supported by priests, secret societies, and social organizations that probably predated the rise of the monarchy and were used to check the power of the political chiefs.

From the Luba homeland near the Upemba depression, Luba culture and institutions were spread by trade routes linking the rainforest in the north to the copper belt of the southern savanna. The court grew wealthy from tribute exacted from neighboring peoples who had accepted the authority of the Luba kings, but the expansion of Luba power was made possible more by the immense prestige of its ruling dynasty than its military force, which was never very formidable. The extent of Luba influence was constrained, however, by the limited size of the Luba population and the difficulties of travel throughout the central savanna. The prestige of the monarch and his ability to exact tribute from his subjects proportionately diminished with distance from the Luba heartland. To sustain their authority and the allegiance of their tributaries, the Luba kings sent warriors as a last resort to collect tribute from recalcitrant villages. This often failed, but ironically these punitive expeditions played an important role in disseminating the culture and political system of the Luba.

LUNDA

The most profound influence of Luba kingship was among the Lunda chiefdoms to the southwest. The Lunda heartland along the Kasai River possessed few minerals, and its soils were relatively impoverished. The population was not large and consequently was scattered in relatively small chiefdoms. The kingdom of the Lunda first appeared in the Mbuji Mayi River valley during the seventeenth century when a mythical stranger, Cibunda Ilunga (ca. 1600–1630), arrived. A Luba hero, Cibunda Ilunga married the Lunda queen Rweej to establish his dynasty and took the title Mwaant Yav (Lord of the Vipers). He depended, however, on the support of the predynastic Lunda chiefs who, as tax collectors and counselors, became the backbone of the royal administration. Thus, the state evolved into a confederation or commonwealth of chiefdoms paying tribute to the king, who redistributed a portion of his treasury to the provincial chiefs in an exchange that was as much an act of trade as royal largess.

Each new Mwaant Yav was enthroned as the living incarnation of the previous ruler to "become" his successor, thus severing all his existing kinship ties and adopting those of his predecessor to ensure continuity from one Lunda ruler to the next. This produced a durable and powerful system of administration that easily integrated new political communities and resolved the problem of succession that had plagued so many other African states. Perpetual kingship enabled the Lunda system to be grafted onto otherwise unrelated polities, which facilitated the expansion of the nuclear Lunda state to the west into the valleys of the Kasai and Kwango rivers and to the south, along the upper reaches of the Zambezi. Lunda expansion was also facilitated by the increase in long-distance trade across the savanna and by the establishment of flourishing markets from which the Lunda kings extracted their share of the profits. These trading networks extended all the way to the western African coast, from which new prolific food crops from the Americas reached the savanna plains of the interior. Cassava, manioc (*Manihot esculenta*), was introduced from the Amazon by the Portuguese in the sixteenth century and flourished in the Lunda heartlands. It proved durable, nutritious, and relatively easy to grow in the marginal soils of the savanna. When ground, its flour could be stored for months without spoiling. It was easily transported and was a valued commodity for exchange in the marketplace, providing another catalyst for Lunda expansion and a significant increase in the population of central Africa. Although the prosperous Kingdom of Kazembe near Lake Tanganyika and the states of the Yaka to the west and Pende to the north recognized the Mwaant Yav as suzerain and continued to send a nominal, symbolic tribute to the king, the Lunda rulers retained relatively little influence over their satellite states.

LOZI

Perhaps the most remarkable state within the Lunda sphere of influence was the Lozi kingdom far to the south in the western Zambezi valley, whose floodplain enabled its settlers to fish the river and cultivate the land. Unlike the northern savanna, however, the Zambezi valley contained pockets of grasslands free of the tsetse fly, which permitted the domestication of cattle. The ancestors of the Lozi, known as the Luyi, immigrated into the region during the seventeenth century from the Lunda heartland.

Floodplain agriculture offered new challenges and opportunities to these immigrants. The annual inundation flooded virtually the entire plain and required the construction of mounds for villages above the waters. When the waters receded, the inhabitants would plant in the enriched soil. The leaders who built and maintained the raised villages, constructed the dams and weirs for fishing, and mobilized the labor to cultivate and tend the cattle became the rulers of the floodplain. By the end of the seventeenth century, several powerful chiefs had consolidated their authority under a leader known as the

Litunga, whose preeminent position was acknowledged by his title, "Keeper of the Earth," which enabled him to expand his authority over the chiefs and their people while his raiding warriors brought him tribute. His slaves labored on royal plantations. In between lived the free cultivators and fishermen from whom Lozi officials exacted tribute—foodstuffs from the farmers, fish from those by the waters, and wild game, honey, and iron from the peoples of the woodlands above the floodplain.

States of West-Central Africa

North and west of the Lunda diaspora, in a region bordered by the equatorial rainforest to the north and the Atlantic coast on the west, several states evolved with histories similar to those found on the eastern savanna. One of these states, the Kingdom of Kongo, was the best known and the most powerful in west-central Africa at the time the first Portuguese mariners made landfall on the western African coast in the 1480s. South of Kongo, the coastal state of Ndongo was ruled by the Ngola, whose name is remembered by the modern state of Angola. In the northeast on the edge of the rainforest, the Kuba kingdom carried on vigorous trade and accumulated considerable wealth, which enabled its artists to create their renowned sculptures. These west-central African kingdoms, as well as several similar lesser-known states, developed unique institutions and ideologies in response to the opportunities and constraints offered by their northern savanna and forest environments.

As on the eastern central savanna, west-central Africa consists of enclaves of moist fertility in a relatively dry and barren plain. This region was bounded on the north by the great Congo River, whose tributaries, themselves mighty rivers, fan out to the north, east, and south and whose navigable waterways were the great highways for

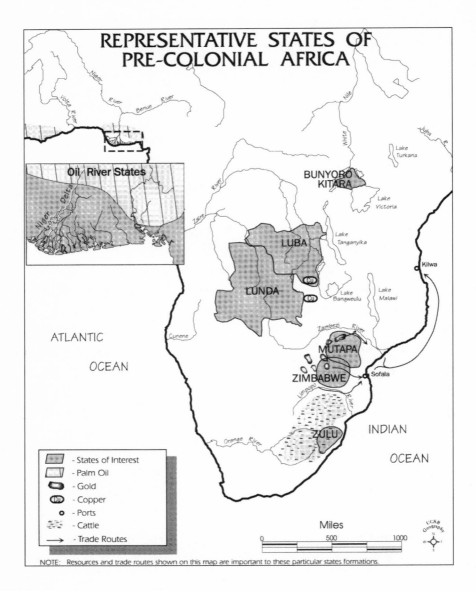

REPRESENTATIVE STATES OF PRE-COLONIAL AFRICA

Oil River States

BUNYORO KITARA

LUBA

LUNDA

MUTAPA

ZIMBABWE

ZULU

ATLANTIC OCEAN

INDIAN OCEAN

Lake Turkana

Lake Victoria

Lake Tanganyika

Lake Bangweulu

Lake Malawi

Kilwa

Sofala

- States of Interest
- Palm Oil
- Gold
- Copper
- Ports
- Cattle
- Trade Routes

Miles
0   500   1000

NOTE: Resources and trade routes shown on this map are important to these particular states formations.

trade and migration. These rivers were filled with fish, and their fertile valleys produced abundant crops for farmers. North of the Congo, the high plateau gives way to the fringes of the equatorial rainforest. South of the river, the terrain divides into three zones that run along a north-south axis. In the far west, the Atlantic coast is a flat, arid plain. To the east, the land rises to a wooded interior plateau. Beyond the highlands lie a higher, more arid plain and the beginning of the central African savanna. The soils of the coast and savanna are particularly poor and for the most part unsuitable for agriculture. However, the plateau and highlands that separate the coastal plain from the savanna are well watered and fertile. The ecological diversity of these regions stimulated economic specialization, and the ease of travel and the transport of goods on the many rivers facilitated local and long-distance trade.

The evolution of complex, stratified societies was, as on the savanna, the result of population growth, technological innovation, and economic specialization. The crucial event in the region, as in all Africa, was the agricultural revolution introduced into all of central Africa by Bantu-speaking farmers, who arrived in the area sometime during the first millennium B.C.E. These early farmers cultivated root crops, such as yams, and other forest crops, such as palm kernels, without the benefit of iron metallurgy. They were soon joined in the region by immigrants from the east who were also members of the Bantu diaspora. These distant eastern cousins brought with them cereal crops, bananas, and, in some places, cattle obtained in eastern Africa that could thrive in the drier regions of the southern plateau.

Like the Bantu on the savannas to the east, the first wave of migrants in west-central Africa settled in those fertile areas most suited to cultivation. Others located on the Atlantic shore, where prolific fishing in the ocean and Congo estuary compensated for the arid conditions of the coastal plain. Later, these fishing communities extracted salt from seawater and briny marshes that was in much demand

and profitably traded for foodstuffs cultivated by the farmers of the interior. In the south near the modern island of Luanda, divers collected the valued *nzimbu* shells (cowries) that became the common currency throughout the region. In the interior, the farmers, who settled on the plateau, in forests, or in fertile river valleys with dependable rainfall, were often separated from one another by large tracts of dry and inhospitable terrain where the hunters and gatherers displaced by the Bantu cultivators still lived. These early settlements of Bantu-speaking peoples were small, isolated communities growing foodstuffs, but as the immigrants adapted to their new environments by utilizing the crops, especially those from the New World, and possessing the iron tools they brought with them, the population increased, the settlements grew larger, and their societies required more complex political organizations in order to take full advantage of their prosperity.

KONGO

When the Portuguese first arrived at the mouth of the Congo River in 1483, the population of the Kingdom of Kongo numbered more than half a million, and the authority of its king, the Mani Kongo, was recognized 200 miles into the interior from the Atlantic shore. The origins of the Kongo kingdom are situated in a small, environmentally attractive niche north of the Congo River called Vungu. Here peoples who shared a common language (KiKongo) and similar culture raised vegetables, yams, and bananas. The Kongo heartland contained deposits of high-grade iron ore and copper, the latter a rare metal in great demand for making jewelry. The early leaders of the Kongo communities were master smiths. As on the savanna to the east, iron working produced a technological revolution among the farmers of west-central Africa. Those who mastered the secrets of its manufacture could exercise control over the weapons, tools, and ornaments that were the principal source of power and wealth among these farming and fishing communities. Traders exchanged the iron of Vungu throughout the region for salt, fish, cloth made from raffia palm, and other goods peculiar to the diverse regions of a growing trade network. One of the traditions of origin claims that the first rulers of the Kongo crossed the Congo River, where they came in contact with Mbundu peoples settled on the interior plateau of modern Angola. Here these KiKongo-speaking immigrants gained a position of influence among the Mbundu lineages, perhaps by intermarriage, possibly through conquest. By their mastery of iron smelting and their control of the copper trade, the Kongo immigrants attracted merchants and supporters to their town of Mbanza Kongo and firmly established themselves as the dominant political and commercial people throughout the region.

The evolution of the Kongo monarchy began with the need for a paramount chief who could provide protection for the mining, manufacture, and trade of copper and iron goods and to keep the peace among the several powerful lineages that controlled them. The new ruler took the title of Mani Kongo, king of the Kongo, and established his dynasty surrounded by an extensive royal family from whom were chosen the key officials at the royal court. The founding of the kingdom was probably in the early fifteenth century. The capital, Mbanza Kongo, was dominated by an aristocracy related and presumably loyal to the Mani Kongo from whom were selected those nobles ordered to conquer the hinterland. In the name of the king, they seized control of the fishing, salt, and seashell industries on the coast and brought the farming and fishing communities in the mountains to the north and east under the rule of the Mani Kongo. They became provincial governors and exacted tribute from the subject peoples, retaining a percentage for themselves and passing along a substantial share to the Mani Kongo and his royal court. In order to increase their own wealth and power, these provincial leaders had every incentive to expand and conquer neighboring peoples on behalf of the Mani Kongo. Since these governors raised their own armies and arranged their own tribute, they exercised a significant degree of autonomy from their ruler at Mbanza Kongo, but when the Portuguese first arrived the Mani Kongo was widely recognized as the supreme ruler over a vast territory stretching from the Atlantic Ocean several hundred miles into the interior. Although the kingdom was sharply divided by social stratification between the nobility, free men, and slaves, its strength resided in the free farmers and merchants and declined when the expansion of the slave trade turned free farmers into slaves or owners of slaves.

NDONGO

South of the Kingdom of Kongo, Mbundu farmers developed their own state that came to be called Ndongo. Here in the central Angolan highlands, several clans came to be recognized as the first and therefore rightful custodians of the land. These farmers experienced recurrent drought on the plateau, and consequently priests responsible in their shrines for the falling rain and abundant fertility shaped the evolution of political institutions. In many places, the invocations of the priests were represented by carved objects called Lunga. The symbolism of the Lunga defined a spiritual and political identity that was connected to a fixed territory, such as a riverbed or an outcrop. The custodians of the Lunga shrines, which were usually situated in the most fertile and well-watered lands, could employ their religious authority to acquire political power by demanding tribute, taxes, and support from their religious followers. Early Mbundu political rulers were religious leaders who controlled the regimen of the agricultural season and received their resources from its harvest. The religious monopoly of authority by the priests was challenged by the ironsmiths and their masters, who arrived among the Mbundu from the north. These were the same craftsmen whose secret societies enabled them to produce and share technologies that dramatically changed the waging of war and the cultivation of the soil. Their authority was represented by the ironsmiths called Ngola. Unlike the Lunga, the Ngola were mobile, for they had no shrines, only easily transportable iron-smelting furnaces, and their secretive powers produced tangible results that challenged the local, sedentary religious authority of the old order. Eventually, the prestige of these master smiths came to supersede that of the original Lunga-based clans, and their chief smith took the name Ngola a kiluanje, the conquering Ngola, which the Portuguese transcribed as Angola.

States of Southern Africa

Geography and climate have had a profound influence on the human experience in southern Africa. The high veld is a plateau of 3,000 to 5,000 feet in height that rises to a chain of mountains with various names, but in the aggregate it is called the Great Escarpment and separates the interior plateau from the coastal plain of the eastern African coast. This unbroken procession of ridges reaches its height in the peaks of the Drakensberg Mountains (9,000 to 11,000 feet). The fertile coastal belt between the Great Escarpment and the Indian Ocean sweeps around southern Africa, ranging from 30 to 150 miles wide. There it is commonly known as the low veld, as the mountain ridges, now no more than 3,000 feet above sea level, merge with the interior plateau. The rolling grasslands of the high veld are broken by isolated outcrops, kopjes, and rocky ridges, such as the Witwatersrand, which are watersheds for the rivers of the plateau and the repository of gold and precious stones. The vast grassland plateau slopes gently to the west, becoming ever-more dry where it turns into the scrublands of the Great Karoo and ultimately into the sands of the Kalahari Desert. Rainfall and water have determined life in southern Africa since the first hominoids began to roam its savanna grasslands. The coastal plain and interior highlands get rain from the annual monsoon that blows in from the Indian Ocean each November. As the rain clouds move westward across the plain, they rise to meet the ridges of the Great Escarpment and the peaks of the Drakensberg Mountains, forming a rain shadow that creates an increasingly arid expanse as the carrying capacity of the moisture-laden Indian Ocean cumulus steadily diminishes on their westward course over the Karoo to die in the Kalahari.

About 300 C.E. new communities appeared on the fertile eastern coast of southern Africa separated from the cape by hundreds of miles of semiarid grasslands and deserts. These Africans, unlike the Khosian people, made their own iron tools and weapons. They lived in agricultural settlements, where they grew a variety of food crops, including sorghum, beans, millet, and cowpeas, but they also raised goats, sheep, and cattle. These agro-pastoralists even hunted and gathered and fished in order to supplement their diet and livelihood, for they were, in fact, the vanguard of the Bantu migration from the Great Lakes region of East Africa and spoke languages that have their roots in the Bantu linguistics of the East African Lake Plateau.

The success and growing dependence of these Bantu-speaking agro-pastoralists on cattle produced a dramatic transformation of their communities. Between 700 and 1200 their settlement sites became ever-more crowded as communities packed together to pro-tect their cattle from predators. Some of these cattlemen cultivators moved away from the richest farmlands to less attractive, even stony, hilltop settlements better situated for defense and keeping watch over their herds. This explosion in cattle-keeping decisively changed almost every aspect of their social and cultural life. Caring for the cat-tle became the sole responsibility of men, and women were expected to undertake the more arduous task of raising crops in addition to their domestic and maternal duties. Cattle became the standard of wealth and consequently the only acceptable currency by which a man could purchase wives. The men rich in cattle were able to establish large families, social standing in the community, and political authority over those less well endowed. With large herds, they could loan cattle to younger, poorer men in exchange for support and services. Ownership of cattle encouraged the emergence of paternalistic, socially stratified communities in which labor and authority were severely divided between men and women and between those who were rich in cattle and those who were not.

MAPUNGUBWE

The socially and economically stratified communities of southern Africa were involved in local and long-distance trade and were scattered all over southern Africa after 1000. By 900 one of the earliest settlements located in the Toutswemogola region of Botswana on the edge of the Kalahari Desert numbered over 1,000 inhabitants. On a small hill overlooking the high veld, the Toutswe herders could tend their cattle and watch for thieves and predators. Although Toutswemogola was abandoned in the thirteenth century, it had exchanged goods for over a century with a similar settlement to the east at Mapungubwe Hill. Here near the confluence of the Limpopo and Shashi rivers, the nearby settlement of Bambandyanalo, founded sometime around 1000, was abandoned at the beginning of the thirteenth century in favor of the high, steep-sided sandstone hill of Mapungubwe. Unlike the more arid climate around Toutswemogola suited only for grazing and marginal agriculture, the valley of the Limpopo possessed rich, well-watered alluvial soils that permitted both abundant cultivation and the raising of livestock. Mapungubwe artisans produced pottery, ivory, and bone carvings, and its smiths created iron tools and weapons. By 1200 its merchants sent gold and ivory to the coastal towns in exchange for the glass beads, porcelain, and cloth of the Indian Ocean trade. Gold was melted and poured into molds to make jewelry and ornamentation for the elites, including a small golden rhinoceros dated to the thirteenth century, the earliest evidence of gold working in southern Africa.

Long-distance trade introduced the elites in settlements like Toutswemogola and Mapungubwe to previously unknown luxury goods such as beads and porcelain that generated disparities of wealth. Those elites who owned and controlled the distribution of these new riches were able to establish their authority in an unprecedented degree over their followers and to fabricate rudimentary political systems. Although cattle and crops remained the fundamental resources of the community, most men could raise several cattle and grow sufficient sorghum and millet to sustain their families and even have a surplus, but the wealth in foreign trade goods was easily monopolized by the few who used their new power to wield political authority. Trade, particularly the long-distance ivory trade, made possible the development of a powerful, centralized polity dominated by an elite ruling class whose authority over their more numerous followers grazing their herds and tilling the soil at the base of the hill was symbolized by the elaborate stone structures on the summit. At the end of the thirteenth century Mapungubwe collapsed.

ZIMBABWE

The decline of Mapungubwe coincided with the rise of Zimbabwe to the north, with its capital at Great Zimbabwe (Cishona, *dzimba dza mabwe*, houses of stone) on the southern edge of the Zimbabwe Plateau. The rise of Zimbabwe has been attributed to its abundance of gold by which Great Zimbabwe was able to seize control of the Indian Ocean trade and the wealth and political authority it produced. The ivory of Mapungubwe could not compete with the gold of Zimbabwe in the international markets on the coast, and Mapungubwe never recovered from its loss. The original inhabitants of Great Zimbabwe practiced the mixed economy of agriculture and pastoralism that characterized most of the communities throughout southern Africa. Zimbabwe as a state emerged from its settled agro-pastoralist communities during the thirteenth century with its center on a hill rising 260 feet above the plain. The southeastern region of the Zimbabwe Plateau was well watered, with fertile soil for cultivation and ample pastureland for cattle free of the tsetse fly. Located near the Sabi River, Great Zimbabwe was situated on an important trade route linking the gold fields of the interior with the important East African coastal emporium of Kilwa. The Africans of Great Zimbabwe became wealthy in cattle and gold and built a circumscribed empire that came to dominate the Zimbabwe Plateau for 200 years. By the twelfth century, Great Zimbabwe was trading gold and ivory in exchange for a variety of exotic wares from the coast, including Chinese porcelains and beads from India. Control of these scarce goods enabled the elite to amass wealth and authority and to develop a political system that could mobilize the human and material resources of the state to construct the magnificent stone structures that are the monuments of this civilization.

Great Zimbabwe occupies 180 acres, the core of which is a hilltop structure known as the acropolis, a large area enclosed by massive stone walls to the south called the Great Enclosure, and a network of settlements adjacent to and outside the walls. These intimidating walls clearly served no military function, for their construction was so refined that mortar was unnecessary. They must have represented the determination by the ruling class to erect an edifice that symbolized their authority and prestige and the mighty, sacred power of their ruler. The walls were built to shelter the elite in spacious living quarters, surrounded by foreign luxury goods and consuming prodigious amounts of beef. Even more important, however, the walls demonstrated the exclusive social status of those who lived within them. In the eastern enclosure on the hilltop was the meeting place of an exclusive religious cult presided over by the stunning Zimbabwe birds carved in soapstone. In the valley below lived the more modest members of society, huddled in densely packed settlements far removed from the elite lifestyle of their social superiors and the sacred and secular power of their rulers.

Great Zimbabwe was not an isolated city-state but the center of an expansive economic and political network of lesser enclosures on the Zimbabwe Plateau that constituted the core of this empire, which stretched east toward the coast and south across the Limpopo. The more than 300 inhabitants within these walled enclosures, similar in architecture and construction, owed their allegiance to Great Zimbabwe, and some of these city-states appear to have been provincial administrative and commercial towns of the state. Between 1420 and 1450 the ruling class had lost control of the coastal trade, which had sustained their conspicuous lifestyle, and they had to revert to their dependency on the agricultural and pastoral economic foundations of the state at a time when the environmental degradation of Zimbabwe had gradually pushed the agricultural and pastoral productivity of the state into depression. When the Portuguese established trading stations in the Zambezi Valley to the north in the fifteenth century, they diverted the flow of gold and goods from Great Zimbabwe, which encouraged the political fragmentation of the state by its provincial communities. The demise of Great Zimbabwe, however, cannot be attributed solely to its economic and political disintegration, for there had been a steady environmental degradation by deforestation, soil erosion, and overgrazing by its more humble citizens on the plains below the escarpment.

MUTAPA

The Mutapa state (ca. 1450–1760) of the Munhumutapa (king) was a provincial community on the northern edge of the Zimbabwe Plateau in the fertile Mazoe Valley. Here on the slopes of Mount Fura (5,000 feet), the inhabitants built circular stone enclosures of rough walls with loopholes, in contrast to the more stylized stonework of

Great Zimbabwe. According to tradition, a heroic emissary from Great Zimbabwe named Nyatsimbe Mutota appeared in the early fifteenth century and founded a new kingdom. His successors took the title Munhumutapa (Cishona, Ravager of the Lands). The Munhumutapa lived with his extended family, advisers, and religious and military functionaries and ruled over his provincial chiefs, whom the Portuguese called governors. He received his revenue from the coastal trade, agriculture, pastoralism, and mining, which were the economic foundations of this powerful state, as well as from the tribute from his subject peoples. Although the Portuguese first arrived in the sixteenth century, they were content to establish only markets (*feira*), but by the seventeenth century they had gained control over the gold and ivory trade to reduce the Munhumutapa to a Portuguese puppet. Although the Muhumutapa appears to have reasserted his control over his kingdom sometime after 1663 when the Portuguese withdrew from the upper Zambezi, he was unable to recapture the peripheral tributaries or to suppress internal insurrections that forced the state into a steady decline and finally to disappear.

CHAPTER FOUR

Europeans, Slavery, and the Slave Trade

18th centuy print: West Africa

Portuguese Explorations of the West and East African Coasts

Although Africa north of the Sahara and the coasts of the Red Sea and East Africa were well known to the ancient Mediterranean world, Africa south of the desert was not. By the fifteenth century, knowledge of sub-Saharan Africa by informed Europeans was shrouded in myths and distorted by legends. The land was inhabited, they believed, by ferocious peoples with bizarre physical features. Africans were collectively called Ethiopians, a pejorative term having nothing to do with the Ethiopians of northeast Africa. Elephants were one of the few things that were described accurately. From the middle of the sixteenth century, the dramatic "discovery" of Africa by Europeans was made possible by the heroic Portuguese voyages of exploration down and around the African coast begun under the direction of Prince Henry (1394–1460), later known as the Navigator. In the 1430s Henry became aware that the gold and slaves of West Africa carried by camels and marched across the Sahara by Muslim Berbers and Arabs could be diverted to Portuguese merchants reaching the West African coast by sea. As Grand Master of the Order of Christ, he possessed the resources to organize the exploration of the African coast and the way to the Orient. At his residence in Sargas near Cape Vincent, he was determined to "build the best sailing ships afloat" and provide the motives, inspiration, and resources for Portuguese exploration until and after his death in 1460.[1]

The Portuguese had ample reasons in the fifteenth century to launch this remarkable program for the systematic exploration of the western African coast. The Portuguese monarchy had captured the last Muslim stronghold in Portugal in 1249 and in 1385 had stabilized political life under a new dynasty, the House of Avis, isolated on the western coast of Europe with a powerful and suspicious Spain as its neighbor to the east. The gold of Africa would provide the resources to defend the kingdom and finance Portuguese expeditions around Africa to the Indian Ocean in order to divert the wealth of the Orient, controlled by the Arabs of the eastern Mediterranean and North Africa, to the kingdom of Portugal. Moreover, beyond the Sahara Desert lived the non-Muslim West Africans who, perhaps, could be converted to Christianity and enlisted in the crusade against the Muslims, which Portugal had been waging with tenacity for more than a century. And then there was the compelling legend of Prester John, a beleaguered Christian monarch mythically located in Ethiopia whose Christian subjects were defending the faith against the jihad, holy war, of Islam. No Portuguese king, noble, or peasant could resist the religious responsibility to come to the aid of Prester John and his besieged Christians, wherever they might be.

Prince Henry and his captains knew that to traverse the Atlantic required new ships, sophisticated maritime technologies, and great courage. The new ship was the round-bottom caravel, at most sixty feet long and twenty feet wide, with two or three masts with lateen and later square sails that enabled it to tack into the wind and whose shallow draft could easily maneuver around the shoals of the western African coast. Navigation was more difficult. Unlike the Mediterranean, the high seas of the Atlantic required knowing the ship's position east and west (longitude) and north and south (latitude). Not until the eighteenth century could an accurate chronometer, fixed at Greenwich, England, give a horizontal location around the globe. However, the crude sextant of the fifteenth century could determine the angle of the sun on any given day to establish the vertical location of the ship at its latitude. Knowing the ship's position north or south of the equator, the captain could sail into the ocean beyond the shore and then turn at the appropriate latitude to sail east, confident that he would meet the coast of western Africa, but to do so required the captains and crews of these tiny caravels to have faith in their instruments and indomitable personal courage.

In 1442 two captains returned from the West African coast with gold, salt, and ten slaves, and from that year there was no turning back. Since the African trade was a royal monopoly in which the monarchy received 20 percent of the profits, Prince Henry controlled the terms by which Portuguese merchants could engage in African commercial exploration. Driven by commerce, Christianity, and the technological improvements in navigation and ships, after 1444 the pace of exploration rapidly accelerated. Between 1450 and 1458 a dozen ships left Portugal for West Africa to return with a profit of between 50 and 800 percent in gold, slaves, and spices. The Portuguese traders brought cloth, silver, hardware, maize (corn), and horses, which were particularly in great demand, in return for hides, beeswax, fish, and ostrich eggs, which were additions to the principals of trade—gold and slaves.

After Prince Henry the Navigator died in 1460, a wealthy Lisbon merchant, Fernão Gomes, was given exclusive rights to explore and trade in Africa. Fernão Gomes represented a new generation of entrepreneurs who were to capitalize on the vision of Prince Henry, the improvements in maritime technology, and the insatiable European demand for the human and material wealth of Africa. His well-organized expeditions swept along the coast where the Portuguese constructed their great trading fort of São Jorge da Mina, Elmina, the Mine, in 1482, to which the Akan now brought their gold hitherto carried across the Sahara to North Africa. By the fifteenth century the Portuguese sea-borne trade was annually exporting half a ton of bullion to Europe, which financed further Portuguese explorations to the Indian Ocean and the Orient. These were extraordinary accomplishments, for the currents that carried the caravels down the African coast frustrated their return. There was no polar star to guide them. The mists, sandbars, and shoals of the West African coast were treacherous.

Under the command of Diogo Cão (d. 1486), an old associate of Prince Henry, two ships discovered the Nzadi, the great river, which Luis Vaz de Camoëns, in his great epic poem, *The Lusiad*, called Zaire and is known today as the Congo. Diogo Cão erected a *padrão*, a seven-foot stone cross inscribed to God, king, and country, and he established relations with the Mani Kongo, Nzinga Nkuwu, ruler of the Kingdom of Kongo, whose capital was at Mbanza Kongo, thirty miles south of the river. This was the beginning of a long and complicated relationship between Europe and the African kings of Kongo and Angola. In 1485 Diogo Cão returned to try to complete the circumnavigation of Africa. Although he died during this expedition, his last voyage convinced King João II (1481–1495), against the advice from his royal counselors, that the future prosperity of Portugal lie in the expansion of the sea routes to India. Two years later the king ordered Bartolomeu Dias (1450–1500) to complete the circumnavigation of the African continent in search of Prester John and the Indies, which had eluded Diogo Cão. Dias rounded the southern tip of the African continent and on February 3, 1485, made a landfall for freshwater at Cabo de São Bras (Cape St. Blaize, now known as Mossel Bay) before turning back for Portugal. During his voyage, he cast anchor in the great headland he named Cabo de Boa Esperança, the Cape of Good Hope, where another *padrão* was placed. He had confirmed the medieval belief that Africa could indeed be circumnavigated. The way to Prester John and the Indies was now open.

It was another ten years before a major expedition could be launched to complete what Dias had failed to accomplish. On July 8,

1497, a fleet of four caravels departed from Lisbon under the command of Vasco da Gama (1460–1524). In stormy seas, he rounded the Cape of Good Hope, and his three remaining ships sailed up the East African coast on currents and fair winds to encounter the Arab dhows of the Indian Ocean trade, whose pilots had instruments for navigation as good as if not superior to those of the Portuguese. As they proceeded up the Swahili coast, they were entertained by people whose wealth in cloth, gold, and produce surpassed any of the gifts that da Gama had to offer. The Portuguese superiority was in cannons and muskets, not the cloth, gold, or porcelains of the Swahili living on the East African coast. With crusading zeal, the Portuguese bombarded and plundered Mozambique, repelled a Swahili attack at Mombasa, and negotiated with its rival Malindi for a Gujarati pilot and sufficient provisions to reach the port of Calicut in India in the summer of 1498. They returned to Malindi in January 1499 ravaged by scurvy, where da Gama erected his stone *padrão*, which still stands. They then returned with two ships to Portugal, sailing into the Tagus estuary at Lisbon in July and August. It was an epic and heroic journey. Honors were heaped upon da Gama, who had discovered the wealth of East Africa, Asia, and India. Europe, Asia, and particularly Africa would never be the same.

Portuguese explorations had sought to enrich the monarchy and the merchants, promote Christianity, and ultimately to introduce plantation agricultural to meet the insatiable European demand for sugar, which required intensive use of labor supplied by the trade in African slaves. They also introduced diseases from the Old World, however, and crops from the New World that historically had a much greater impact on Africa than European mercantile enterprise or European religion. Disease in Africa was usually carried by resilient members of its rich insect population that multiplied profusely in the tropical environment unchecked by the climatic change of seasons in temperate continents. The tropics have been the home of the greatest diversity of living organisms—animal, mammal, and vegetable—and the parasites that are carried from one host to another. Until the twentieth century, the means of infection remained obscure and treatment more spiritual than medicinal. The diseases were many. One source lists 296 infectious diseases, but there were three that accounted for the most continuous decimation of the African peoples and consequently hindered their ability to populate the vast landmass of the continent—sleeping sickness (trypanosomisis), bilharzias (schistosoma), and the endemic killer, malaria (Italian, *mal'aria*, bad air from swampy vapors near Rome).

The Portuguese, and the English, French, and other Europeans who came after them, carried the diseases of the Old World that were to infect the peoples of Africa and add to their multiplicity of tropical endemic diseases. The virulent variety of smallpox (English, small pockes, "pocke" meaning sac) had been the major killer disease in Europe against which Africans had no natural immunity. As early as 1589, a smallpox epidemic was reported in Mozambique by João dos Santos, and during subsequent centuries epidemics erupted usually during periods of severe drought. From the sixteenth to the nineteenth centuries, epidemics of European smallpox ravaged western Africa, particularly in the equatorial regions of the Kongo in 1560 and Angola between 1625 and 1628. In 1864, 1867, and 1873 the Igbo and others in West Africa were decimated by smallpox; one-quarter of the population of Luanda perished in the epidemic of 1864. Smallpox arrived at Cape Town from Asia with the Dutch in 1713, killing one-quarter of the settlement's population and devastating the Khosian people. Only one in ten is recorded to have survived. The epidemic swept north across the Orange (Gariep) River, and there were extensive outbreaks of smallpox in 1755 and 1767 that proved fatal to unrecorded numbers.

There were other diseases carried out of Europe to which Africans had no natural immunity. Like smallpox, syphilis seems to be indigenous to Africa in a mild form, but with the introduction by Europeans in the sixteenth century of a virulent strain, venereal syphilis became widespread. Typhus and tuberculosis appeared in Africa during the seventeenth century. The desert prevented the pneumonic plague, the Black Death, from advancing into sub-Saharan Africa, but in the seventeenth century it arrived in the Kongo and Angola via the Atlantic slave trade and appeared in Senegal and Guinea in the eighteenth century. Disease was the principal inhibiting factor for the African population to expand at the same rate as humans in more temperate climates, and the arrival of the Europeans contributed new parasites to which Africans were vulnerable.

Ironically, the arrival of the Europeans in the sixteenth century, particularly the Portuguese, introduced the New World crops of great productivity, which enabled Africans to begin a steady increase in their population to fill a relatively empty continent. Today the major foodstuffs in Africa are both seed and root crops as in the past, but they are not indigenous to Africa. Maize (corn) has replaced sorghum as the preferred grain, and cassava (manioc), not the yam, soon became the dominant African tuber food. Maize (*Zea mays*) originated in the coastal regions of Peru and was cultivated for over two millennia in Mexico, from where it reached Spain and was brought to Delagoa Bay in Angola by the Portuguese in the sixteenth century. Maize grows well in humid and sunny weather, and its adoption spread erratically but steadily from southern and central Africa to all the grasslands of the continent by the nineteenth century. Its high yields, twice as many calories as millet and 50 percent more than sorghum, and taste made it the staple, prestigious grain food in Africa. Unlike flowering sorghum, the compact corncob is sheathed, its defense against voracious birds, and corn is easily stored in cribs, compared to the seeds from the sorghum plant, which are kept in fragile baskets. Corn became the standard food for the itinerant trader over long distances.

The cassava plant is only a few feet high, but it produces fat roots of varying length. Cassava (manioc, *Manihot esculenta*) was carried by the Portuguese from the Amazon in Brazil to Africa also, like maize, in the sixteenth century. Transplanted to West Africa and the Congo rainforest, it flourished in the heat, humidity, and poor soils to become the staple tuber crop. Cassava produces 150 percent more calories than maize and, like maize, had spread throughout most of sub-Saharan Africa by the nineteenth century. Its tubers are prolific and low in protein, but they require, like the banana, little land and labor compared to sorghum and maize. Cassava was an efficient food in regions of dense population and could survive drought to become insurance against famine.

These new staples, maize and cassava, that began to change the demography of Africa should not diminish the importance of other New World crops, most of them brought by the Portuguese, that have contributed to the increase in the population of the African continent during the last 400 years. There were beans of all varieties—kidney, lima, navy—that grow well where there is water. Like maize, beans were first domesticated by the Indians of the Americas. Ancient Peruvian pottery inscriptions portray Indians holding beans in one hand and maize in the other to acknowledge their dependence upon them. The Spanish carried beans to the Philippines and Asia. The Portuguese transplanted them to Africa, and other varieties came during the Atlantic slave trade, the lima bean from Brazil. Sweet potatoes were popular and widely grown throughout Africa. Another crop from the Indians in the valleys of the Andes, the potato, found its way to Africa via Florida, Spain, and England in the eighteenth century. Other New World crops were brought to Africa during the Atlantic slave trade. Peanuts, first domesticated from the wild in Brazil and Paraguay, spread northward through Central America and Mexico. The Spanish brought them to Iberia, and the Portuguese introduced them to West Africa in the sixteenth century, where they flourished and spread throughout the continent. The tomato also arrived in Africa from South and Central America along the same route. Peas, sesame, and sugarcane came from Asia carried by Asian and European merchants in the globalization of international trade that followed the Portuguese pioneering voyages of discovery.

Slavery in Africa

Slavery in Africa has been recorded during the past 5,000 years and remains today an institution no longer acceptable but existing in various forms of servile labor. Although it made possible the trade in slaves to other continents, African slavery existed long before slaves became the principal African export down the Nile, across the Sahara Desert, or over the Indian and Atlantic oceans. The oldest known accounts of the enslavement of Africans are the carvings and inscriptions at the second cataract of the Nile representing Pharaoh Djer of the first Egyptian dynasty of the Old Kingdom taking slaves in a boat from Nubia to Egypt in 2900 B.C.E. Five thousand years later there are today voluminous accounts by journalists, academics, and investigators from numerous nongovernmental agencies, such as Human Rights Watch, describing contemporary African slavery as well as reports of slavery in specific countries, such as those by the United States Abolition Committee in 2002 for Mauritania, Niger, and the Sudan.

Who is a slave? There are endless arguments, some blunt, others subtle, to define the status of slavery, "that peculiar institution." Is a slave a chattel, a concubine, a eunuch, a domestic, a field hand, a herdsman, a soldier, or a powerful official? There are those who argue that migrant workers and illegal immigrants are treated as slaves. The literature defining slavery is enormous and often creates more confusion than clarity by presenting conundrums as to who is a slave. There

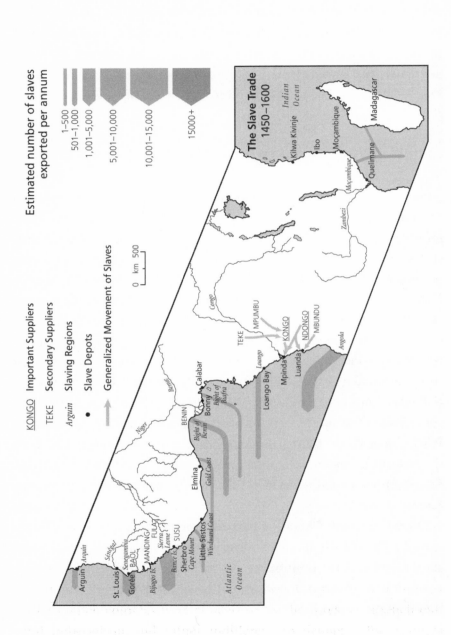

The Slave Trade
1450–1600

Estimated number of slaves
exported per annum

1–500
501–1,000
1,001–5,000
5,001–10,000
10,001–15,000
15000+

KONGO   Important Suppliers
TEKE   Secondary Suppliers
Arguin   Slaving Regions
  •   Slave Depots
         Generalized Movement of Slaves

0   km   500

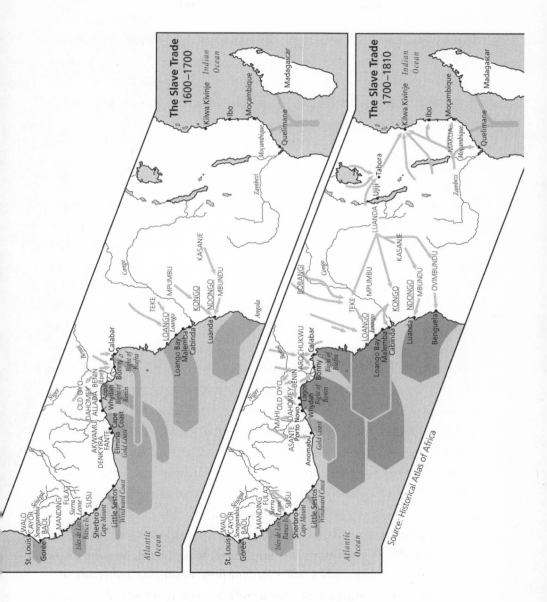

The Slave Trade
1600–1700

The Slave Trade
1700–1810

Source: Historical Atlas of Africa

is, however, one fundamental definition that cuts through the variety of relationships between master and slave. Slavery is "involuntary servitude" in which one human being is in control of another. Throughout history there are endless examples of slaves regarded as members of the owner's family, as willing sexual partners, and as those upon whom their masters were completely dependent, but none of these euphemistic rationalizations can disguise the ultimate claim of dominance by the owner.

There were infinite variations of African slavery, but slavery and its justification fall within general categories that were universally applied by those who accepted, approved, and practiced the institution. Slaves in Africa were property, chattels, to be bought and sold like horses or cattle, but unlike animals, a slave is distinguished by intelligence. If the master was to utilize the slave efficiently, it implied the recognition of the slave's capabilities, so that there was a frequent relaxation of the obligations to obedience by the slave. There were often restrictions on the sale of slaves, but slaves were still considered a commodity that was sharply defined by the power of emancipation that made them free. Among numerous African societies, there were religious restrictions, particularly among Muslims in regard to other Muslims or among traditional religions, that governed the sale of the slaves' offspring and kin. Whether the relationship between master and slave was simple or complex, however, that relationship was ultimately based upon one person having control of another. The sale of a slave to another owner was determined by innumerable reasons ranging from need to contentious behavior, but from which the original owner sought to profit in goods or cash.

Although the treatment of slaves in Africa varied from the brutal to the benign, the severity of punishment usually diminished from one slave generation to another as the community became more accustomed to the slaves. Assimilated by language and culture into that of the master, the offspring of slaves, who no longer possessed a memory of their past freedom, more readily assimilated the language and culture of the master than their parents, which made these off-spring more acceptable to the community. The constraints of nature and disease that limited population growth throughout Africa dis-couraged the sale of slaves either temporarily or permanently, for the needs, social status, and importance of the master could best be satis-fied by large numbers of slaves. Slaves, of course, represented wealth, and wealth created inequalities within the ethnic community. As early as the eleventh century there were merchants in the trans-Saharan trade who owned more than 1,000 slaves. In southern Nigeria at the end of the nineteenth century, wealthy merchants often possessed 1,000 or more slaves. In northern Nigeria by the 1850s, 50 percent of the inhabitants of the Sultanate of Sokoto were slaves, a pattern that continued into the twentieth century. In the French territories of the western Sudan, French officials estimated that 30 to 50 percent of the African population, or some five million people, were slaves. Farther east in the great basin of Lake Chad in the states of Kanem-Bornu, Bagirmi, and Wadai, the percentages were much the same.

The long history of slavery in West Africa before the coming of the Europeans and the development of the Atlantic slave trade has often obscured the institution of slavery among the societies of central and southern Africa. Before the arrival of the Portuguese, three kingdoms had emerged north and south of the Congo River—Loango, Tio, and Kongo—in which both the free commoners and the nobility owned slaves taken as captives in the wars of consolidation or by the slave raid. The Mani-Kongo (King of the Kongo) had a standing army of 16,000 to 20,000 slave soldiers who sustained and expanded the king-dom. As an accepted institution, a commodity to be sold, and a resource for the king, nobility, and commoners, slaves soon became the principal article of trade upon the arrival of the Portuguese, by which the Mani-Kongo was ironically able to increase the central authority of the state by the sale of its principal resource.

Most slaves were taken in wars or slave raids, the *razzia*, or kid-napping, and consequently they were outsiders who were particular-ly vulnerable to the demands and exploitation by those of different ethnicity who had acquired them. There were many reasons to declare war, but war prisoners were a ready sale that helped defray the cost of the military expeditions. Kings made wars in the name of the state, but many of these hostilities were an ill-disguised excuse to raid for slaves. In the fifteenth century, the larger kingdom of Jolof in the Senegal valley on the frontier of Islam disintegrated before the assaults of Wolof warlords and their armies of mounted pagan slaves (*ceddo, tyeddo*). African kings in time of war had the right to demand military service from the nobility, who were the aristocratic heads of clans. They were, as in Europe, notoriously unreliable when called to honor their allegiance and fight for the king, who consequently came to rely increasingly on slave soldiers who had no loyalties to ethnici-ty, clan, or kin, only to their master. Throughout history, these slave troops formed the core of the royal armies in dynastic Egypt, the Kingdom of Kush, the empires of the western Sudan, and the Kingdoms of Ashanti, Benin, Dahomey, the Kongo, Bagirmi, and the Luba-Lunda of Central Africa. The king provided arms and horses. The armed slaves were fed at the master's expense or were bil-leted in the villages, ready to march immediately at the king's com-mand.

If a slave shared the same language without accent, culture, reli-gion, and politics of the owner, he or she would usually be accepted as part of the family but not a member of the kinship or lineage. There were those, however, who belonged to the same ethnic group but became outsiders when they were regarded by the community as undesirable—criminals for murder, theft, adultery, sorcery; inflicted with a deforming disease, particularly the hated leprosy; or accused of other antisocial activities. Those upon whom society imposed its sanctions were at times victims of ritual sacrifice, as in Benin, but most undesirables were more easily eliminated by a profitable sale to foreign traders for transportation to the New World or Asia. Slavery in Africa was the means to cleanse and protect society, and consequently the expendable were sold to other Africans long before the introduction of the Atlantic and Asian export slave trade, which precluded the institutional system of imprisonment established in Europe and America. African slavery purged the unwanted from society—the old, widows, the feeble-minded, the destitute, debtors, and the homeless in search of food in times of famine, during which Africans chose to enslave themselves in return for food to survive.

This benign view of slavery as a criminal justice system was not, however, the reality. Coercion by the master was usually administered in one of two ways, the brutal and the subtle. To ensure obedience, discipline, and service, slaves were intimidated by flogging, dismemberment, castration, and sacrifice to gods or as spectacle for the crowds. The use of force was historically common in all slave societies and not peculiar to Africa. There was, however, an equally powerful psychological means of coercion that resulted in the meek acceptance of servitude. Insubordinate or hostile slaves ran the risk of sale into situations, such as ritual sacrifice, that were worse than their present servitude. This imminent threat for many slaves was more powerful than harsh punishment because it was always present and its results uncertain.

If slaves were property, and indeed they were, owners were reluctant to lose their means of production or reproduction. The number of slaves was the demonstration of their wealth, and the size of their retinue served as an important symbol of their prestige in society. As an instrument of labor, the slave was a nonperson who must carry out the master's orders, from the most menial to those that often involved great risk in which the slave had no choice but to obey or be punished. If slaves could be assigned any task, however, they could also be given significant positions of authority as agents, officials, or warriors.

They could acquire great wealth and own slaves in their own right. Unless given freedom or manumission upon the death of the owner, the descendants of slaves remained slaves. Manumission was not uncommon, particularly among African Muslims, where Islamic jurisprudence had long established that children of concubines by the owner were free. Most slaves, however, were passed on to the heirs of their masters along with the land and livestock, the men as laborers, soldiers, or retainers, the women as household domestics, cultivators, concubines, or wives.

Slavery in Africa took many forms depending on the needs and occupations of the slave owners, and often the work of slaves was hardly distinguishable from that of free Africans in the society— those who were serfs, those who labored for wages, artisans, or those working on traditional communal lands or pastures. Yet all of these workers had, theoretically, the freedom to walk away, a choice that the slave did not possess. Slave owners controlled the sexual and reproductive capacities as well as the physical and mental lives of their slaves. Demand, largely regulated by the marketplace, determined the price of male and female African slaves. Sexually attractive women and young girls commanded high prices compared to men and boys of similar ages. The right of the master to have sexual access drove up the price of female slaves to twice that of a male of comparable age. Moreover, she had to have the consent of her master to have sex with another, and her children became his property. There were often strong bonds of affection between owners and their slaves, whether male or female, but in the end the master controlled the reward system. In Africa, as in the Americas and Asia, the short life-span of a slave, largely from overwork, and the very low birthrate among slave women who did not wish to bear children their master would own were the driving forces to seek new sources of slaves by warfare, *razzia*, or trade.

Of all African slaves, the eunuch was the most highly prized and the most expensive. The demand for eunuchs always exceeded the supply, and consequently their price in the African slave markets could often be ten times that of a prime female slave. The making of a eunuch by castration has historically been extremely hazardous, with an estimated mortality of 70 to 90 percent, depending on whom was performing the operation. In the literature and mythology of the West, the eunuch was the guardian of the ruler's harem, but in fact the primary role of the eunuch was not protecting the concubines, who were usually quite capable of looking after their own interests, but as political advisers to the rulers whether in the African kingdoms of Ashanti, Oyo, Dahomey, Bagirmi or the Arab, Turkish, and Persian empires of the Middle East or the Tang and Ming dynasties of China. The eunuch was the quintessential slave. He could not pass on life, goods, titles, or functions. He was beholden to no clan, chief, or noble. He remained aloof from the intrigues of imperial courtesans and was not dependent upon the supplications of the king's own family and kin.

After the eunuch, women were the most desirable slaves, for they could perform more functions than any male. They could cook at the hearth, cultivate and carry, provide sex, bear children, conduct business, and themselves often dealt in slaves. The average estimated demand for female to male slaves over time and place in Africa was usually two to one, which was reflected in numbers and price. Women were brought up to be more submissive and docile than men, an erroneous assumption of female inferiority that was pervasive in most societies in Africa, Asia, and the Americas. Female slaves were often purchased for their ability to reproduce, but it proved a bad investment and a mistake to regard them strictly in biological terms. Female slaves in Africa had few children, for the child would be a slave never fully admitted into the close kinship relations so essential to acceptability in African society. The relationship between male masters and female slaves was usually fragile. Abortions were commonplace. If female slaves were not the solution to reproduction, their place was in the fields of production.

In the past and today, women in Africa performed 60 to 70 percent of the agricultural labor, all the housekeeping, but none of the pastoral work. In the history of Africa, women have been the producers not just in the fields but in labor-intensive crafts like weaving. The men did the heavy work of clearing and planting, but it was woman's work to cultivate the crop, weed, and prepare for the harvest. Since women did the agricultural field work in free African societies, they were expected to do the same as slaves and consequently were worth twice the price in the marketplace. Young girls throughout the centuries to the present were frequently used in the form of slavery known as "pawning," whereby the slave was "pawned" by a parent or seller to a creditor in return for cash to be recovered on repayment that seldom ever occurred. Young girls were also given to reward soldiers or as booty, payment of fines, and bride wealth. In some African societies, women were also warriors. Within the markets of the continent, the slave was the most convertible of all currencies, more so than gold or cowries. They became the essential medium in the transactions of the internal trade. The buying and selling of slaves was not a male monopoly. Female owners and traders in slaves were not uncommon. They were free women who kept their property separate from husbands and men according to local customs and traditions. The female head of the house dominated and controlled the household slaves. She did not let the bonds of same sex restrain her from exploiting female African slaves in the pursuit of commercial profit. Female slaves were sought for their labor because they were more submissive than men, particularly if the slave owner was a woman, for in many African societies, particularly in West Africa, there was a long and respected tradition of female mercantile entrepreneurs.

Many of these African businesswomen were the offspring of transient European male traders and African women from the social elite, who have been given the name Eurafricans by the historian George E. Brooks. Cultivated, entrepreneurial, and multilingual, they were slave owners who played a crucial role in the commercial and social relations between Africans and European merchants, keeping the Europeans physically and mentally healthy. They often practiced Catholicism without abandoning their traditional religious rituals. These African and Eurafrican women who owned slaves could prosper by marrying a male slave and becoming the recipient of his labor. Marriage between two women was widespread, in which the female slave owner assumed the role of legal genitor whereby all the children of the younger female slaves belonged to their female partner. There is a Igbo saying that "those who have people are wealthier than those with money."

Ironically, the abolition of the Atlantic slave trade in the nineteenth century produced a dramatic increase of slavery within Africa. There were more slaves in Africa than outside. When they could no longer be exported, the institution of slavery expanded into the interior regions of the continent, where slaving and slavery had hitherto been of little importance. The Mossi on the Upper Volta River and the Luba and the Ovambo in the interior of Angola were now enslaved by African slave traders. No longer exportable, the number of slaves in Africa increased, and their masters now feared that the concentration of slaves in their territory, most of whom were men, would overwhelm them in times of trouble. There were slave rebellions in the Futa Jalon, the Niger Delta, and among the Yoruba, the suppression of which was accompanied by an increase in ritual human sacrifice, often perfunctory but usually attached to a festival, funeral, or a religious rite.

Slavery in Africa was a historic and accepted institution whose numbers undoubtedly surpassed throughout the millennia the estimated sixteen and a half million slaves who were forcefully exported out of Africa between the seventeenth and twentieth centuries to the

Americas and Asia. What the sterile statistics do not record and the factual descriptions of slavery often fail to emphasize is the indescribable amount of suffering—physical, psychological, emotional— of the slaves who were the victims of this system that, until the nineteenth century, was universally accepted. A few slaves survived to enjoy positions of power and pleasure. Those who did not perish when captured or during transport to the slave markets no longer possessed their own person. They were transformed into dehumanized beings to serve their masters. No words can convey the enormous and tragic loss to humankind of this "peculiar institution."

Atlantic Slave Trade

Although slavery had been an established institution in Africa for over a millennium, and the trans-Saharan, Red Sea, and East African slave trade had been pervasive for many more centuries, the Atlantic slave trade differed from them by its numbers, intensity, and the changes it produced within the societies of the African continent. More than eleven million Africans were exported to the Americas from the coast of western Africa. This Atlantic slave trade was mostly conducted in just 300 years and was concentrated in specific regions during different centuries that created an uneven disruption of African societies along the coast. Over half the trade took place in the eighteenth century, principally from the Gold Coast and the Bights of Benin and Biafra. In response to the Atlantic slave trade, Africans developed new forms of political and social organizations, but the skills and equipment that made possible the transatlantic trade accelerated the growing technological gap between Africa and Europe. The demand for slaves increased the institution of slavery in Africa, contributed to the disruption of traditional cultures, and confirmed the growth of a callous disregard for human life as persons became property. The brutality that accompanied the capture, sale, service, and ultimately transport across the Atlantic of Africans produced a great misery that cannot be ignored by the fact that the human resiliency of Africans and their institutions survived the suffering.

In 1492 Columbus "discovered" the Caribbean islands for Spain; in 1500 Pedro Álvares Cabral "discovered" Brazil for Portugal. Both regions were admirably suited to the cultivation of sugar on large plantations. Europe had an insatiable taste for sugar, the plantations an insatiable demand for the labor to produce it. The first cargo of African slaves to arrive in the Americas came from Spain on a Spanish ship in 1501, followed by a second shipment of seventeen slaves in 1505, but it was not until 1518 that the first cargo of slaves reached the Caribbean directly from Africa. At first the nascent plantations had been worked by American Indians, but by the middle of the sixteenth century their population had been decimated by European and African diseases. The indigenous people were replaced by Africans to meet the increasing demand for labor from plantation owners. By the end of the sixteenth century, the volume of the Atlantic slave trade totaled about 10,000 slaves exported annually. This number remained steady until the mid-seventeenth century, when the Dutch supplied slaves at cheaper prices for the owners of new plantations in the Americas. The dramatic increase and subsequent profits in the Dutch trade in the latter half of the seventeenth century naturally attracted their fierce mercantile rivals, the British and the French. These interlopers had been active in the trade in the past, but between 1650 and 1700 they gradually overwhelmed the Dutch by organizing companies under royal charters and later by private individual British and French merchants working out of Liverpool, Nantes, and other Atlantic coast ports that specialized in the slave trade. During the seventeenth century, the trade's trajectory peaked at 18,680 per year. Between 1601 and 1700, 1,348,000 slaves had landed in the Americas, but this number was only a stream that was soon to become a mighty river in the eighteenth century.[2]

The eighteenth century experienced the zenith of the slave trade during which the annual trajectory continued upward to a height of 61,330 slaves per year. The focus of the Atlantic trade moved steadily down the coast from the Senegambia, where it began, to Upper Guinea and the Windward Coast and then to the Gold Coast, the Bights of Benin and Biafra, and finally west-central Africa. Over six million slaves, or 54 percent of the total during 450 years (1450–1900), were exported from these four regions in just one century, but by far the greatest number, 2,331,800 (38 percent), were taken from the west-central African coast, particularly Angola.[3]

In the last quarter of the eighteenth century, the annual supply of slaves increased to 78,000 from the 30,900 exported annually during a comparable period in the seventeenth century. There appears little doubt that the demand of the marketplace encouraged a rise in price, which contributed to the acceptance of the slave trade as a legitimate institution of investment. There is a commonly held belief that the slaves were acquired with worthless items of conspicuous consumption—liquor, beads, trinkets. That is a myth. To purchase slaves on the western African coast for the Atlantic trade, cash was preferred—cowries, silver coins, gold bullion. But quality goods—textiles, iron, copper, bars and wire of brass, firearms, fine glass beads, and porcelain—were readily accessible. During the rapid expansion of the Atlantic slave trade in the eighteenth century, military hardware, muskets and flintlocks, became the principal article of trade preferred by British merchants. In 1730 over 180,000 guns were imported; from 1750 to 1800 the annual average fluctuated between 283,000 and 394,000. By the end of the eighteenth century, an estimated twenty million guns had been sold to Africans, along with another 22,000 tons of gunpowder.[4] There is the simplistic theory of the "gun-slave cycle," whereby guns and luxury goods were sold to encourage

enslavement. This hypothesis fails to take into account the complexities of the slave trade in which the powerful African rulers, chiefs, and
wealthy merchants set the terms of trade for what they perceived as
their own best interests. They were all committed to slavery, and hence
to the slave trade, and required no guns or goods to convince them to
be enthusiastically involved in the trade.

Profits from the slave trade depended upon the prompt sale of a
valuable but perishable commodity before slaves died or escaped.
Until the arrival of a European buyer anchoring in roadstead or harbor, the slaves were incarcerated in barracks known as "Traders
Houses" or barracoons, where they were reasonably well treated, fed,
and oiled in anticipation for a quick sale. When slave ships did not
promptly arrive, however, the slaves would attempt to escape or sometimes rebel, which usually ended in savage suppression. The European
merchants in associations operated from permanent coastal trading
forts, known as "factories," or more likely they were private traders
cruising along the coast purchasing slaves until they filled their ships.
Most of the elaborate negotiations with European merchants were
conducted by coastal middlemen, whose main concern, besides profit,
was to keep the Europeans from the interior and the African rulers in
the hinterland from direct access to the coast. These middlemen were
mostly Africans, but some were Afro-Europeans, and the subsequent
negotiations with the European sea-merchants were accompanied by
lengthy haggling, expansive hospitality, bribery, abundant quantities
of alcohol, and frequently trust and good faith between individuals
who had conducted business in the past and who expected to continue in the future, from which they expected substantial profits.

Unlike the internal slave trade within African societies or across the
Sahara, where the demand for female slaves outnumbered the males
two to one, the Atlantic trade was almost exactly the opposite. Women
were unsuited for the very heavy, intensive labor required to plant and
harvest the cane on the sugar plantations of the Americas. European

agents on the coast were given precise instructions to purchase young men in their prime and were reluctant to take children under fifteen years of age, but more children could be packed into the ships than adults at less cost. These children would soon reach maturity, which would ultimately justify the cheaper investment for their purchase.

Having been sold, slaves were branded as in Roman times with the mark of their owners and marched or taken in canoes in chains to the hold of the slave ship. By the eighteenth century, the typical slave ship was not specifically built for the trade but was a converted wooden cargo ship with square sails and three masts and armed with muskets and cannons. More than half of the British slave ships of that century had been obtained by capture during the European mercantile wars. The remainder came from several British and French shipyards that specifically designed and built ships for the trade. Slave ships were short-lived. No owner expected a slave ship to be seaworthy for more than ten years, and few European ships made more than six transatlantic voyages. The number of officers and crew varied throughout the century, averaging about thirty officers and sailors in their twenties, often recruited while drunk in the local taverns of the European ports that catered to the trade. They were harshly disciplined in the violent world of a slave ship, where it was not unusual for 20 percent of the crew to die during a voyage. But the survivors were well paid, with bonuses for the number of slaves delivered alive. Freed African slaves were often sailors, and sometimes slaves were rented out by their owners as crew.

The slaves were terrified of the vast, mysterious sea, and many, especially those from the interior, believed that the crew were cannibals whose red wine was African blood and whose gunpowder was crushed African bones. Once under way and with a steady flow from the southeast trade winds and high pressure in the mid-Atlantic, the average time in the eighteenth century to cross the Middle Passage was thirty days. In 1754 the *Saint-Phillippe of Nantes* carrying 460

Africans from Whydah established a record of twenty-five days. In 1727 the *Sainte-Anne*, also from Nantes, established another record of nine months from Whydah to Saint-Domingue, during which fifty-five slaves were lost.[5] Below decks a slave was "tightly packed" into a space normally five feet high and four feet wide, with the sexes separated as much to prevent the women from inciting the men to rebel as to prevent sexual intercourse. The quantity was limited, for the more space given to supplies of food and water, the less room there was for slaves. The eatables varied with the nationality of the ship. On Portuguese slavers, cassava was the staple food. British ships carried maize, and French ships carried oats. The daily ration averaged about three pounds, accompanied by a few ounces of flour, beans, and salted beef. A greater problem was space for drinking water. Water is heavy and cumbersome, and it requires a lot of room, yet water more than food determined the success of a slave voyage, success measured by the number of slaves who survived. Slave voyages were hot and crowded, and many slaves suffered from dysentery, the "flux," and its dehydration, which claimed a third of the dead from disease on any one voyage. Smallpox, scurvy, and a variety of other tropical diseases accounted for the remainder. In the sixteenth century, the loss of slaves during the passage was as high as 20 percent; with better food, this loss was halved to 10 percent by the nineteenth century. Many deaths were the result of violence, particularly rebellions. Insurrections were common on slave ships of every nationality, estimated at one in every eight or ten voyages. They almost always occurred during embarkation, before sailing or when the ship was still in sight of the coast. Most mutinies were promptly suppressed, for the crews were always alert and well armed when loading slaves or taking meals on deck. All hands not involved in distributing the food stood to arms with cannon loaded and aimed at the crowded, hungry, and hostile slaves.

At the end of the eighteenth century, the Atlantic slave trade represented the largest involuntary migration in human history. It also witnessed the mass movement known as abolition to end the slave trade. Motivated by moral, political, and economic considerations, the reformers demanded that the European nations outlaw the slave trade. These laws were not easy to pass and difficult to enforce against clever smugglers. Britain launched a sustained diplomatic assault to convince all nations to abandon the trade and to support diplomacy, and the Royal Navy was sent to patrol the West African coast to intercept illegal slave ships. Their frigates were joined by ships from the U.S. and French navies, but they largely failed to contain the privateers until after the 1840s. The crews of the anti–slave trade squadron suffered devastating losses from disease on the West African coast, and the region soon became known prophetically as "the White Man's Grave."

Despite these setbacks, the reformers had ignited a moral consciousness that abolished the slave trade and ultimately slavery without fully realizing the consequences of what they had accomplished. The abolitionists were convinced and took heart that the economic loss from the slave trade would be replaced by what facilely became known to them and historians as the "legitimate trade" in nonslave goods—ivory, peanuts, palm oil, gold, rubber, cloves, hides, ostrich feathers, beeswax, and gum Arabic. The abolitionists argued that legitimate trade was not only the substitute for the slave trade but would end slavery itself. In nineteenth-century Africa, the contradiction between the ubiquitous system of slavery on the one hand and the increasing determination of the abolitionists to bring an end to slavery on the other resulted in the hitherto unknown European intervention into the interior of Africa that ultimately contributed to the imposition of colonialism. True to their abolitionist tradition, the European colonial administrators of the twentieth century firmly suppressed the African trade in slaves, but they refrained from rigorously imposing their own prohibitions against slavery, fearing that to do so would precipitate the widespread disruption of African societies, which would make their burden of European colonial administration all the more difficult. Thus, the institution of slavery did not disappear, and involuntary servitude continues to this day under a variety of euphemistic disguises.

During the 450 years of the Atlantic slave trade, an estimated 11,313,000 Africans were exported to the Americas, but these statistics do not record the incredible human suffering of those transported to the New World where, however, their African resiliency enabled them to survive and multiply to make their contribution in the forging of new societies.

TABLE 1

Estimated Slave Exports from Africa across the Atlantic, 1450–1900

Date	Number	Percentage of Total Atlantic Trade
1450–1600	409,000	3.6%
1601–1700	1,348,000	11.9%
1701–1800	6,090,000	53.8%
1801–1900	3,466,000	30.6%
Total	11,313,000	100.0%

Source: Lovejoy, *Transformations in Slavery*, Table 1.1.

Asian Slave Trade

There can be no reasonable estimate of the number of slaves exported from Africa to the Mediterranean basin, the Middle East, and the Indian Ocean before the arrival of the Arabs in Africa during the seventh century. Between 800 and 1600 the evidence for the estimated volume of slaves is more intuitive than empirical but better than none at all. One can only surmise that during the previous 4,000 years, when slavery was a common and accepted institution in most African societies, those slaves marched across the Sahara or transported over the Red Sea and the Indian Ocean to Asia during these eight centuries must have, cumulatively, amounted to a very considerable number of slaves. Until the seventeenth century, the evidence is derived mostly from literary sources, and maximum and minimum numbers must at best be extrapolated given the paucity of direct data. There is a considerable amount of indirect evidence from accounts of the trade and the numbers of black slaves demanded by the rulers of North Africa for military service from which general but not unreasonable estimates of the Asian slave trade can be proposed.

When European states directly entered the world of international slave trade in the seventeenth century, the estimates of the number of slaves become increasingly reliable. There is a striking similarity between the total estimated number of slaves exported across the Atlantic and those sent to Asia. The transatlantic trade carried an estimated 11,313,000 million slaves from 1450 to 1900. The Asian trade numbered an estimated total of 12,580,000 slaves from 800 to 1900. The important difference between the Atlantic and the Asia slave trade, however, is the time span in which the exportation of slaves took place. The more than 11,000,000 slaves of the Atlantic trade were exported to the Americas in only 400 years, an intensity that had dramatic effects on the African societies engaged in the trade. The 12,580,000 slaves exported to Asia during eleven centuries obviously did not have the same traumatic impact on the western African coast. During the 300 years, 1600–1900, for which there is more credible evidence, the volume of the Asian trade is estimated at 5,510,000 slaves, half that of the Atlantic trade. At the end of the Napoleonic wars during the first half of the nineteenth century, an extensive plantation economy was developed on the East African coast and on the islands of Zanzibar, Pemba, and the Mascarenes in the Indian Ocean that required greater numbers of slaves from the interior. In a brief spasm of fifty years, until the impact of the European abolitionists after 1860 dramatically restrained and then ended the trade to Asia, the eastern African slave trade was more reminiscent of the western African experience than in any of the preceding centuries.

Until the arrival of the Portuguese on the coasts of sub-Saharan Africa in the fifteenth century, Islam was the only ideology to introduce a more systematic regulation of slavery in Africa. By the tenth century, the Arabs, who had conquered North Africa, the Middle East, and Persia, had absorbed the historic institution of slavery, but as Muslims they shaped the ancient traditions of slavery to conform to the religious laws and practices of Islam. Their legal definitions and treatment of slaves, however, were more a modification in the status and function of a slave than any fundamental change in the practice of involuntary servitude. The slave remained property to be used as the master wished—as an agricultural laborer, soldier, domestic, concubine, or even a high official, a *wazir*. Thousands of slaves were taken in the holy wars, jihad, during the expansion of the Islamic world, for their enslavement was legally and morally justified because they were not Muslims but unbelievers (*kafirin*) expected to abandon their traditional religions and embrace in slavery the true faith. Islam recognized that Christians, Jews, and Zoroastrians required a special status. They were "People of the Book"—the Bible, the Talmud, or the Avesta (Pure Instruction)—who acknowledged one supreme deity, God, Jehovah, or Ahura Mazda. Consequently, they were regarded as protected minorities (*dhimmis*) who were not to be enslaved, their property was safeguarded, and they were permitted to practice their religion freely so long as they paid a special tax (*jizya*). In reality, Christians, Jews, and Zoroastrians were regularly enslaved in the tumult of war, raids, or piracy, where legal distinctions disappeared before passion, bigotry, and avarice.

As the Islamic empire expanded, slaves came increasingly from conquests of non-Muslim Africans on the frontiers of Islam for slave markets in the Arab Middle East, where women and children were more pliable and therefore more likely to accept Islam. Young women became domestics or concubines for the harem; young men were trained for military or administrative service. Except for the constant demand of the Moroccan sultans in the seventeenth and eighteenth centuries for young men as slave soldiers, mature males and women were preferred to perform the menial tasks of field and household under harsh conditions. Given their short life spans, these slaves had to be continuously replaced by newly acquired slaves, preferably females.

Since the young were absorbed into Muslim society and the old perished, the need for constant replenishment of slaves was not impeded by race or color. The only criterion for the Muslim was that the slave be pagan, and since African traditional religions were unacceptable, sub-Saharan Africa became the most important source of slaves for Muslim merchants. These merchants established elaborate commercial networks to transport the slaves out of Africa across the Sahara, the Red Sea, and the Indian Ocean. In order to justify slavery, Europeans frequently argued that conversion to Christianity, the religion of the plantation owners, would by example bring civilization and salvation to slaves otherwise condemned to eternal damnation. Islam, however, imposed upon the Muslim master an obligation to convert non-Muslims slaves in order for them to become members of the greater Islamic society in which the beneficence of the afterlife was assumed. Indeed, the daily observance of the well-defined Islamic religious rituals was the symbolic and outward manifestation of the inward conversion without which emancipation was impossible. Unlike in Christianity and African religions, Islamic legal tradition explicitly enabled the slave to become immediately free rather than undergo the lengthy African generational process of acceptance by social assimilation. Conversion also enabled slaves to perform different functions unknown in the slavery of the New World. The Arab conquests had produced a far-flung empire of many ethnicities, whose common denominator was Islam administered by a vast bureaucracy that required slave officials and slave soldiers loyal to the state, for their status was dependent upon their master and his or her religion. These slave officials were frequently empowered to have authority over free members of the state. Often Muslim slaves became highly specialized in commerce and industry through the acquisition of skills in the more advanced technology of the Islamic world compared to Africa or even the sugar plantations of the Americas.

Women also occupied a different status in Islam than in African or Atlantic slavery. Islamic law limited the number of legal wives to four, the sexual appetite of men being satisfied by the number of concubines they could afford. Slave women were given as concubines to other slaves, to freed slaves, or to the master's sons. The relationship between the male master and the female slave, however, was clearly defined in theory by the legal Islamic sanctions that applied to emancipation. A concubine became legally free upon the death of her owner. If she bore him children, she could not be sold and her children were free, but in practice they had a lower status than children of free wives.

Trans-Saharan Slave Trade

Until the fifteenth century, the export of slaves across the Sahara, the Red Sea, and the Indian Ocean was believed to be relatively constant, numbering between 5,000 and 10,000 annually throughout these many centuries. Such modest numbers mitigated the impact of the demographic loss among African societies. The estimated number of slaves, 4,670,000, exported across the Sahara between 800 and 1600 can only be but a reasonable guess based on diffuse direct and indirect evidence acceptable for lack of a better figure. Whether more or less, there was a demonstrable demand for slaves from sub-Saharan Africa that resulted in continuous contact between Muslim merchants, who organized the trans-Saharan slave trade, and the rulers of the Sudanic states, who supplied them. The presence of Muslim traders had a profound influence at the courts of African kings. The merchants not only conducted commerce but also introduced literacy and Islamic law as it pertained to their transactions, principally slaves.

Although the Bilad al-Sudan stretched from the Atlantic Ocean to the Red Sea, there were only six established vertical routes across the Sahara that resulted in well-defined markets at each terminus south of the Sahara and in North Africa. There was the Walata Road from ancient Ghana to Sijilmasa in Morocco; the Taghaza Trail from Timbuktu at the great bend of the Niger north to Taghaza and Sijilmasa or to Tuwat and Tunis; the Ghadames Road from Gao on the lower Niger to Agades, Ghat, Ghadames, and Tripoli; the Bilma Trail, or the Garamantian Road, from the Hausa states at Kano and Lake Chad to Bilma, Murzuk in the Fezzan, and on to Tripoli; the Forty Days Road, the Darb al-Arbain, from El Fasher in Darfur north to the Nile at Asuyt; and the route farthest east that began at Suakin on the Red Sea, swung southwest to Sennar on the Blue Nile, and thence followed the Nile to Egypt. As in the Atlantic trade, the largest number of slaves did not come from the same region throughout the millennium of the trans-Saharan trade, and although a very important source of revenue, the savanna states of the western and central Sudan were not dependent upon the slave trade for their rise, expansion, and decline. They were important suppliers of slaves but not at the expense of their political and cultural development.

During the seventeenth and eighteenth centuries, the trans-Saharan trade steadily increased to some 700,000 in each century, or 67 percent of the total exported across the Sahara in the preceding

800 years. This estimated average of 7,000 per year for these two centuries, based on limited evidence, may be greater than the real numbers, but the indirect evidence reasonably concludes that there was a considerable supply of slaves from the savanna and Sahel because of drought and warfare. When the rains did not come, for instance, during 1639–1643, 1711–1716, 1738–1756, and 1770–1771, the fields were barren and the free cultivators vulnerable to slavers when wandering the countryside in search of food. In order to survive, they often chose to enslave themselves to those who could supply food.

These two centuries also experienced the dissolution of the old Sudanic empires into petty states, whose warlords carried on interminable warfare with local rivals that produced an abundance of captives who became slaves. The extent of suffering from drought or war was painfully measured by the increase in the number of slaves during these two centuries. The wars that followed the fragmentation of the old empires were characterized by Muslims against non-Muslims, Muslims who claimed to be Muslims but did not practice orthodox Islam, and Islamic jihads led by holy men against infidels and those they regarded as renegade Muslims. The historic goal of Muslims was to convert unbelievers to Islam, and the enslavement of unbelievers for conversion was both legally and morally correct. These reasons, however, were often a euphemistic rationale for the warlord, Muslim or non-Muslim, to resolve the problem of replacing the natural loss of his slaves by exploiting new sources for his own use or sale in order to provide revenue for himself and the state. The organized *razzia* became commonplace with a variety of official names, *ghazwa* or salatiya in Darfur and Sennar, for instance, to be carried out more often than not by slave soldiers. Some of the enslaved were retained—women as concubines, men as soldiers or agricultural laborers—but a far greater number were sold. For most warlords, after direct taxes, slaves were the greatest source of their revenue.

The reduction in the number of slaves crossing the desert that accompanied the steady decline of the established trans-Saharan trade in the nineteenth century was offset by the astonishing growth of the Nilotic slave trade. In 1820 the army of the able and dynamic ruler of Egypt, Muhammad Ali, invaded the Sudan to enslave the pagan Sudanese to rebuild his army. Hitherto the Funj Kingdom of Sennar had exported some 1,500 slaves per year to Egypt. Muhammad Ali wanted 20,000. A military training camp and a special depot to receive slaves from the Sudan at Aswan were constructed at Isna. From the administrative capital at Khartoum, the Egyptian governor-general organized military expeditions up the Blue and White Niles to enslave Africans. Despite heavy losses from disease and exhaustion on the march down the Nile and across the Nubian Desert, by 1838, 10,000 to 12,000 slaves reached Egypt every year. During the 1870s, tens of thousands of slaves were exported to Egypt and to Arabia from ports on the Red Sea. This exporting of slaves only came to an end after the Anglo-Egyptian conquest of the Sudan in 1898.

Red Sea Slave Trade

The Red Sea slave trade was older than the trans-Saharan. The dynastic Egyptians regularly sent expeditions to the Land of Punt, the coasts of the Red Sea, and northern Somalia, to return with ivory, perfumes, and slaves. Slaves were undoubtedly among the commodities exported from Africa to Arabia across the Red Sea and the Gulf of Arabia during the centuries of Greek and Roman rule in Egypt. Although the direct evidence remains scanty, between 800 and 1600 the numbers of slaves transported to Arabia to Arabia were not large. The markets were few, and the conduct of the trade was more casual compared to the well-organized sales in West and North Africa. An estimated 1,600,000 slaves were exported during this period, or an annual average of 2,000 slaves. The sources of slaves for the Red Sea trade were limited to Nubia, the Nile north of its confluence at the modern capital of Khartoum, and Ethiopia, but the total Red Sea trade amounted to only 34 percent of the trans-Saharan trade during these same 800 years. The ports were few: Aidhab in Egypt until destroyed by the Ottoman Turks in 1416, Suakin in the Sudan, and Adulis (Massawa) in Ethiopia. During the seventeenth century, the Red Sea export trade appears to have involved a steady but modest number of 1,000 slaves per year. The estimated number of slaves increased in the eighteenth century to some 2,000 slaves annually from Ethiopia and the Nile Valley. That number was, however, only a symbolically small portion of the increasing worldwide export of African slaves that continued into the nineteenth century. Throughout the eighteenth and early nineteenth centuries, Darfur in the Nile basin sent several thousand slaves per year to Egypt but also to the Red Sea through Sennar on the Blue Nile and thence east along the established trade route to Suakin.

East Africa and the Indian Ocean Slave Trade

Although Arabic, Persian, and Chinese documentation and the writings of Arab geographers and travelers about East Africa and its trade exist, there is little direct evidence as to the number of slaves exported to Asia until the nineteenth century. By extrapolation from the numbers involved in the slave trade in the Red Sea, until the nineteenth century the exportation of an estimated 1,000 slaves per year does not appear unreasonable. At the end of the eighteenth century, there are records of the number of slaves (2,500 per year) from the mainland who passed through Kilwa to the French sugar and coffee plantations on the Mascarene Islands, and slaves exported from Mozambique to Cape Town and Brazil add another 4,000 to 5,000 annually from the historic ports of the East African coast.[vi] This was a dramatic increase from the last three decades of the eighteenth century but only the harbinger of the massive numbers exported during the first half of the nineteenth century.

In the first decade of the nineteenth century, 80,000 slaves are estimated to have been brought to the East African coast from the interior. Over one-third (30,000) were retained on the coast; the other 50,000 were shipped to the Asian mainland (Arabia, Persia, and India), the Mascarene Islands, and the Americas. During the next four decades, the decline in the Mascarene trade was offset by a regular increase in the number of slaves sent to the Americas, mainly Brazil, which reached a high of 100,000 per decade during the 1830s and 1840s, thereafter to experience a drastic decrease to a trickle by midcentury. During this same half-century, the export trade from the East African coast to the Asian mainland experienced a modest but firm increase to a high of 65,000 slaves per decade in the 1850s and 1860s until 1873, when the sultan of Zanzibar was forced by the British government and its Royal Navy to ban all trade in slaves by sea. This spectacular increase in the nineteenth-century East African slave trade was caused by the development of plantations that required large numbers of slave labor on the islands of Zanzibar and Pemba, where Swahili entrepreneurs from the mainland and Arab immigrants from the Hadhramaut and Omanhad planted extensive plantations of cloves, coconuts, and grain. Cloves were being exported from Zanzibar by 1827, and thereafter the island became the principal supplier to the international market. The clove, like cotton, is a labor-intensive crop that required an ever-increasing supply of slaves, and it is no coincidence that the demand for slaves was greatest during the peak of clove production in the 1860s and 1870s.

TABLE 2

Estimated Slave Exports across the Sahara, Red Sea, East Africa, and the Indian Ocean, 800–1900 and 1600–1900.

	Trans-Saharan	Red Sea	East Africa and Indian Ocean
800–1600	4,670,000	1,600,000	800,000
1601–1800	1,400,000	300,000	500,000
1801–1900	1,200,000	492,000	1,618,000
Total	7,270,000	2,392,000	2,918,000

Slave Exports from the Sahara, Red Sea, and East Africa and Indian Ocean, 800–1900. Total 12,580,000

Slave Exports from the Sahara, Red Sea, and East Africa and Indian Ocean, 1600–1900. Total 5,510,000

Source: Lovejoy, *Transformation in Slavery*, Tables 2.1, 2.2, 3.7, 7.1, 7.7.

A Summing Up

The history of slavery in Africa and the slave trade cannot be measured only in terms of numbers or statistics, which obscure the complexities of the system and the enormity of the misery that accompanied the institution. Yet numbers do serve their purpose, for they quantify to give a means, no matter how sterile, to understand this otherwise incomprehensible human tragedy of humankind. There are pitfalls to avoid in reading the numbers. There was, of course, no trade with the Americas until after Europeans arrived there at the end of the fifteenth century, yet slaves had been taken out of Africa across the Sahara, the Red Sea, and East Africa for many centuries before Columbus. Their numbers can only be estimated, precariously, from indirect evidence and extrapolation after the coming of the Arabs from 800 to the great surge in the Atlantic slave trade in the seventeenth century at some 7,000,000, or less than 9,000 per year. This figure is not very helpful, for the number of slaves taken to the Mediterranean and Asia varied dramatically in time and place. Not until the seventeenth century did evidence, direct and indirect, permit greater certainty as to the estimated numbers of slaves taken out of Africa. From 1600 to 1900, the Atlantic and the Asian slave trades together systematically exported 16,414,000 slaves from Africa, including 10,904,000 slaves to the Americas and 5,510,00 slaves to the Indian Ocean islands and Asia. This represents an average of 54,713 slaves per year, or more than 36,347 slaves exported cross the Atlantic and another 18,367 to Asia.

Although there are no statistics, many accounts and oral traditions confirm that the slave trade and slavery were very much a part of African life until the 1930s. Thereafter, numerous incidents of slavery have been reported to the present day, and involuntary servitude remains under new names, but after 5,000 years the institution of slavery as a system has come to an end. The historic focus on the Atlantic slave trade and on slavery in the Americas has often obscured the trade to Asia and slavery within Africa. Indigenous to Africa as well as to Europe and Asia, slavery was an institution in most African societies, and its abolition came later than in the Americas. The international system of slavery tied the Americas, Africa, and Asia together, and the task of emancipation was not complete until slaves were as free in Africa as in the Americas.

Notes

1. Ca'da Mosto quoted in Hugh Thomas, *The Slave Trade: The Story of the Atlantic Slave Trade: 1440–1870* (New York: Simon and Schuster, 1997), 53.

2. Paul E. Lovejoy, *Transformations in Slavery: A History of Slavery in Africa*, 2nd ed. (Cambridge: Cambridge University Press, 2000), 46–49.

3. Lovejoy, *Transformations in Slavery*, 46–50.

4. Lovejoy, *Transformations in Slavery*, 109.

5. Thomas, *Slave Trade*, 411.

6. Lovejoy, *Transformations in Slavery*

CHAPTER FIVE

European Conquest and Colonization of Sub-Saharan Africa

Court of King Makoko, 1880

Prelude to the Conquest

There was no reason for Europeans of any nationality to disrupt an efficient, customary, and highly profitable commercial relationship with Africans for slaves in western Africa. Even if the Europeans had sought to challenge the African authorities beyond the coast to change the terms of trade, they did not have the motivation or the resources to do so. Before the nineteenth century, the European technology was not that superior to the African, particularly in warfare, and certainly the high rate of European mortality from African diseases did not encourage any exploration or invasion into the interior, where it was thought the loss of life would be even greater than on the coast. Thus the centuries slipped by while the commercial success of the systematic trade in slaves convinced the Europeans it was to their advantage to remain contentedly in their enclaves. Suddenly, in the first half of the nineteenth century, the interior of Africa was opened by European explorers. These explorers were followed by Christian missionaries and merchants, but no European government contemplated or imagined rushing into Africa. Who were these men and women in the first three-quarters of the nineteenth century who became the agents of intervention when their governments had no interest in imperial expansion on the African continent?

The explorers were mostly British, French, and German with very complex personalities, but all had similar characteristics. Most had been wanderers who had traveled extensively before launching into

Africa. They possessed a curiosity of the unknown that was made legitimate by appeals to science, despite the fact that few had the rigor of a scientific education. Some of them, like the saintly missionary Dr. David Livingstone or even a tough journalist like Henry Morton Stanley, were driven by the humanitarian mission of the abolitionist to end the African slave trade and open Africa to commerce, Christianity, and civilization. Their books were avidly read by Europeans, particularly the English and the Americans, for they were an irresistible combination of exotic landscapes, fauna, flora, and, of course, "savage" Africans. In return, these European explorers hoped to reap the rewards of discovery—fame for many, the redemption of a hitherto aimless personal life for some, and a fortune for a few. Exploration was hard and dangerous work, but it was heady stuff and an exhilarating escape from the humdrum of an oppressive class system in European society. Most of the explorers were hopelessly romantic misfits searching for their own identity in Africa, which had eluded them in Europe.

Although the age of the European exploration of Africa was associated with Victorian England of the nineteenth century, it was the great crusade of the abolitionists at the end of the eighteenth century and throughout most of the nineteenth that focused public attention on Africa and particularly on West Africa. The abolitionists bound Africa to Europe ever more closely, but when arguing for the continued presence of the Royal Naval Squadron on the coast of West Africa, they never perceived that their efforts would lead to the intervention and conquest of the interior of the continent in the last quarter of the nineteenth century. It was, however, the culmination and final triumph of the abolitionist crusade begun a hundred years earlier in West Africa when Dr. David Livingstone exposed the vigorous trade in slaves in East Africa that prepared the way for the European conquest of Africa. If Livingstone was a missionary general to show the way into Africa, there were many other missionaries more concerned with conversion to Christianity than exploration. The teachings and preaching by Protestant evangelicals in the eighteenth century had given spiritual relief to the grinding poverty and harsh working conditions in the new urban cities of the Industrial Revolution. The foundation of the evangelical movement was built on populist principles and led by the charisma and character of common men and women rather than the elite Catholic brotherhoods or the established Protestant Church of England dominated by the monarchy and landed nobility.

Each of the evangelical churches organized its own missionary societies during the early nineteenth century. These churches were financially supported by their large constituencies in Europe, particularly Great Britain, that could not be politically ignored or their motivations criticized. All had close ties with the influential British and other European abolitionists whose secular principles were synonymous with their religious ideology. Although the Europeans had been trading on the West African coast for 300 years, they were confined to their ships or their coastal trading forts. They knew little of the African societies and, more important, of the traditional religions with which Christianity would have to compete in order to replace them as the true faith. It was not surprising, therefore, that the European missionaries in the first half of the nineteenth century perceived that their success depended on the conversion and training of an African clergy who in turn would be the vanguard in the spread of Christianity throughout the continent. The arrival of European and African Christian missionaries created a dilemma for the African authorities and their subjects. The Africans may have been indifferent to the Christian message, but they could not and did not want to ignore the skills of the European missionaries or their African disciples. Africans wanted the talents and material goods of the European missionaries, the price for which was often acceptance of the Christian faith.

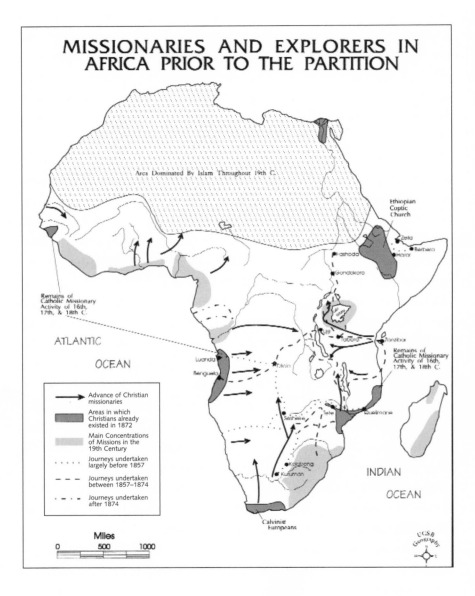

MISSIONARIES AND EXPLORERS IN
AFRICA PRIOR TO THE PARTITION

A pervasive and powerful force, the missionaries who brought a new religion and the skills necessary to use it slowly made their way into the interior of Africa. In many regions they were in advance of the merchants and the military, but if the missionaries were the new harbingers of change by faith in nineteenth-century Africa, European traders had been transforming African coastal societies by the trade in slaves since the end of the sixteenth century. Throughout 400 years of West African trade, the mercantile interests of the European merchants and the African traders remained the same. In the first twenty years of the nineteenth century, however, this historic commercial contract came to an end with the abolition of the slave trade. British merchants who had to abandon the trade now sought to extend what was known as "legitimate" commerce into the populous interior of Africa being opened by European explorers and Christian missionaries. They were encouraged by the free trade principles of the British government, combined with the systematic application of quinine, which allowed European entrepreneurs to follow the explorers and missionaries for commercial exploitation and to advance national interests without the state having to occupy unwanted territory or creating troublesome military and administrative responsibilities at great expense.

European Conquest of African States from the Sahel to the Southern Savanna

The European conquest of Africa during the last quarter of the nineteenth century was so abrupt and unexpected that its causes were puzzling to contemporaries at the time and remain to this day a source of controversy and debate among historians. At the beginning of the twentieth century, it had become increasingly clear that the changing equilibrium between Africa and Europe, which had drawn

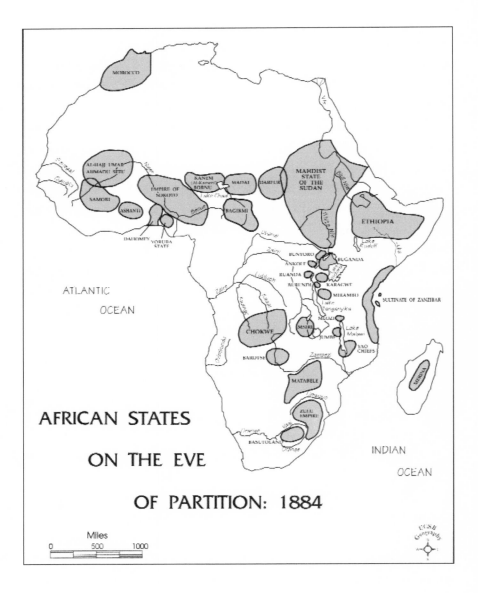

AFRICAN STATES

ON THE EVE

OF PARTITION: 1884

Europeans into the heart of Africa and its affairs in the nineteenth century, had collapsed, but to those bewildered observers in the last quarter of that century the sudden conquest of the African continent by European nation-states was a frantic, unexpected, and often unseemly scramble for African territory. Between 1878 and 1898 virtually the entire continent was partitioned by European states that during the previous 400 years had paid scant attention to Africa beyond its coastline. It was all very perplexing, perhaps frivolous, but best explained by the eminent British historian Sir John R. Seeley in 1883 that the empire had been acquired "in a fit of absence of mind," a cryptic phrase that became as famous as it was simplistic.[1] The conquest of Africa was made possible by the dramatic technological disparity between Europe and Africa that had its origins in the Enlightenment and the Industrial Revolution. There had to be, of course, the political will and public acceptance for the conquest and for the establishment of colonies inhabited by millions of Africans hitherto free of European governance, but the expansion of European empires in Africa could not have been accomplished without the new scientific and technical inventions that transformed European society and redistributed power and authority.

Steamboats, railways, and the telegraph certainly facilitated the European conquest of Africa, but the most decisive difference between the forces of Africa and Europe in the nineteenth century was the revolution in firearms. In the 1860s the muzzle-loading musket of the Napoleonic era was replaced by the single breech-loader, which by the 1880s had become the magazine repeating rifle. In 1885 Hiram S. Maxim (1840–1916) took the logic of the repeating rifle one step further by binding them into a revolving column, the Maxim gun, the prototype of the modern machine gun, against which Africans had no defense. All of these instruments of empire building would have remained useless so long as disease implacably struck down the European invaders. There were numerous diseases—yellow

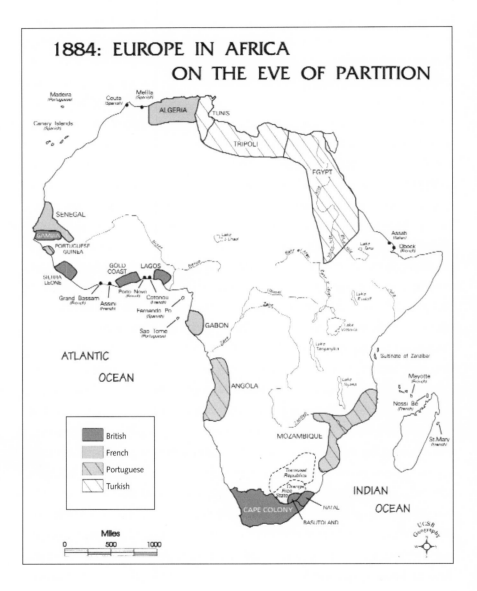

1884: EUROPE IN AFRICA
ON THE EVE OF PARTITION

fever, sleeping sickness, yaws, endemic syphilis, leprosy—but the greatest killer for Africans and particularly Europeans, who unlike some Africans had no immunities, was endemic malaria. By the 1860s and 1870s, however, the prophylactic quinine was in regular use by European missionaries, merchants, and soldiers. As much as steam, telegraphy, and firearms, quinine made possible the new imperialism in tropical Africa.

The new imperialism of the nineteenth century was accompanied by a new European self-confidence, which cannot be measured like ships, guns, or quinine but whose pervasive power enabled the Europeans to control continents, command millions, and harness knowledge for prosperity, progress, and prestige. Was it not their duty, indeed moral obligation, to promote the advancement of European civilization in Africa? Were they not ordained to bring light to those living in darkness and to march with the civilized vanguard of humanity motivated by a supreme calling, the "white man's burden"? This crusade could justify the imposition upon Africans of a new and presumably a better way of living by the extension of empire, even if it required the slaughter of those who refused to accept an alien culture and its civilization. The manifestation of this powerful force remains with us to this very day in different forms, mutations, and institutions, usually expressed in the most compelling appeals for humanitarian assistance but frequently as the affirmation of national greatness by the neo-imperialists of the twenty-first century.

The new technology and self-confidence of the Victorian era found their expression in nationalism. France and Great Britain were old countries with old empires. Germany and Italy, ambitious nations created in the last quarter of the nineteenth century, were to make their own significant contributions to the new imperialism and the conquest of Africa. In January 1871 Germany had become unified under Otto von Bismarck (1815–1898) by blood and iron and was now determined to confirm its military domination in Europe by acquiring empire abroad, beginning in Africa. Italy also became a unified nation-state in 1866. Like the Germans, the Italians sought to prove their rightful place in the African sun by staking out their claims for colonies in Ethiopia and the Horn of Africa. The aggressive new nationalism that had built states in Europe was soon turned loose to create new empires in Africa.

The new technology and medicine made the European conquest of Africa possible. The new nationalism bestowed upon the statesmen of Europe the incentives, approval, and authority to do so. The drama, speed, and success of the European conquest of this vast and relatively unknown continent have often diminished and even obscured the crucial role played by Africans in the history of their subjugation. During the conquest, many Africans, both rulers and subjects, had much to lose; others perceived they had much to gain. African resistance to the invaders was sometimes feeble, often heroic, but Africans throughout the continent frequently determined the pace, the character, and the reality of the European invasion. Other Africans decided there was more to be gained by cooperation than hostility and readily allied with the invaders and in their own way deeply influenced the European conquest of the continent.

The swift defeat of African armies by British forces has produced among the public and historians alike the false impression that the African armies gained little by their futile resistance, but upon closer examination this does not prove to be the case. At no time in the ensuing conflicts did the superiority of the new technology replace the skill, determination, courage, and resourcefulness of individual African and European adversaries. In our appreciation of nineteenth-century technology and the awe that sophisticated science has instilled in our minds at the beginning of the twenty-first, one forgets that the skirmishes, battles, and warfare during the European conquest of Africa were intensely personal. The conduct of warfare in Africa was left largely "to the man on the spot," whether a European invader or an African defender. Individuals made choices that often had little to do with their means to make war or their ideologies but certainly shaped the nature of the conflict and its outcome. The individual in history is often overwhelmed by the sweeping drama of men at war driven by honor, country, machines, and God, but it was the individual judgment, often instant, frequently erratic, by European traders, officers, and soldiers that conditioned those decisions made in their capitals by men who often knew little of combat and less of Africa and Africans. The African defenders were no different. They weighed the prospects to resist, collaborate, or remain aloof that shaped the conquest of Africa as surely as their European counterparts on the other side of the barricade considered their actions.

If British conquests in West and East Africa and later in the Sudan were relatively swift, those of the French in the western Sudan proved long and painful in the face of African resistance. From the beginning of aggressive French military activity after the Battle of Medina in 1857 until the fall of Timbuktu in 1893 and the capture of Samori Turé (1830–1900) in 1898, the French had to engage in many hard-fought battles to complete the conquest of their western Sudanic empire. After 1870, the forward advance of the French in the search for greatness in the hinterland of the western Sudan accelerated, but its pace was still agonizingly slow. Despite the best efforts of the French commanders known as the Officiers Sudanais, who became infamous for regularly ignoring orders from Paris to employ diplomacy rather than force, and their struggling columns of African troops, the Tiraileurs Sénégalais, equipped with repeating rifles and artillery, it still required another thirty years to subdue the warrior chiefs of the western Sudan and their armies of *sofas* equipped with rifles, swords, and daggers.

The rulers of Europe gave the orders to conquer Africa, and their officers were expected to carry out those commands to victory, but it was the black African soldier, not white continental troops, who did most of the fighting for the Europeans. They were not only five times less susceptible to tropical diseases and much cheaper, but trained in European military techniques they became disciplined and resilient fighters. Belonging to neither traditional African societies nor socially accepted by Europeans, the composition and motivations of these African troopers were strikingly similar. They were often marginalized members of their societies or bound by personal friendship or ethnic ties to accept the pay, prestige, and security of the battalion in return for their submission to European discipline, demands, and their lives in combat against other Africans. Many learned skills for later civilian employment after demobilization. Others established family traditions for sons to follow fathers in the colonial and, after independence, the national armed forces.

Technology, nationalism, and African troops may have made the invasion of Africa possible, but there were three critical events in three years—1865, 1867, and 1869—that precipitated the conquest. In 1865 Leopold II (r. 1865–1909) became king of the Belgians. King Leopold was determined to carve out a personal empire from what he called that "Magnificent African Cake." Obsessed with Africa, intelligent, mystically romantic, and rich, King Leopold was a very dangerous man not only to young European women but also to adult Africans. Two years later in 1867, a small Boer girl playing in the dry bed of the Orange River picked up a glittering stone the size of a hazel nut, a diamond of twenty-one carats worth £500. By 1871 there were 5,000 miners at Kimberley from Great Britain, Ireland, continental Europe, North America, and Australia working 700 claims and exporting over one million carats worth a total of £1.6 million. The race for the mineral wealth of Africa became a stampede from which no British government could profit except by incorporation into the empire. In 1869 the Khedive of Egypt, Ismail Pasha (1830–1895), opened the Suez Canal with panache and splendor. It was a grand event that in one stroke dramatically changed the global defensive strategy of the British Empire, since Africa no longer had to be circumnavigated. Suddenly, the Suez Canal became the linchpin of the vast Oriental estate of Great Britain.

King Leopold was the first to take the initiative to acquire an African empire. In 1876 he established the Comate des Etudes due Haut Congo (Committee for the Study of the Upper Congo) to further his more ambitious schemes for outright ownership of African territory. Leopold promptly hired the famous explorer Henry Morton Stanley, ostensibly to curtail the slave trade but in reality to make treaties with the Congo chiefs by which they granted full sovereignty of their territory to Leopold's scientific committee. Leopold used all his prestige as a relatively powerless king of little Belgium presumably interested only in the advancement of science and the abolition of the slave trade and slavery. He lobbied the courts of Europe with vigor, officials with flattery, humanitarians with tirades against the slave trade, and impecunious but influential journalists with cash. A year later Leopold was to receive his reward, the Congo, as his personal fief with accountability to no one but himself.

Although the British had long been fascinated by Egypt, their interests were largely concerned with its dynastic monuments, its cotton for the textile mills of Lancashire, and its strategic location in the eastern Mediterranean. In 1882, when Egyptian nationalists led by Colonel Arabic Pasha (1839–1896) threatened to seize the Suez Canal, a British expeditionary force landed at Ismailia, destroyed the Egyptian army at Tel el-Kefir, and occupied Egypt. The British occupation ensured control of the Suez Canal. The security of the canal was subject to whomever ruled at Cairo, however, and their control was totally dependent upon the waters of the Nile, whose source was 4,000 miles in the heart of Africa. The British soon realized that to protect Suez they had to secure the Nile waters for Egypt. Reluctantly but relentlessly, the British in Egypt proceeded to acquire over a million square miles of African territory in eastern Africa and the Sudan to protect the Nile waters. By 1889, twenty years after the opening of the Suez Canal, the British were completely committed to employ all their considerable military, diplomatic, and economic power to exclude any European or African state from the Nile basin in order to secure Egypt and Suez.

When British prime minister Lord Salisbury (1830–1903) became convinced that no European power should be allowed access to the Nile waters, as also Britain's foreign minister, he used all his diplomatic skills to defend the Nile and Suez. In 1890 Germany agreed to have no further interest in the Nile waters in return for the Germanic island of Heliogland in the North Sea, and the following year Italy promised not to interfere with the natural flow of the Blue Nile in return for British neutrality in the Italian invasion of Ethiopia. On March 1, 1896, Salisbury's policy to let the Italians defend the eastern approach to the Nile collapsed when Emperor Menelik II and his Ethiopian host destroyed the Italian army of General Oreste Baratieri (1841–1901) at the Battle of Adua. This dramatic victory by a technically inferior African nation against the army of a European invader had a profound and lasting impact on Africa. It is remembered throughout Africa today. March 1 is the Ethiopian national holiday, and Addis Ababa is the headquarters of the African Union. The Italian defeat opened the way for French expeditions from Ethiopia and another under Captain Jean-Baptiste Marchand to seize the upper Nile waters at Fashoda and challenge British control in Egypt and at the Suez Canal.

When in the spring of 1897 British intelligence reported Marchand astride the Congo-Nile watershed and heading for Fashoda, the British prime minister ordered General Horatio Herbert Kitchener (1850–1916) and his Anglo-Egyptian army to Khartoum. The British won the river war of 1897–1898, the most massive European military intervention in the conquest of Africa, by logistics, technical superiority, discipline, and the training of the Anglo-Egyptian forces. The

Khalifa Abdallahi (1846–1899), ruler of the Mahdist State, responded to the invasion by concentrating his armies at the capital of Omdurman at the confluence of the Blue and White Niles. On the nearby plains of Karari, his overwhelming forces would fall upon the invaders, presumably exhausted from their long march from Egypt, and destroy them in one apocalyptic battle. On September 2, 1898, some 26,000 British, Egyptian, and Sudanese infantry, supported by gunboats and Maxim guns, engaged the Khalifa's army, consisting of some 70,000 Mahdist Ansar. By noon the Khalifa's army was destroyed. Kitchener, accompanied by a flotilla of gunboats and steamers carrying two British battalions, confronted Marchand at Fashoda three weeks later. The British government absolutely refused to concede the Nile waters to France and prepared for war, but the French army and navy were in no condition to fight for Fashoda. Marchand was recalled. The crisis was over and with it the "scramble" for Africa by the Europeans, who now had to complete and consolidate their conquests. From its source to its mouth, the Nile was firmly British, as were the territories in southern and central Africa acquired by Cecil Rhodes. Africa was securely partitioned among the European powers. They now had to contemplate the distasteful business of suppressing African resistance in their new colonial acquisitions and the more disturbing question of governing Africans while exploiting their human and material resources.

European Conquest of Southern Africa

Unlike the brief spasm of the European scramble for sub-Saharan Africa in the north at the end of the nineteenth century, the European conquest of South Africa required nearly 400 years. It was fiercely contested by Africans in a complex struggle characterized by European settlement, enslavement, economic domination, and cultur-

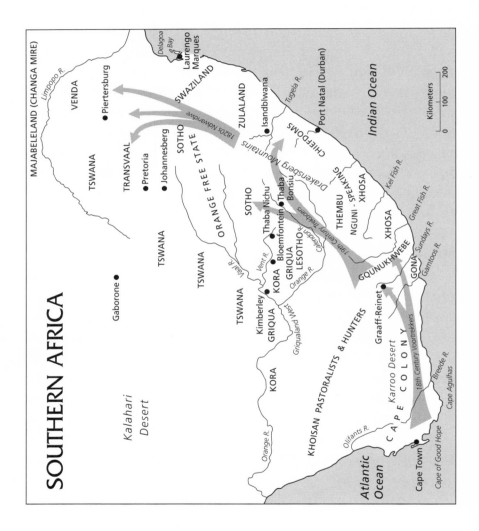

SOUTHERN AFRICA

al and sexual intercourse that produced mixed communities of Afro-Europeans. In 1649 a stranded Dutchman who had wintered at Table Bay convinced the Dutch East India Company (Dutch Vereenigde Oost-Indisch Compagnie, V.O.C.) to establish a settlement to reprovision its ships on the long voyage to and from Asia. Three years later Jan van Riebeeck (1619–1677) arrived in command of eighty company employees to build a fort and supply their ships. In 1657 the company began to release its employees from their contracts and give them land as free burghers to be boers (Dutch: farmers). Their numbers increased throughout the seventeenth and eighteenth centuries by immigration from the Netherlands and from French Protestant refugees fleeing from Catholic persecution, the Huguenots, who were soon assimilated into Dutch culture, language, and the religion of the Dutch Reform Church. The indigenous Khoi and San surrounding the Cape were unwilling to become slave labor for these Dutch farmers, who consequently imported slaves. The first shipment of slaves arrived in 1658 from Dahomey in West Africa, but thereafter the slaves came from the Dutch East Indies, Ceylon, India, and Madagascar, bringing with them a rich cultural, linguistic, and religious diversity. The company and the free burghers were soon dependent upon slave labor, and by the eighteenth century the distinctive characteristics of slavery at the Cape had become solidified. By 1711 slaves outnumbered the free burghers, but only a few officials and farmers owned more than a hundred slaves, several burghers possessed fewer than fifty, and half of them no more than six.

Any expansion by the Dutch at the Cape had at first been contained by the Khoi and the arid Karoo, the vast scrubland that stretched to the north and east. Gradually and throughout the eighteenth century, younger sons of farmers and landless settlers began to make their way through the Khoi territories and across the Karoo to the more attractive grasslands that lay beyond. They drifted into the interior, living by herding and hunting, to become increasingly removed from life at the Cape. These white pastoralists, called *trek-boers* (Dutch: migrant farmers), lived the independent, Spartan, and often violent life of the frontier, which included sexual intercourse with Africans, slave and free. Such a life frequently brought them into conflict with Khoi pastoralists and San hunter-gatherers, who in turn would rustle their cattle and sheep and even attack the homes of white farmers. The *trekboers* retaliated by organizing their own military operation, called a commando. By the end of the eighteenth century, the commandos had enslaved the indigenous peoples of southwestern Africa, except those who fled for safety into the interior to become mixed communities who called themselves by a variety of names, including Baastards and Griqua. During this same period, a similar community of mixed parentage of those who had remained behind in the Cape Colony, known as the Cape Coloured, emerged as a distinctive society.

Far to the east of the Cape on the high plateau of southern Africa lived Bantu-speaking communities divided by language, material culture, and political organization, but this diversity was relatively superficial and frequently concealed the fundamental continuities that bound them together. All spoke languages of the Bantu branch (Benue-Congo) of the greater Niger-Congo language family and engaged in agriculture, including keeping livestock, especially cattle. The first of them to encounter the advancing white Dutch *trekboers* were the Xhosa, the southernmost of the Nguni communities.

By 1800 the *trekboers* had been checked by the Xhosa in the east, and at the Cape memories of the glorious Dutch past had faded. Cape Town had settled into a sleepy existence as just another port of call in a declining empire. The French Revolution and the subsequent Napoleonic wars, however, suddenly revealed the enormous strategic importance of the Cape peninsula to Great Britain, now the world's dominant sea power. Great Britain occupied the Cape in 1806, only to be confronted by incredibly complex problems of governance.

On the one hand, the British presence stimulated a sluggish local economy. On the other, English, and no longer Dutch, became the official language of government; English common law began to take precedence over the codified Dutch Roman law; and the languid, inefficient Dutch administration was replaced by a modern, reliable bureaucracy that was reluctant to take on new administrative responsibilities on the eastern frontier. Finally, the British promulgated in 1828 the Fiftieth Ordinance, giving the Khoi and "free people of colour" equality with whites before the law, to be followed in 1833 by the emancipation of slaves throughout the British Empire, both of which produced outrage and hostility among the Dutch. Discontent ran deep and was symbolized by the Dutch adopting the name of Boer, and later Afrikaner, to distinguish themselves from the English. In the tradition of the eighteenth-century *trekboers*, the Boers were determined to protect their spiritual beliefs, their material culture, and their property by moving from the Cape beyond the control of misguided and oppressive British authority.

At the end of the eighteenth century, the northern Nguni living in the hills and valleys and on the adjacent coastal plain between the Drakensberg Mountains and the Indian Ocean were organized into small chiefdoms. A generation later, by the 1830s, the northern Nguni had undergone a dramatic cultural, political, and social transformation. The reasons for this revolution of Nguni society remain unclear to this day, but by 1820 Shaka (ca. 1790–1828) and his Zulu armies controlled the coastal plain of southeast Africa. The Zulu kingdom of Shaka was a state organized for war, with a permanent standing army of some 40,000 warriors dedicated to the expansion of the Zulu empire. Warfare no longer involved disputes over grass, water, and cows but the means by which to acquire vast amounts of territory, incorporate defeated chiefdoms, and seize large quantities of confiscated food and cattle as booty. Not surprisingly, there was deep disaffection and frequent rebellions throughout the 1820s against Shaka,

who brutally suppressed them by merciless Zulu campaigns that produced a massive migration of refugees, many miles of despoiled
lands, and widespread destruction. This period was often called "the
time of troubles" (Zulu: *Mfecame*; Sesotho: *Difaqane*). Many of these
refugees organized their own militant bands and employed Nguni
military tactics and administrative techniques to carry out their own
plunder and conquest. Some crossed the Drakensbergs to the high
veld in the west, establishing themselves by force of arms among the
Sotho-Tswana communities. Others headed south among the Xhosa,
ultimately destabilizing their frontier with the Cape Colony. One
group, led by the Zulu leader Mzilikazi (ca. 1790–1868), embarked in
1821 on a long odyssey throughout the high veld, eventually settling
in the western region of modern Zimbabwe, where he founded the
Ndebele kingdom. The Sotho leader Moshoeshoe (1786–1870) gathered together the refugees in the Caledon River valley on the mesa
called Thaba Bosiu, who repulsed the Ndebele warriors of Mzilikazi
and established the present-day Kingdom of Lesotho. In the mountains northwest of Zululand, Sobhuza (1780–1839) laid the foundations for the Kingdom of Swaziland. Shaka did not live to see the end
of this traumatic restructuring of African society throughout much
of southern Africa; he was assassinated by his half-brother, Dingane
(ca. 1795–1840), on September 24, 1828, who became the new king of
the Zulu.

Descriptions of the fertile lands of the coastal plain depopulated
by Zulu raiders attracted the attention of the Cape Afrikaner population who detested British rule and, in the traditional fashion of the
trekboers, were seeking new lands far beyond the reach of the British
authorities. Parties of *voortrekkers* were soon on the move in what
came to be known as the Great Trek. By 1840 some 6,000 Afrikaners,
10 percent of the white population of the Cape, had marched into the
interior. There they were confronted by the Ndebele warriors of
Mzilikazi, against whom the guns of the *voortrekkers* prevailed.

Alarmed by the defeat of the Ndebele and threatened by those *voortrekkers* now descending from the high veld into Natal, Dingane launched his Zulu regiments against them on February 6, 1838, killing many and capturing large herds of cattle and sheep. When news of the massacre reached Natal, a *voortrekker* commando led by Andries Pretorius (1798–1853) was mobilized to seek vengeance. On December 15, 1838, Pretorius and 500 men encircled their wagons at the Ncome River (later renamed Blood River by the *voortrekkers*). With incomparable courage, 10,000 Zulu attacked, only to retreat before *voortrekker* guns, leaving behind some 3,000 dead. The Afrikaners suffered not a single casualty. This was the first and most dramatic example in Africa of the power of the new European technology that was to be relentlessly employed against African military forces until the end of the European conquest. In the aftermath of Blood River, the Zulu kingdom declined into disarray as the *voortrekkers* established their supremacy in Natal south of the Tugela River.

British officials at the Cape watched the expansion of the *trekboers* with considerable trepidation, fearing that conflict in the far interior between *voortrekkers* and Africans would require British intervention. The conflict appeared to have been resolved in 1854 when the Cape government officially recognized the autonomy of the two largest *voortrekker* settlements, the Orange Free State north of the Orange (Gariep) River and the South African Republic beyond the Vaal. By the middle of the nineteenth century, the historical mixing of the diverse communities of southern Africa—Khoi, Boer, Briton, Bantu, and Griqua—emboldened the original white Europeans, the Dutch and now their displaced *voortrekker* descendants, to forge a new sense of identity to preserve their cultural heritage. The Great Trek and the victory over the Zulu at Blood River became the source for historical traditions that linked the *voortrekkers* into what they perceived as their national struggle against Africans and the British, and by the end of the nineteenth century the Dutch and Boers had become

Afrikaners. By 1862 two centuries of European settlement in southern Africa had destroyed some indigenous societies and transformed others, but beyond the Cape Colony settler control over African communities was tenuous. Powerful African states on the high veld, in Natal and Zululand, had contained the insatiable territorial ambitions of the Afrikaners in an uneasy equilibrium. This was soon upset by the South African mineral revolution, which proved a greater threat to African societies than European farmers and pastoralists and ultimately determined the success of white domination throughout southern Africa.

In 1867, on the northern border of the Cape Colony, alluvial diamonds were discovered on a *trekboer* farm. By 1872, 20,000 whites and 30,000 blacks were engaged as independent miners or the employees of white miners in the extraction of diamonds on the site they called Kimberley. Since the diamonds lay in shallow clay beds, they could initially be mined by simple tools, which enabled Africans to extract the diamonds. The soon outnumbered white miners formed "digger committees," which used threats and violence to prevent Africans from owning their diggings, thereby forcing them to labor in white mines on white miners' terms. Having dubiously annexed Kimberley, the British left labor relations, for which the Cape government was responsible, to the digger committees, whose industrial rules defined and hardened the racism of the Dutch agrarian settlers. Kimberley quickly became a rough-and-ready frontier town with a plethora of competing, often petty claims that within a decade had been consolidated into the mining monopoly of De Beers Consolidated Mines led by Cecil Rhodes (1853–1902), Alfred Beit (1853–1906), and Barney Barnato (1852–1897).

The discovery of diamonds had produced a massive influx of immigrants and wealth into southern Africa. The newcomers were miners whose interests, outlooks, and industrial pursuits were drastically different from the agrarian, pastoral Afrikaners and completely ignored the independent and powerful African states—the Xhosa chiefdoms; the Zulu kingdom; the Afrikaner republics of the Orange Free State and the South African Republic, commonly known as the Transvaal; and the British-dominated Cape and Natal. In 1866 the remnants of the Xhosa chieftaincies were incorporated into the Cape Colony. The Zulu kingdom was next. In 1872 Cetshwayo (1832–1884) became king of the Zulu. He was determined to restore his authority and that of his central government and to revive the Zulu to the glorious days of Shaka. The powerful secretary of Native affairs and British agent in Natal, Theophilus Shepstone (1817–1893), had annexed the Transvaal to the British Crown in 1877. To secure the support of the Afrikaners for his policy of humbling Cetshwayo and containing the Zulu, he encouraged their insatiable demands for Zulu territory. The following year Shepstone and his officials in Natal had become convinced that only by the destruction of Zulu independence would the mighty Zulu warriors be reduced to wage laborers. Shepstone demanded Cetshwayo disband the Zulu army. The king refused and mobilized 30,000 Zulu warriors, who massacred 1,600 British troops on January 22, 1879, at the highland pass of Isandhlwana. It was the greatest British military defeat since the Crimean War. British reinforcements were rushed to Natal and after heavy fighting captured the Zulu capital of Ulundi in July. The Zulu kingdom never recovered and was officially annexed between the British and the Transvaal in 1887.

Once the Zulu threat had been broken, in 1881 the Afrikaners in the Transvaal, chafing under British governance, once again proclaimed their independence. After the Afrikaner victory over a British force at Majuba Hill, the British government conceded self-government to the Transvaal but retained control of the republic's foreign policy and Native affairs. The British might have possibly remained satisfied with this somewhat ambiguous relationship if not for the discovery of the world's largest deposits of gold in 1886 at Witwatersrand in the heart of the Transvaal forty miles south of the capital, Pretoria. The phenomenal wealth of Witwatersrand, however, threatened to upset the balance of power in southern Africa. Efforts by British officials to draw the Transvaal into closer union with the Cape proved fruitless, and a filibustering raid in 1896 led by Dr. Leander Starr Jameson (1856–1917) on behalf of Rhodes and his British South African Company utterly failed to overthrow the Transvaal government. Three years later the Orange Free State and the Transvaal had become convinced that the British government was determined to destroy the independence of the Transvaal. On October 11, 1899, the war began, called the Boer War by the British, the Second War of Freedom by the Afrikaners, and the South African War by historians today.

For two and a half years 88,000 fighting Afrikaners were able to defeat, harass, and hold in check 450,000 British troops and their imperial allies from Canada, Australia, and New Zealand. British victory was ultimately achieved after Lord Kitchener of Khartoum introduced scorched-earth policies that destroyed over 30,000 Afrikaner farms and established camps where the civilian population was concentrated. Nearly 28,000 Afrikaner women and children died of disease at these camps. Overwhelmed by death, disease, and desertions, the Afrikaner armies surrendered, and their commando officers signed the Peace of Vereeniging on May 31, 1902.

In defeat, the Afrikaners were more united and more committed to Afrikaner nationalism than ever before. They were determined to insist on the clause in the Peace of Vereeniging that granted the white Afrikaners of the Transvaal and Orange Free States the right to decide if their black African subjects would be permitted to vote, which everyone knew would never happen. Afrikaner solidarity was accompanied by postwar disenchantment with South Africa in England, which convinced the British government to appease the Afrikaners in order to protect its financial, mining, and business interests. The Transvaal and the Orange River Colony were granted self-government in 1907, which ensured the vote only for whites, including British South Africans, most of whom now supported the Afrikaners. When the South African Party came to power in the Cape with the support of the Afrikaner Bond, the principal organization to promote the cause of the Afrikaners, it became increasingly clear that British material interests and the islands of white South Africans surrounded by a sea of blacks could only be protected by some sort of a political union. The nineteenth-century vision of an imperial confederation and schemes by Cecil Rhodes for a British southern Africa from the Cape to the Zambezi had never died, and in October 1908 the all-white national constitutional convention for a united South Africa was convened in Durban. The constitution they drafted was overwhelmingly approved by the individual colonial governments, and on May 31, 1910, eight years to the day after the Afrikaner military forces had surrendered, the four colonies of the Transvaal, Orange River, Natal, and the Cape became the Union of South Africa.

European Colonial Rule in Africa

European colonial rule in Africa was relatively brief. Most of the colonies conquered or annexed after 1885 were independent less than eighty years later, yet this brisk episode produced a massive disruption of African societies and left a legacy of strong, centralized, authoritarian governments. European colonial states differed dramatically from the traditional political systems Africans had developed during their long precolonial history. Not surprisingly, most Africans regarded them as the imposition of an unfamiliar, unwanted, and unnecessary means of governance. Within a generation, discontented Africans began to organize movements that soon demanded national liberation and ultimately independence, but by then the European ideas of

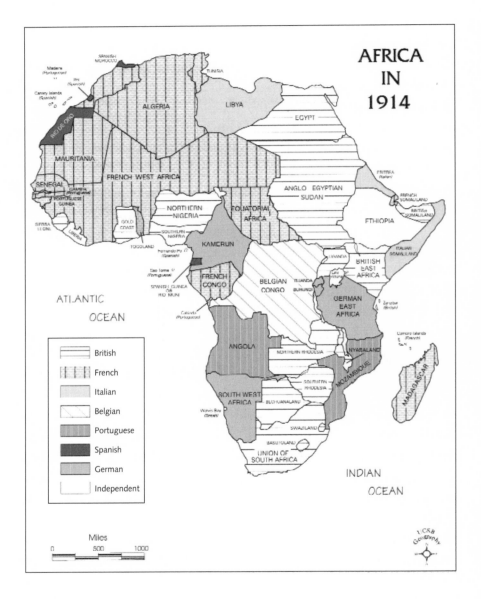

AFRICA
IN
1914

Legend:

- British
- French
- Italian
- Belgian
- Portuguese
- Spanish
- German
- Independent

ATLANTIC OCEAN

INDIAN OCEAN

Miles

0   500   1000

strong, protective governments had become so deeply entrenched that the new leaders of independent African states ironically embraced the colonial state system they had vowed to dismantle. Today the structure of administration in most African states has changed little from that bequeathed to them by their European conquerors. Although that European inheritance differed according to the traditions of law and government introduced by French, British, Portuguese, Belgian, German, and Italian officials into their African colonies, the diverse methods of administration employed by these imperial rulers shared some fundamental common features.

Like the nation-states of nineteenth-century Europe, European African colonies were demarcated, at least on maps if not always on the ground, by territorial boundaries, while the division of precolonial African states was more closely associated with communities of people in which networks of lineage and kinship defined the borders. Some Africans now found themselves associated with peoples with whom they had little or no previous contact, and other homogeneous ethnic groups discovered themselves divided between two alien rulers by a boundary that for them made no sense and created a great deal of inconvenience if not hardship. The colonial borders, largely drafted in the staterooms of Europe, ensured that few colonies would have a linguistically homogeneous population and guaranteed that most would contain a bewildering array of ethnically diverse Africans. Upon independence, African leaders, fearing that the redrafting of boundaries would lead to endless and even bloody boundary disputes, retained this European legacy that is today the jigsaw political geography of modern Africa.

Another common feature of European colonial rule was the ability of each nation to extend its authority throughout the colony by the sophisticated toolbox of industrial technology—telegraphs, railways, steamboats, and repeating rifles—that enabled the Europeans to impose an unprecedented degree of communication, coercion, and centralization. Although there were remote pockets of unknown Africans that the colonial administration never reached and isolated communities that never fully submitted to the new European order, European technologies and the colonial armies equipped with them imposed and enforced an unprecedented degree of political consolidation of hitherto diverse African polities.

Moreover, the European conquest of Africa was carried out without any preparation, planning, or even an ideology by which to establish the governance of colonies once pacified. The result in virtually every colony was a jerry-built administrative structure that was the product of ad hoc decisions to grapple with the many unexpected challenges of ruling vast regions of the Africa continent. Administration was left largely to the European officials on the ground—usually white officers leading African armies—who determined the methods by which to administer the new colonies. This may explain the diversity and national peculiarities of each colonial administration and the fact that the development of more systematic colonial administration with rational regulations and defined objectives only came after the pacification of the colony. It fails to explain, however, why little thought was given to the administration of future colonies before the conquest, except for the piratical assumption that their resources were naturally to be exploited.

Although the colonial rulers came to Africa with different European national cultures, they all would agree that their colonies should be financially self-sufficient and most certainly not a burden on domestic taxpayers, many of whom were very ambivalent about the imperial mission of their governments. On the one hand, this principle required colonial governments to practice a frugality that precluded the recruitment of a sufficient number of expensive European officials to administer vast territories inhabited by different Africans with differing needs. On the other, the thin khaki line of colonial administrators that arrived in Africa was expected to extract as much desperately needed revenue as possible with only a casual regard for the most egregious and visible human abuses.

Consequently, the colonial governments were staffed by a very small number of European officials who held all the principal political administrative positions and most of the military ranks above captain in the officer crops of the colonial armies. Therefore, the colonial bureaucracies soon came to be dependent upon Africans to act as interpreters, policemen, clerks, and typists and to perform a variety of other menial jobs in the colonial service. In return for low pay, long hours, and few psychological rewards, these recruits, who often had some training in a mission school, learned linguistic, clerical, and technical skills that set them apart from those who remained with their cattle in the pastures. Within less than a generation, this colonial system had created a class of Western-educated men, for virtually all of them were men, who were often scornfully referred to by their white superiors as "half-educated" but who had achieved an understanding of the workings of the colonial state.

This cadre of minor civil servants was necessary to make the colonial administration function, but they could not become and were never considered political leaders. With limited resources and few European political and administrative officials, all colonial governments were therefore forced to rely on the traditional or accepted African leaders to carry out colonial policy and practice. During and after the conquest and pacification, the administration sought the cooperation of the existing African political leaders by flattery, bribery, rewards, and threats. When collaboration of a traditional leader was not forthcoming, a pliant nonentity was often given a position of authority and expected to execute the wishes of his white political overseers. The British in Africa enthusiastically embraced this concept of ruling through "Native authorities" as "indirect rule," which evolved quite rationally from preexisting British domestic and imperial institutions.

The indirect rule of 129 million subjects of British colonial Africa required the cooperation of the traditional authorities or their pliable surrogates who would employ traditional laws and customs that encouraged subject peoples to associate closely with their own ethnic identity, often in competition with neighboring ethnic communities. They would be advised by a British official who knew the language and, hopefully, the laws and customs of the people under his tutelage. In theory, indirect rule would cause the least possible disruption in the lives of Africans during a time of gradual change by allowing their traditional leaders to administer justice, collect taxes, and implement the policies of the colonial government. In practice, however, indirect rule contained numerous inherent contradictions that unintentionally transformed African custom, law, and politics.

First, the system confirmed traditional rulers in their positions of leadership. At the same time, however, the British adviser demanded that the chiefs undertake a host of new and unpopular responsibilities that included recruiting soldiers for colonial service, collecting new taxes, and providing laborers for public works or for European farms. Chiefs charged with imposing these new demands on their subjects often became lightning rods for public dissent. Second, indirect rule aspired to govern Africans through their own laws in Native courts, but that "customary law" was inevitably transformed when traditional rulers could no longer use the "barbaric customs" to eliminate rivals and malcontents or to overawe and intimidate their subjects. Such "customs" had been essential instruments to maintain political and social order. African jurisprudence was also changed by the simple act of codifying and standardizing "customary law." In the non-Muslim African kingdoms, custom and law were part of an oral tradition that was constantly being subject to interpretation to meet new circumstances and could vary widely within a single linguistic or ethnic community. The very act of writing down "customary laws," however, made them uniform, static, and unable to respond to changing conditions, which ensured the privileges and interests of those Africans whose version happened to be the one that was codified. The status of women was acutely affected by this codification of "customary law," for the patriarchal authority of males in African society was reinforced and fixed in place, solidifying the second-class status of women in African societies.

Although every colonial power at one time or another contemplated, imposed, or abandoned some variant of British indirect rule, the French at first experimented with a policy of "assimilation," which has left a deep and influential legacy throughout Francophone Africa to the present day. Like British indirect rule, the French policy of assimilation was the product of French history, its revolutionary and imperial institutions, and its political traditions. The French Revolution had translated the philosophical beliefs of the eighteenth-century Enlightenment about the universality of man into practical ideas of action in the *Declaration of the Rights of Man and of the Citizen* of 1789. This document triumphantly proclaimed that all men, not just Frenchmen, are born and live free and equal in rights. These egalitarian principles obviously had to apply to the inhabitants of the French colonies, and throughout the nineteenth century France aspired to assimilate its colonial subjects through French language and culture. French enthusiasm for creating an empire of "100 million Frenchmen" was rooted in the egalitarian traditions of the French Revolution but also in the imperial heritage of Napoleon to spread the ideas of the revolution founded on the superiority of French culture.

On the surface, indirect rule and assimilation appeared dramatically different. Indirect rule assumed that Europeans and Africans had separate capabilities and destinies. Assimilation assumed that French culture was accessible to all peoples regardless of "race," which appeared to render it less overtly racists than indirect rule. However, it also presumed that French culture was superior and therefore preferable to the diverse African cultures to be found in the colonies. Although the idea of assimilation remained the theoretical framework for French colonial policy throughout the nineteenth century, there were growing doubts. By the end of the century, several of the most famous French empire-builders, Louis Faidherbe (1818–1889) in the Senegal, Joseph Gallieni (1849–1916) in Indo-China and Madagascar, and Louis Lyautey (1854–1934) in Morocco, realized that millions of Africans and Asians were not about to become French. At the end of the First World War, during which the public experienced the practical and racial problems of the presence of large numbers of Africans fighting for France on the western front, French officials embraced a policy of "association." Law and order at little expense was now to be achieved by French collaboration with the traditional authorities, accompanied by respect for their language, customs, and institutions. In theory, "association" was not much different from British indirect rule.

Many French officials believed that association was little more than assimilation disguised by the cloak of hypocrisy in which it was wrapped. French officials continued to maintain complete control of the administration of their colonies, unchecked by the chiefs who had been converted into convenient petty officials rather than representatives of their people. French administrators had no illusions about this contradiction but were quite content to ignore it in order to replace African customs, for which they had little more than contempt, by the relentless dissemination of the French language and culture. A greater percentage of French Africans learned to speak the language of their masters than their neighbors in the British colonies. During the 1930s, when African leaders in the British colonies were agitating for greater political influence in government, their cohorts in the French colonies were concerned by the threat of French cultural imperialism and rather indifferent to demands for political rights. It is no coincidence that the political movement for Pan-

African unity was born and promulgated from the British colonies, while their African intellectual counterparts in the French colonies debated the validity of "Negritude" as a cultural identity to oppose the pervasive spread of French assimilation.

Colonial Legacy

Colonialism is a discrete brand of imperialism by which a state imposes its administrative control over peoples of another culture who are manipulated for the needs of their colonial rulers with little regard for the indigenous cultures and, in Africa, a firm belief in European cultural superiority. It has always been challenged by political theorists and most demonstrably by thousands of Africans who fought and died physically resisting the imposition of colonial rule. Others, particularly Europeans at the end of the nineteenth and in the early twentieth century, sincerely believed in the virtues and obligations of colonialism, the "white man's burden," to replace slavery, tyranny, and backwardness in Africa with European commerce, Christianity, and civilization. Consequently, colonial enterprise has been both condemned as exploitive and praised as innovative. The West Indian scholar Walter Rodney asserted that Europe, beginning with the slave trade, corrupted African elites by commercial means to which they became addicted, which stifled African economic growth and led to the "underdevelopment" of Africa. Many Europeans, however, perceived colonialism as a profitable field for capital investment that would enrich themselves and develop Africa for the benefit of Africans. Others thought colonialism was the result of European strategic and geopolitical considerations. Some argued that colonialism provided legitimate employment for a declining European aristocracy. At the beginning of the twenty-first century, the controversy remains at the center of vigorous academic and journalistic debate, but there are certain aspects of European colonialism in Africa upon which the protagonists agree. European conquest and colonialism dramatically transformed Africa and Africans, played a critical role in shaping the nature of colonialism, and exposed its limitations.

The colonial experience in Africa can be roughly divided into discrete periods. At the start of the twentieth century, the beginnings of colonialism in Africa were characterized by the systematic forceful imposition of European administration, accompanied by violent economic expropriation, which Africans resisted, fled, or accommodated themselves. By the end of the First World War, the excessive abuse of Africans during the preceding decades had elicited a reaction by the European public that such behavior by colonial officials would no longer be tolerated. During the interwar years, the British and the French fumbled with their policies of indirect rule and assimilation, respectively, in futile attempts to transform African societies according to their models. Their efforts were further compromised by the world economic depression of the 1930s that produced a colonial crisis at the end of the Second World War precipitated by those allies, the United States and the Soviet Union, whose war aims included "self-determination" for the European colonies and demands for independence by the growing African political opposition. To respond to their critics, the British in 1940 and the French in 1946 launched programs for "development" that would mobilize African resources to restore African economies but also provide employment and improved conditions for African wage laborers. When it became increasingly clear that these plans for economic revitalization from the top down had failed to transform the colonial economic structure, European rulers had no other alternatives but to use massive force, which they could financially and morally ill-afford, or to grant independence, which suddenly appeared the lesser of two evils.

From their beginnings, the European colonies in Africa were governed by two institutions—the colonial economy and the colonial state. The first demand by the colonial rulers from African economies was sufficient revenue to pay for their administration. The second objective was to encourage or compel Africans to provide foodstuffs and raw materials to feed European industries and their workers and in return consume European manufactured goods. The colonial authorities, desperately in search of revenue, soon concentrated on the promotion of African cash crops best adapted to the specialized environments of individual colonies—cocoa in the Gold Coast and the Côte d'Ivoire; peanuts in Senegal and the Gambia; cotton in Tanganyika, Mozambique, Uganda, and the Anglo-Egyptian Sudan; rubber in King Leopold's Congo Free State. Raw materials were in even greater demand—copper in the southern Congo and northern Rhodesia (Zambia).

In order to generate further revenues to support the colonial state and secure a supply of valued foodstuffs, European governments encouraged their citizens to emigrate to those colonies with an environment suitable for European settlement—the British in Kenya, Tanzania, and the Rhodesias; the French in the Côte d'Ivoire; the Portuguese in Angola and Mozambique. The European settlers were mostly large plantation owners, not small farmers. Some arrived in Africa with their own considerable wealth to invest, others with only modest sums, but all were supported by the colonial state that expropriated large tracts of land for their commercial plantations or for individual farms. Land grants in extensive areas of Kenya, Tanzania, and southern Rhodesia in particular were made or sold at nominal prices to white farmers, while large tracts of the French and Belgian Congo were given to financially secure European concession companies. Land grants in Angola and the *prazo* plantation system in Mozambique had been the fundamental economic policy of Portugal since the seventeenth century.

During the European colonial period, however, labor had been and remained Africa's principal commodity. The Atlantic and Asian slave trade had been brought to an end, but slavery in its many manifestations remained widespread throughout Africa. Although European colonial policy was committed to end that "peculiar institution," colonial officials were not prepared to precipitate the social dislocation that sweeping emancipation of slavery would, they firmly believed, create. When an African slave asked for his freedom, for example, a certificate of manumission would usually be granted, but most officials did little more to transform slaves into workers. In fact, the economic policy of the colonial state was dependent upon harnessing African labor, by force if necessary, to build the infrastructure for military and political control and upon cheap workers for export-oriented industries and settler farms.

Economic and political control by the colonial state could be achieved by the construction of an elaborate infrastructure, which only European technology and capital could build. The exploitation of Africa's abundant but heavy agricultural and mineral commodities could best be made profitable from cheap transportation by railways, steamships, and roads, all of which produced dramatic changes in traditional African societies. Demands by the colonial state and the introduction of a cash economy, however, also created new responsibilities, opportunities, and lifestyles for Africans. Many African men could only fulfill their new obligation to pay a head or hut tax by finding work in domestic service, agriculture, the mines, or the colonial civil and military service. There were few workers who could perform such services and remain in their villages, and whole communities lost their male workforce for many months and often years. In this new economic environment, the young men, now engaged in wage labor, had the resources and the opportunities to challenge or ignore established hierarchies in their traditional societies. In most African communities, the dominance of older men was based on their control of land, cattle, and women. The colonial economy made it possible for these young men to circumvent these hierarchies by acquiring capital and social advancement outside of the authority of the elders. In addition, with their new wealth, there was now the prospect of land, cattle, and multiple marriages.

The participation by African males in the wage economy transformed the African roles of gender, those appropriate masculine and feminine social practices that had been negotiated and renegotiated for generations in precolonial societies. The economic and social policies imposed by the colonial state virtually excluded women from colonial employment. In many instances, these colonial views of gender enabled men in African societies to increase their patriarchal control over women. This inflation of male prestige, assisted by the colonial authorities, was not without its contradictions, for the massive labor migrations set in motion by colonial economic policies inadvertently created greater burdens and responsibilities but also new opportunities for African women. Many colonial officials, and particularly their wives, thought that African women should play a greater role in the transformation of their societies as homemakers, like middle-class European women, in addition to their traditional role as the mainstay of agricultural production. Colonialism thus placed a double burden on African women by expecting them to embrace a European cult of respectability, while at the same time encouraging the construction of migratory labor industries that further increased their responsibility for rural agricultural production.

Colonial rule also introduced profound changes in the way African peoples identified themselves. Precolonial Africans defined their identity by the ties of family, clan, and lineage, but colonial authorities sought to understand who they ruled by a census in which their new subjects were listed by discrete ethnic communities. The assumption that all Africans must belong to a "tribe" conditioned virtually every aspect by which colonial rulers administered their subjects and solidified an official identity for Africans that hitherto had been more flexible. Ethnic identity was also given greater definition by the logistics of migrant laborers, who were issued passes giving an official imprimatur to one's identity. This practice encouraged a sense of belonging to a distinct "tribe," which engendered brotherhood and pride in the bewildering melting pot of the mining townships and a strategy to maintain their ties to their rural homelands.

European colonial rule in Africa also encouraged the spread of the two great religions of the book, Christianity and Islam. Both religions had ancient roots in Africa before the colonial era, and both had witnessed dramatic expansion in the decades preceding the colonial conquest. Both religions were also able to spread more widely under the umbrella of patronage and protection by the colonial administrations at the expense of traditional African religions, but Christianity proved sufficiently elastic for many Africans to include revered aspects of their pre-Christian religious traditions in the new rituals of the missionaries. In southern and central Africa, spontaneous religious movements emerged in the twentieth century that synthesized aspects of Christian and non-Christian beliefs. While many African Christians joined the traditional Catholic and Protestant religious hierarchies of the European Christian tradition, many more followed the teachings of African preachers who founded their own dissenting Christian denominations. These zealous converts and their religious enthusiasm were regarded by concerned colonial officials as a potentially destabilizing force in African society.

Ironically, Islam expanded rapidly in those African territories under Christian colonial rulers that lay on the frontiers of Islam. Europeans had a long history of conflict with Muslims and did not want to jeopardize their fragile colonial administrations by provoking the African Muslim community. They recognized the Muslim rulers as "traditional" authorities, particularly in the western Sudan, despite the fact that many of them had only seized power by their recent jihads, holy wars, in the eighteenth and nineteenth centuries. The Muslim leaders now had the tacit support of colonial officials to encourage the conversion of Africans to Islam. Moreover, Islam was untainted by any association with European colonialism, its historical adversary. Unlike Christianity, whose missionaries were largely European or American, virtually all Muslim missionaries were Africans. Islam, like Christianity, also opened for Africans membership in a powerful, global religious tradition, but it did not require Africans to abandon their indigenous social and cultural practices, particularly polygamy.

Western education was first introduced into Africa by Christian missionaries, who continued to monopolize education in the early decades of colonial rule in Africa. After the First World War, colonial governments could no longer remain aloof from providing education for Africans. There had been increasing criticism of missionary education that was concerned more with prayer than reading, writing, and arithmetic. African elites, who at first had shunned Western education, now perceived that it was an avenue to social and political advancement and demanded that the colonial state build schools and train teachers. Secular government elementary and secondary schools were established, to which the chiefs in service to the colonial state sent their sons, who would be needed to assist the colonial bureaucracy govern a rapidly expanding population.

Despite the massive destruction and dislocation of Africans that had accompanied the European conquest of Africa, the population of Africa began to experience an extraordinary increase after the First World War, from an estimated 120 million in 1885 to 142 million in 1920. Thereafter, the population exploded, reaching 165 million by 1935 and 200 million after the Second World War. In little more than a decade, in 1960, the year of African independence, the estimated population of Africa had reached nearly 300 million. Some attribute this dramatic growth to Africans abandoning traditional constraints on births, to the end of slavery, and to better food; others attribute the astonishing increase to the introduction by colonial authorities of the means to transport food to areas in need, the containment of epidemics, and the improvement of African public health and personal hygiene made possible by colonial innovations in tropical medicine.

Modern Western media—motion pictures, phonographs, radios, and newspapers—also introduced urban Africans to the world beyond their borders. After the end of the First World War, radios and phonographs became more widely available in cities and towns, where the influence of the American cinema among urban Africans was well established by the 1920s. At the end of the Second World War, radio networks programmed for African audiences had spread throughout the continent. Over their airwaves, American jazz became a staple of urban township life. The flood of Western media soon produced the synthesis of African and American musical traditions in the development of new forms of African popular music. The evolution of highlife music in the Gold Coast was influenced by European ballroom music, Soukous in the Congo by Afro-Cuban jazz, and Isicathamiya music in South Africa by African American gospel traditions. The impact of these new forms of communication, creativity, and entertainment rapidly percolated into rural villages, for urban migration was for the most part transitory, with workers maintaining residences in both rural and urban environments and commuting between them in the expectation of retiring to their home villages.

European colonial rule also influenced Africans in less conspicuous ways. Whether to convert, commercialize, or train a civil servant, the colonial administration treated their African subjects as individuals rather than as members of corporate entities. The colonial authorities insisted that the individual rather than kin-group be held responsible for taxes, criminal and civil prosecution, debts, and job performance. This emphasis on individual responsibility was consistent with the acceptance of capitalism and Christianity, which were part and parcel of the colonial project in Africa. But perhaps the most intangible, enduring legacy of colonial rule was the psychological impact of the colonial experience, the "colonization of the mind," which had a profound influence particularly on middle-class Africans. Every colony had a small but growing number of Africans who shamelessly adopted European dress, diet, and culture. They were the first in their communities to take European names, to speak a European language, and to dress in European clothes. Many assumed the European characterization of African culture as "primitive" and believed that Africans eventually would adopt European beliefs, customs, and languages. Not all educated Africans accepted these views, but the influence of European culture was a powerful teacher and indelibly shaped the class that would take power in Africa after independence.

Note

1. John R. Seeley, *England: Two Courses of Lecturers* (London: MacMillan, 1883).

CHAPTER SIX

Independent Africa

Yomo Kenyatta

Nationalism and Independence

Today, the movement for African independence appears to have been inevitable, but no one, African or European, anticipated the course or the pace of events precipitated by the First World War that would lead to the end of European colonial empires in Africa forty years later. Even before the war, they had failed to recognize that the Europeans were inadvertently sowing the seeds of their own demise. Colonialism had already introduced new ideologies, technologies, and administrative forms of governance that Africans could easily use against the continuation of European imperial domination in Africa. Colonial rule inexorably alienated its subject peoples by its despotic, condescending, and racist policies, which were often accompanied by brutal practices. This growing anger began to appear, coalesce, and become a social and political force during the upheavals of the First World War.

The First World War relentlessly dragged the European conflict into Africa as colonial powers sought to occupy the territory of their imperial rivals. This affected every European colony but some more than others, particularly German East Africa. The war's insatiable appetite for raw materials to feed Europeans and their factories necessitated unprecedented demands on Europe's African subjects. Forced labor and requisitioned foodstuffs brought privation to Africans, most of whom were subsistence farmers and herdsmen with little surplus for Europe let alone for themselves. Even those African colonies far removed from the actual fighting experienced the relentless demands of war. All of the colonial governments arbitrarily requisitioned men into service as soldiers and laborers. France was particularly aggressive and determined to recruit Africans to fight in Europe to replace the devastating losses suffered by the French army on the western front. Many villages in the western Sudan lost most of their agricultural laborers. This loss of workers created severe scarcity and hardships for many communities that precipitated demonstrations and several rebellions. Those soldiers and workers who survived the fierce fighting in Europe often returned to African village life no longer in awe or fear of their colonial rulers. Many of them had witnessed the unprecedented scenes of Europeans killing Europeans in France and in Africa that inevitably undermined the moral authority, aura of invincibility, and the belief in the racial superiority of white Europeans.

The end of the war and subsequent peace treaty introduced significant changes in the international order that altered the colonial composition of Africa. Justified by the victors on the grounds that Germans were simply unfit to rule Africans, Germany's African colonies were transferred to France, Belgium, and Great Britain. The war also saw the emergence of two new great powers—the United States and the Soviet Union—that dominated world affairs in the latter half of the twentieth century. Although both countries became ardent opponents of European imperialism for ideologically opposite reasons, the immediate impact on Africa of their anticolonialism was limited, for both the United States and the Soviet Union during the interwar years were much too absorbed in their own internal affairs to express their hostility toward European imperialism in Africa. Moreover, an increasing number of European intellectuals had themselves begun to question the ideologies of imperialism. After the war, public enthusiasm had disappeared for many of those ideologies—

including militarism, nationalism, and social Darwinism—that had made the conquest of Africa morally acceptable.

Hard times for Africans did not end with the war in 1918. The demobilization of soldiers and laborers produced high unemployment in Africa as well as in Europe, and the painful transition from war to peace by the European economies contributed to postwar inflation and the shortage of basic European commodities imported to Africa. During the 1920s, local grievances galvanized into demonstrations and strikes that symbolized a wider condemnation of colonial rule by the new urban African workers than just anger about their working conditions in the nascent industrial economy. Such resistance was often ruthlessly suppressed by the colonial authorities, for virtually all strikes were illegal. Punitive raids against rebellious rural subjects often resulted in the destruction of villages and the slaughter of their inhabitants. These futile outbursts of discontent did not threaten the domination of colonial government in Africa, but collectively they remained a residual of smoldering resentment that later stoked the flames of broader political movements.

During the 1930s, a small group of educated Africans and trade union leaders began forming associations to increase their role in colonial governance. The most influential of these organizations were in the British West African colonies, for the British policy of indirect rule through the traditional African authorities, a policy educated Africans condemned, was predicated on the assumption that British colonies were politically separate and not a part of the national government in London. This distinction contrasted sharply with the policies of the French and Portuguese, who regarded their African possessions as overseas provinces with representation in the legislatures of Paris and Lisbon. Consequently, British West African politicians could discuss political autonomy without fear of being arrested for sedition, and British officials in the Gold Coast and Nigeria were prepared to tolerate a degree of political criticism that would not be countenanced by colonial officials in the French or Portuguese colonies. Many of the emerging African elite were more ambitious, hoping to replace the colonial order with a Pan-African union of all the former colonies and not just independent sovereign states. Not surprisingly, Pan-Africanism had its greatest following among English-speaking Africans, in contrast to those French-speakers who throughout the Francophile Africa diaspora regarded the regeneration of black Africa as more cultural than political. The French policy of assimilation was creating ambivalent concerns among many of African French-speaking intellectuals, who feared their African cultural identity would be subsumed by language and culture into an enlarged France. To counter this spread of French cultural assimilation, they advocated the concept of "Negritude," a unique black identity shared by all peoples in the African diaspora.

Of greater concern for most Africans was the beginning of the global depression in 1929, which quickly had a devastating impact on the fragile economies of every colony in the continent. Ironically, the arrival of the depression in Africa occurred at a time when the colonial authorities were finally establishing effective administration over their African subjects. By 1929 even the most isolated communities had become integrated into the colonial administrative system, and many villagers found themselves for the first time accountable to colonial tax collectors, police, and the courts. In order to meet the new obligations of hut and poll taxes, African farmers were pulled, usually with great reluctance, into the colonial economy as cash-crop farmers, miners, plantation laborers, and service workers in the rapidly expanding colonial cities. Thus, when the depression struck, vast numbers of Africans dependent on the export economy for their livelihood were thrust into poverty. African farmers and herdsmen found international demand for their crops drastically curtailed. African dockworkers became unemployed. African clerks were the first to be laid off when colonial bureaucracies retrenched. African miners could no longer expect a steady demand for their labor. Rural agrarian and urban industrial Africans were becoming increasingly frustrated by a colonial system that required more drastic change than simple reform.

By the eve of the Second World War, however, no coherent organization or movement had emerged to bind these inchoate interests and grievances into a common cause. Political associations, where they existed before 1940, were dominated by the few educated Africans who lobbied for some influence over state policy. Their demands were usually ignored by colonial officials, but their superiors in London and Paris were more sensitive to the events of the interwar years. They abandoned the illusion that the colonies should be economically self-sufficient and began to contemplate minor reforms when the Second World War and its aftermath demanded major changes in imperial policy. After the fall of France in 1940, Great Britain mobilized all the resources of its empire to fight both Germany and Japan, and British African colonies instantly became vital economic and strategic assets. Minerals from African mines, foods from African farms, and soldiers from African villages were desperately needed to make war, but those African chiefs, farmers, laborers, and soldiers would have to be given visible incentives to support the Allied cause. Local newspapers, radio, and the cinema disseminated British propaganda that victory would lead to better economic opportunities and improved political status for Great Britain's African subjects. In August 1941 U.S. president Franklin Delano Roosevelt (1882–1945) and British prime minister Winston Churchill (1874–1965) signed the Atlantic Charter, proclaiming that the war was being fought "to liberate subject peoples." Although Churchill, desperate for American support, reluctantly agreed "to liberate subject peoples," he interpreted this declaration to apply only to the people of occupied Europe, but many Africans anticipated that the charter would bring important changes for Africa at the end of the war.

When the war ended in 1945, the colonial powers had emerged victorious in no small part because of the contributions from their African empires. Although few observers in 1945 were prepared to accept a foreseeable end to colonial rule in Africa, there was general agreement that some transformation of colonialism was necessary. France abolished the hated *corvée*, or forced labor, and publicly acknowledged that Africans had earned the right to a reform of colonial administration. Britain introduced new constitutions into their West African colonies. African politicians, however, disdainfully regarded these "reforms" as mere symbols of British illusions rather than an acceptable response to the aspirations of their subjects. In October 1945 the Pan-African conference in Manchester, England, had called for the "complete and absolute independence of the people of West Africa," and in the late 1940s a small group of politicians in the Gold Coast created the United Gold Coast Convention (UGCC) and invited Kwame Nkrumah (1909–1972) to return from Britain to lead them. Nkrumah soon emerged as a powerful spokesman against colonialism at the same time that the relationship between Europe and Africa had reached a crossroads. Virtually everyone agreed that the war and its aftermath precluded any return to the colonialism of the past, but there was a deep division of opinion as to the nature of any new relationship between Europe and Africa.

The British and the French envisaged that change would come gradually by the combination of limited constitutional reforms and state-sponsored economic development. To African nationalists, this renewed commitment in London and Paris appeared little more than heavy-handed paternalism that did not address Africa's postwar problems, and it drove many rural Africans into alliance with urban leaders who offered appealing and understandable solutions. Kwame Nkrumah was one of the first to recognize that the simple demand for independence could mobilize the African masses in the countryside as well as in the cities. When more moderate politicians and elites were agitating for greater influence over colonial policies, Nkrumah electrified African crowds with the tantalizing prospect of an immediate end to British rule, which would resolve all of the postwar grievances—the tyranny of "traditional" authorities, inflation, shortages of basic goods, colonial marketing boards that paid cheap prices for farm produce, and unemployment. In the press and on the platform, Nkrumah egregiously promoted unrealistic, exaggerated expectations, believing that the problems of the people of the Gold Coast could only be properly resolved when addressed by an independent African government.

The transformation of the Gold Coast from colony to the nation of Ghana in 1957 and the powerful example of European colonies in Asia becoming independent sovereign states launched the other African colonies on their own paths to independence. Once Ghana had become independent, it became impossible for British and French negotiators to convince most African politicians to settle for something less. In 1960 British prime minister Harold Macmillan (1894–1986) delivered a speech in the South African Parliament that warned of the "winds of change" sweeping the continent. In that same year France granted independence to all of its sub-Saharan possessions, and within five years Great Britain had relinquished control over all of its colonies. In both the French and British territories, the transfer of power was peaceful, the result of protracted negotiations throughout the decade following the war, culminating in elections to a parliament and concluding with a grand ceremony celebrating the passage from colony to independent sovereign state. Unfortunately, Africans living under other colonial regimes would experience a much more difficult road during their journey to independence.

Apartheid State of South Africa

In 1910 the modern state of South Africa, the Union of South Africa, was founded after several years of hard bargaining between the Afrikaner leaders of the Dutch republics and the British government who had conquered them in the South African War (1899–1902). The settlement created a single state, a union, from the territories of Natal, Cape Colony, the Orange Free State, and the South African Republic, usually referred to as the Transvaal. Like other political combinations being forged in Nigeria and northern Rhodesia, the Union of South Africa embraced disparate communities differentiated by culture, ethnicity, and race into a geographical configuration defined by arbitrary boundaries and called a state. Unlike Nigeria and northern Rhodesia, however, South Africa included a large and diverse European population. The Union immediately became the wealthiest state on the African continent by a combination of political stability guaranteed by Great Britain and the gold industry of the Transvaal and the diamond mines of Kimberly that secured economic prosperity. Mining attracted a steady flow of investment, which produced urbanization and the many businesses required to sustain the cities that in turn stimulated the demand for foodstuffs, cattle, and sheep from the farms, fruit from the orchards, and wine from the vineyards of the Cape. This vigorous combination of the mine, the factory, and the farm endowed South Africa with a diverse and thriving internal and export economy.

Once established, the Union government began chipping away at the limited rights that Africans had enjoyed in the different provinces. The relentless passage of this repressive legislation did not go unchallenged. In 1912 the South African Native National Congress was founded by a group of mission-educated African reformers who advocated political equality for all "civilized" men. Renamed the African National Congress (ANC) in 1925, its agenda was encapsulated in the famous aphorism by Cecil Rhodes—"Equal rights for all civilized men south of the Zambezi." Having no access to the public forum, the ANC printed its own newspaper, the *Abantu-Batho* (The People), to publish its views and platform in Tswana, Xhosa, Sotho, and Zulu as well as English. As the legislation against non-Europeans became ever more numerous and restrictive, the ANC began to be regarded as a venerable but the least effective of the nascent nationalist movements in Africa. It had failed to appeal to the mass of African laborers. It also remained aloof from the Cape coloureds (Africans of mixed marriages), who had formed their own African Political Organization (APO) under Dr. Abdullah Abdurahman (1872–1940) as early as 1902, and the growing communities of South Asian immigrants, whose plight was vigorously adopted by a young Indian lawyer named Mohandas K. Gandhi (Mahatma, 1869–1948). His campaigns of nonviolent protest, or *satyagraha*, launched in 1906 against these abuses filled the jails with his followers and forced the Union government to repeal its discriminatory legislation.

Although many trace the beginnings of Afrikaner nationalism to the Great Trek of 1836–1854, its roots were firmly planted during the brutal treatment of Afrikaner civilians in the Transvaal and Orange Free State during the South African War. The preservation of Afrikaner culture and the recognition of equality with English for the Afrikaner language were paramount demands by the Afrikaner politicians during the contentious negotiations for the Union. Afrikaner leaders were also deeply concerned about the plight of "poor whites," landless Afrikaners in the countryside and unskilled Afrikaner white workers in the city who now had to face fierce competition for jobs from blacks and coloureds.

Like the rest of colonial Africa, South Africa was not immune from the economic depression at the end of the First World War. Demobilized soldiers flooded the job market, and shortages of imports produced spiraling inflation. Economic hardships had precipitated the dockworkers strike of 1919. The low price of gold and the high cost of mining at great depth for low-grade ore had produced financial losses for the mine owners best resolved by replacing white workers, whose wages were fifteen times those of blacks, with lesser-paid Africans. To preserve their jobs, the white miners of Johannesburg went on strike, which effectively closed the gold mines. Martial law was declared and the strike broken, but the violence convinced both the government and the mine owners to retain and eventually strengthen segregation in the mining industry. The white miners had demonstrated that they were a powerful political force. The number of poor white Afrikaners on farms, in the mines, and in urban industries continued to grow in the postwar era. Each represented a powerful constituency in the Union, determined to preserve white privilege and political power. In response, Union politicians passed new legislation in 1926 to reinforce segregation in the mines. In 1934 Daniel F. Malan (1874–1959) organized a group of Afrikaner politicians into a *gesuiwerde* (purified) National Party to promote an exclusive party of only Afrikaner workers, professionals, businessmen, and financiers.

The Great Depression of 1929 ravaged social and economic life throughout the world, but South Africa survived better than most countries. South African gold mining was one of the few industries that prospered; gold was in constant demand, even more so in the depression. After South Africa went off of the gold standard in 1932, its export products became more attractive to foreign buyers. In 1934 the high price of gold produced significant revenues. In the same year, Jan Smuts (1870–1950) and James Hertzog (1866–1942) founded the United Party (UP), which ruled South Africa until 1948 and presided over a spectacular economic recovery. The government invested heavily in steel and electrical industries and encouraged light manufacturing, whose products were South African substitutes for American and British imports. Although Smuts was able to muster the votes to support Great Britain and declare war on Germany in September 1939, Hertzog resigned, and many Afrikaners openly sympathized with Germany. They deeply admired the Nazi Germany of Adolph Hitler and considered the ethnic purity advocated by his racist National Socialist Party as a model for South Africa. Nevertheless, South African combat troops fought in East and North Africa and in Italy. As in the First World War, the colored and African volunteers were confined to noncombat roles in labor battalions and to serving as transport drivers.

The war further stimulated the buoyant South African economy, creating unique opportunities for entrepreneurs to invest in new industries, particularly in Natal and the Cape. South African factories produced steel and munitions; its mines, coal and strategic minerals such as gold, platinum, and uranium; its farms, foodstuffs to replenish the huge convoys making their way around the Cape of Good Hope to the Orient and the Pacific. This rapid economic expansion produced a tidal wave of over half a million blacks fleeing the poverty of the reserves and whites abandoning the harsh life of the farms. These migrants crashed on the concrete of the cities to create new problems. The pass system, which had been implemented to keep Africans in the rural areas, proved unenforceable in the face of this massive migration to the cities, and the burgeoning numbers of whites, blacks, and coloureds now packed together in adjacent neighborhoods eroded the hitherto strict urban segregation. White voters watched the segregation of the past steadily dissolve in the turmoil of the cities to challenge their privileged status and economic future. The old cliché of political equality for all "civilized" men had now very little appeal. The new solution for social dislocation was the program advocated by the Afrikaner National Party called "apartness," popularly known by its Afrikaans word, "apartheid." Afrikaner intellectuals had developed this concept during the 1930s. Rooted in social Darwinism, the doctrine held that each race had a distinct culture, heritage, and spiritual and biological characteristics. To protect its own unique way of life and to ensure its destiny, each race should be permitted to develop its own distinctive qualities independent of others or their influence.

In 1948 the National Party defeated the ruling United Party of the moderate Jan Smuts on a platform of apartheid that had produced an alliance of both rural and urban Afrikaners. During the next two decades, the party effectively segregated all aspects of South African society into white and nonwhite—residential and rural lands, education, and public services. Pass laws were strictly enforced. Black trade unions were denied legal recognition. The Suppression of Communism Act of 1950 was used to intimidate African nationalists, socialists, and even liberals. Between 1958 and 1966, ten zones of rural poverty were designated as "homelands," or "Bantu Nations," for the vast majority of black Africans. Black Africans from the squatter camps that surrounded the urban areas were forcibly removed and dumped into these overcrowded and environmentally degraded reserves that were pretentiously declared independent Bantustans. The introduction of a rigorously segregated society dominated by white Afrikaner power was made largely possible by the continuing and extraordinary rate of economic growth of 6 percent per year during the high-water mark of apartheid from 1963 to 1972. Very little of this economic expansion trickled down to nonwhite Africans, however, as the chasm in the standard of living between blacks and whites virtually eliminated the "poor white problem" of the Afrikaners that had haunted every Union government since 1902.

The election of the National Party on its platform of apartheid convinced the radical faction of the ANC, led by Walter Sisal (1912–), Oliver Tambour (1917–1943), and Nelson Mandela (1918–), that there could no longer be reform of the system, only fundamental change, national freedom, and an end to white domination. The ANC allied with the South African Indian Congress in a defiance campaign of passive resistance against discriminatory laws, which led to the Congress Alliance consisting of the ANC, the South African Indian Congress, the Congress of Democrats (white leftists), the Coloured People's Congress, and the South African Congress of Trade Unions. At first this grand coalition attracted massive nonwhite support, but by the end of the decade its protests lost their momentum because of the arrest of most of their leaders on charges of high treason and because of internal tensions between the "non-African" and the "Africanized" members who broke with the ANC to organize the independent Pan-Africanize Congress (PAC). On March 21, 1960, several thousand PAC members without passes marched to the Orlando police station in the Revenging township of Sharpeville. The police met the crowd with a hail of gunfire, killing 69 and wounding 186, most of whom were shot in the back. In retrospect, Sharpeville was the turning point in the liberation movement and a watershed in the history of South Africa. Both the leadership of the ANC and PAC realized that only militant insurgency, not civil disobedience, would achieve their objectives. The government fiercely retaliated. The ANC and PAC activists and their leaders were arrested, convicted of treason, and imprisoned on Robben Island four miles offshore from Cape Town. By the end of 1963, violent resistance was over, and South Africa remained quiescent, enabling its white citizens to enjoy their unprecedented prosperity and contemplate their fate as a pariah state.

By the early 1970s, the pace of economic growth began to slacken. The international recession precipitated by the dramatic rise in the price of oil after 1973 quickly depressed the South African economic boom. Having no sustainable reserves of fuel, the increased cost of manufacturing and government tariffs and subsidies to white enterprises made South African goods less competitive in the world market and increased the nation's dependence on imported technology and capital. The determination by the National Party to prevent the emergence of a black skilled labor force in South Africa resulted in the emergence instead of an increasing number of black semiskilled and unskilled workers bound together by a class consciousness. Their grievances, produced by inflation and unemployment, resulted in a wave of strikes from which sprouted dynamic black trade unionism. Black consciousness soon permeated into the urban schools, where it was eagerly adopted by black students. On June 16, 1976, thousands of black schoolchildren in Soweto demonstrated against the language of instruction, Afrikaans, the language of the oppressor. The student protests swept through the nation only to be brutally suppressed.

By 1985 South Africa was overwhelmed by the rising tide of black civil society—the youth, the women, and civic associations in black townships. The ANC returned to the center of domestic politics, its exiled leaders regarded as a government-in-waiting, and its Umkhonto we Sizwe (MK) guerrillas carrying out spectacular sabotage. The government of President P. W. Botha (1916–) met the escalation of violence with even greater force. A state of emergency was declared on July 20, 1985, followed by massive repression—arrests, detentions, torture, and the assassination of antiapartheid activists—that momentarily gave the illusion of peace but at great cost. Capital fled, the rand collapsed, and international bankers refused credit. Leading businessmen, African academics, and church leaders were meeting with the exiled leaders of the ANC in Lusaka, London, and Paris, and the monolithic facade of the National Party cracked. Although confronted by protracted economic decline, the National Party government still commanded the formidable military and security forces of the state, but it had virtually no influence over the liberation movement, led by the ANC, that could mobilize the masses.

On February 2, 1990, President F. W. De Clerk (1936–) delivered a historic speech in parliament to announce lifting the bans on the ANC, PAC, and the South African Communist Party; removing restrictions on suspect organizations and trade unions; and freeing political prisoners, including Nelson Mandela, who from prison had recently proposed negotiations between the ANC and the government. Complex and protracted negotiations began in December 1991. Two years later they produced an interim constitution, creating a multiparty democracy based on universal suffrage, proportional representation, a separation of powers, and a bill of rights. When elections were finally held in April 1994, the ANC carried the electorate with 62.7 percent of the vote, followed by 20.4 percent for the National Party; 10.5 percent for the Inkatha Freedom Party (IFP), which represented the national aspirations of the Zulu; and the remainder to the other lesser parties. The ANC's popularity was largely attributed to its leadership. Men such as Nelson Mandela and Thabo Mbeki (1942—) had made great personal sacrifices on behalf of the freedom struggle, earning them enormous credibility among a wide spectrum of the diverse South African electorate. On May 10, 1994, 342 years after the Dutch East India Company had established its settlement at the Cape of Good Hope, which led to the importation of slaves and the conquest of the indigenous Africans, Nelson Mandela took the presidential oath of office.

The 1994 election that brought Nelson Mandela to power was the culmination of the long march of African independence throughout the continent in the twentieth century. Although it was almost four decades after the independence of the Gold Coast, the white South Africans who had conceded power to the African majority in 1994 did so on terms that would have seemed familiar to British officials during the 1950s and early 1960s. Mandela was a mission-educated African nationalist who promised to respect the rule of law and protect private property. He was yet another in a long line of African leaders who could articulate his arguments for democracy and social equality that appealed to Western leaders. In 1994, however, South Africa was a society that would require a long time to recover from the trauma of apartheid. The crimes committed under the apartheid state will hopefully be resolved by the Truth and Reconciliation Committee with justice and the passage of time, but the wrongs of the past will not disappear until the rest of the nation begins to share in the wealth of the privileged white minority.

Decade of Expectations

In only twenty-three years after the independence of Ghana, every colony on the continent had become independent, as the vast African empires of Belgium, Great Britain, France, and Portugal disintegrated into a checkerboard of sovereign states. These new nations were dramatically different in size, population, economic development, and natural environments. The tiny territories of Togo, Benin, and Equatorial Guinea were dwarfed by giant states like the Congo and Sudan. The population of Nigeria alone accounted for nearly 20 percent of the continent, while the inhabitants of the Kingdom of Swaziland amounted to less than 1 percent. Economically, there was little industrial development outside of South Africa. The Congo and Zambia had extensive mining industries, but the economies of the remaining new states of Africa were predominantly agricultural. Some, such as Ghana, Senegal, Kenya, and Uganda, possessed pockets of fertile agricultural land that supported a vibrant export economy. Other new states survived more on subsistence than cash crops and had little to offer from their regional economies other than the export of human labor. Many straddled diverse ecological and geographic zones. Yet despite all these many differences, the leaders of these new states shared a common goal—to replace European colonial with sovereign, independent nations under their authority.

The men who seized power after 1957 were towering figures whose shadows continue to sprawl across Africa today. They were charismatic, intelligent, often inspiring leaders. Many of them had spent time in colonial prisons for their nationalist activities. Almost all were products of a Western education. Kwame Nkrumah of Ghana, Nnamdi Azikiwe of Nigeria, Leopold Senghor of Senegal, and Jomo Kenyatta of Kenya were among the new heads of state who had attended universities overseas. Others were the graduates of mission schools within their home colony. All were proficient in the language of their colonial masters. All had justified their independence struggle in the language of liberalism and nationalism, and all took power as the heads of parliamentary democracies. As a group, however, they ultimately proved more proficient organizing a revolution than ruling a nation. One by one the leaders of the liberation struggle were cast aside by less glamorous but often more practical and astute soldiers and politicians. The very traits and training that had made them such a success when dealing with European colonial officials for self-government and independence ultimately alienated them from their African supporters.

Since the end of the Second World War, the industrial nations of the world—in North America, Western Europe, and behind the iron curtain—had increasingly perceived the state as the primary engine of economic development. Socialist ideology combined with political self-interest in postwar Europe dominated the French and British colonial policies that required more direct intervention in the economies of their African colonies. They introduced scientific schemes to "modernize" traditional African agricultural practices and promoted the expansion of mining and cash crop production. Virtually every African educated overseas had embraced socialism and often Marxism, whose doctrines placed the state at the very center of economic development. Not surprisingly, the new African leaders continued and reinforced these interventionist policies, which had been a major source of African discontent in the postwar years leading to independence. Ironically, African socialism now became the cornerstone of the economic policies of the new national governments.

However, promises by the nationalist leaders for better jobs, schools, hospitals, and roads created unrealistic expectations for the new regimes, and the economies of even the wealthiest former colonial states were hopelessly inadequate to provide basic services and employment for the vast majority of their African citizens. When the new state could not immediately provide expected services, the disappointment by most Africans became all the more bitter when they realized there was little prospect of any future improvement in their standard of living. Discontent against the new ruling elite, who seemed indifferent to the concerns of the average African, became widespread and certainly contributed to the rapid demise of democracy in postcolonial Africa. Since the army was the only multiethnic national institution in most African states, its officers, often educated and professional, became increasingly exasperated by the failure of the democratically elected leaders to govern. Some of these officers were self-seeking, ruthless thugs, but others were motivated by a sense of responsibility to rectify the mistakes of incompetent politicians.

During the first decade of independent Africa, there was, consequently, a spate of military coup d'états, until there were few states without military governments or authoritarian single-party governments. Governments democratically elected at independence were also threatened by their own civilian rulers who, when confronted by internal opposition, proved as equally willing to subvert the electoral process as the military. Some were influenced by the success of the Russian Communist Party, which had forged the many ethnic groups of Eastern Europe and Central Asia into a one-party state. Others were more concerned about the divisive issue of tribalism, arguing that the nature of African ethnic identities made multiparty politics dangerous and ineffective. There is no doubt that most Africans had not transferred their loyalty from clan, lineage, and ethnicity to the new independent state, which gave African rulers a ready excuse to silence any internal opposition to consolidate their power and that of their supporters.

The rapid disintegration of democratic institutions in Africa during the 1960s was not inevitable. Some states—Botswana, Kenya, Sudan, Tanzania—tolerated opposition parties, but throughout Africa loyalty to the new nation-state was fragile at best and ephemeral at worst. There was the demonstrable popular African enthusiasm for the end of colonial rule, but these arbitrary configurations of the past had little relevance for the future after the colonizers had packed up and gone home. Personal loyalties for most Africans were intricately woven in a network of connections—kinship groups, religious and fraternal organizations, local clients, patrons—all of which transcended the distant and invented nation-state. Cold war competition between the West, specifically the United States, and the Eastern bloc, particularly the Soviet Union, certainly did not encourage the development of democracy. Despite the anticolonial and democratic rhetoric propagated throughout Africa by both the United States and the Soviet Union, each was more concerned to secure loyal clients to protect its own national interests. Some of Africa's new leaders were motivated by ideological principles of socialism and Marxism; others sought to use cold war rivalries to secure their power for their own personal advantage. A few were reduced to serving as pawns in the larger global struggle for the minds of men and women and their material worth.

Ambitious economic policies adopted by some of the new regimes did little to encourage political democracy. In the past, African leaders had denounced many of the colonial economic institutions, such as marketing boards, but after independence the large development projects managed by the state and its principal source of revenue were expanded more for the benefit of the government than its citizens. In a fit of nationalism, a few states—Ghana, Sudan, Zaire—expropriated all foreign-owned businesses to henceforth be managed by African nationals. Although the confiscation of foreign firms produced instant employment, the new owners simply did not have the education or experience to manage them. Corruption became the means to get things done and soon acquired an aura of respectability and acceptance as it became ever more pervasive. In 1960 the economies of the African colonial states were overwhelmingly agricultural and remain so to this day, but in the heady days of independence some of the new leaders educated in the West attributed Western prosperity to industrialization. By contrast, Africa was simply a supplier of primary agricultural produce and was vulnerable to the volatile prices fixed by manufacturing. The desire to emulate the industrial nations was irresistible, particularly when heavy industry was a source of employment and revenue and was a visible symbol of national vigor and economic independence. The creation of mines, dams, ports, and factories was also an important opportunity to reward regions or ethnic groups loyal to the government, which often made the decision to finance and implement development schemes more on a political basis rather than on economics.

If state-sponsored industry proved economically inefficient, the socialist state management and organization of peasant agriculture proved equally unproductive. Scientific and often stern measures to improve peasant farming during the postwar colonial years had little economic success and considerable political failure. More than any other colonial policy, they mobilized conservative rural farmers to protest and demonstrate against colonial rule. Draconian methods to contain disease among livestock and dig contour ridges to curb erosion reminiscent of the prewar hated *corvée* were among the least popular initiatives of the colonial state. Nevertheless, the new African governments in the spirit of African socialism proved equally enthusiastic about imposing a revolution in agriculture introduced and managed by the state from the top down as a spur to development.

The emphasis on the role of the state in economic life made access to the corridors of power essential in obtaining a share of the limited resources available to the independent African governments. Those states, or more accurately those Africans with access to the president and his ministers, would be those most likely to be the beneficiaries of highways, hospitals, schools, and foreign monetary and humanitarian assistance and private foreign investment. Almost every aspect of the new African states was controlled by the central government. The men with the political authority, for there were few women, regulated the revenues from exports, imports, taxes, and customs. They decided who was permitted to travel and who was to study abroad. They controlled the purse and access to the world beyond the borders and jurisdiction of the state. In this environment, politicians developed systems of patronage to reward friends, relatives, and ethnic brothers and were the ones who approved development projects in the regions where they lived. Leaders who had been elected on a national platform now found themselves reverting to becoming tribal chiefs responsible to their ethnic communities and homelands. They did not command the authority of their colonial predecessors, whose self-confidence had been assured by the military and economic power of the metropolitan government. They did not possess the power to govern without the more devious means of corruption, bribery, intimidation, and frequently personal violence that became increasingly accepted and effective so long as the political elite maintained control of the resources flowing into the country from foreign nations, humanitarian organizations, and international corporations.

By the late 1960s the enthusiasm and optimism of the decade of expectations were ebbing like a receding tide. In addition to the military coup d'états, there were three bloody internal secessionist movements in the Sudan, Nigeria, and the Congo. Although these African secessionist struggles riveted the bewildered attention of the outside world, the dramatic decline of the economy of African states attracted less attention. International economic conditions had devalued many African agricultural exports. State bureaucracies, which had become bloated by politicians handing out jobs to supporters, were imposing a heavy burden on fragile revenues. Expensive, unrealistic development projects were now exposed to have failed. In virtually every state democracy had been abandoned in favor of autocracy justified by the demon of tribalism. Foreign patrons and businesspeople evaluated African nations based on stability and the malleability of the ruling class that was often made secure by grotesque human rights violations. When a second wave of African independence movements broke in the mid-1970s, it came in a context that was far removed from the optimism, confidence, and jubilation captured by the newsreels at the independence celebrations in Accra, Ghana, in 1957. The decade of expectations had become the decade of delusion.

Ethnicity and Insurgency in Cold War Africa

The decade of expectations in Africa gave way to two decades of crisis. The optimism that had greeted independence evaporated as economic development stalled, the standard of living declined, and African states and society were threatened by political instability. During the two decades after 1973, governments proved incapable or unwilling to provide good leadership or good government for their subjects, and the opposition to the political ineptitude, corruption, and tyranny divided many of the independent states along ethnic lines. Tribal identities were invoked as a means to resist government policies, to ensure security by ethnic cohesion, and even to mobilize a community for secession. The specter of separatist movements spread rapidly throughout Africa after independence. In response, those African politicians who had most benefited from the African state system left by the colonial powers denounced tribalism as the enemy of the nation to justify their dismantling of democratic institutions in order to mold competing ethnicities into a one-party state. Those ethnic minorities they could not suborn were subject to discrimination, abuse, and even ethnic cleansing in the name of combating tribal resistance to national sovereignty.

The ethnic hostilities of the 1970s and 1980s, however, developed in an entirely different environment than in the past. During these decades, Africa experienced a severe depression in its export of African products, spiraling inflation, relentless population growth, new epidemic diseases, political corruption, and the destabilizing influences of cold war politics. In the cauldron of these crises, the competition for dwindling resources, individual and communal security, and the prospects of employment could best be found in dependable tribal identities. These ethnic identities often had deep roots in African history, but they had been accentuated under colonial rule during which certain tribes were favored over others by colonial officials.

There were very few Africans and non-Africans alike who anticipated the crises of the 1970s, for they were driven by the optimism of independence that appeared to be confirmed by the immediate economic prosperity that coincided with a boom in the world economy. In much of southern Africa, growing demand for maize and other food crops encouraged the expansion of indigenous agricultural production, which enabled farmers to command a price worth growing a surplus. This economic bubble, however, was balanced on very tenuous foundations. Many governments invested the profits from the world commodities boom in unsustainable development projects. All over Africa, independent governments plowed revenues into schemes of modernization that emulated the levels of infrastructure and industrial development of their former colonial masters. These were ambitious, indeed, visionary plans that could not be sustained solely by an agriculture whose development was studiously ignored.

Virtually all the independent African states neglected investing in agriculture, despite the fact that agriculture was practiced by the vast

majority of their citizens, the major source of their revenues, and the pillar of their economies. The official bias against agriculture can be attributed to the views of the urban ruling African elite, who had adopted a preference for modern industrial development from their colonial masters. These leaders tended to see peasant farmers as traditional and backward. These farmers' crops might well be the principal source of revenue for national governments, but agriculture was not the key to the future or a priority in drafting plans for economic development. Consequently, the politicians and planners at the center of power in the capital sought to maximize state revenues from agriculture by employing with ever-greater rigor the unpopular marketing boards inherited from the colonial powers that had the authority to fix the prices paid to farmers for their crops. Not surprisingly, the marketing boards offered the lowest possible price to the farmer, who was in no position to refuse, for the boards were the only permitted buyer. The buyer would then export the crop at the highest possible price on the world market. The extraordinary profits from these sales entered the vaults of the treasury and the pockets of the politicians, leaving the farming communities impoverished and with little or no incentive to expand agricultural production.

In retrospect, it appears that African politicians, the African elite, and foreign experts, both in and out of Africa, learned the wrong lessons from the first decade of independence. African leaders expected capital earned from foreign exports to stimulate the creation of an African industrial economy that would ensure genuine political and economic independence from the West. Ironically, this strategy not only failed to generate increasing autonomy but also dragged the African economies into greater dependency on Western investment and expertise. African leaders perceived, quite correctly, that the conquest of Africa by Europe, the subsequent half-century of colonial rule, and the dominant role of Western influence in postindependent Africa were made possible to a great extent by the vibrant industrial economies of the West. They failed to realize that the chimerical attempt to reproduce similar economies in Africa would ultimately increase the reliance of Africa on Western imports, financial assistance, and technological skills.

The year 1973 was the turning point in world economic history and particularly for independent Africa. When the Arab members of the Organization of Petroleum Exporting Countries (OPEC) imposed a suspension of oil shipments on selected Western countries in retaliation for their support for Israel during the Arab-Israel (Yom Kippur) War of October 1973, the African states firmly supported the embargo. The economies of Europe and the United States were sufficiently resilient to accommodate the loss of Arab oil; the African states were not, forty of them being net importers of oil. The price of Arab oil quadrupled, sending the cost of transportation beyond the reach of many Africans, making the price of African exports no longer competitive in the world market, and raising the cost of imported food, which became increasingly prohibitive except for the elites. The Arab states half-heartedly offered some financial assistance, mostly to countries with Muslim majorities, which did little to assuage the bitter sense of betrayal by African leaders and their citizens for supporting the Arabs.

If Africans and non-Africans could manipulate, for better or for worse, their national economies, nature imperiously controlled Africa's climate. During the period of decolonization and the first decade of independence, Africa enjoyed above-average rainfall. This decade of expanding agricultural production, however, culminated in the onset of a multiyear drought that blistered Africa for twenty years during the 1970s and 1980s. Drought contributed to desertification, which became a major environmental concern during the 1970s, as the need for firewood and cultivation in marginal lands, now with little rain, destroyed a landscape that could not easily be restored.

The central role of the state in economic life also saddled many

African nations with large, unproductive bureaucracies and armies inherited from the colonial era that devoured government revenues. Economic life in the colonial world had been controlled by the European administration. The distribution of land and labor, the pricing of commodities, and the import and export of goods all passed through the hands of colonial officials and the African civil servants who succeeded them after independence. In this environment, it was much easier to enrich oneself through a permanent career in the civil service than as an entrepreneur exposed to the greater risk usually associated with private enterprise. Consequently, the wealthiest and most powerful figures in Africa since independence have been those civil servants who occupied positions with the authority to approve private investment, foreign aid, and humanitarian assistance and the power to channel these resources to favored communities, industries, and regions at a price. The opportunities to augment a minimal government salary were innumerable and irresistible.

In southern Africa, the economic crises of the early 1970s were made worse by the violent struggles against governments controlled by intransigent white minorities. The first cracks in this edifice appeared in 1974, when events in Europe precipitated the sudden dissolution of Portugal's ancient African empire. Led by incompetent generals, ill-equipped, and hopelessly demoralized, the Portuguese army realized that it was fighting a losing war against the nationalist guerrillas in Angola and Mozambique. In Portugal, the Armed Forces Movement of young officers, determined to restore democracy to Portugal, overthrew the fascist government in Lisbon in April 1974 and granted independence to Mozambique in September and Angola in November 1975. When the Portuguese withdrew, Angola erupted into a three-cornered civil war in which each of the protagonists sought to exploit the cold war rivalries of the United States and the Soviet Union for weapons, financing, and even, at times, troops.

Only after long and acrimonious negotiations was a peace agreement finally reached among all the parties in 1988. In Mozambique, a civil war escalated during the 1980s, until both sides were exhausted and without patrons. Once again, after protracted negotiations the People's Republic of Mozambique peacefully became, simply, the Republic of Mozambique in 1990.

The independence of the Portuguese colonies immediately threatened settler rule in neighboring Rhodesia. No longer having access to the Indian Ocean and exposed on its eastern and western borders to hostile neighbors willing to harbor insurgent guerrilla armies, the Rhodesian Front could no longer sustain itself. In September 1979 Great Britain brokered a ceasefire that led to negotiations and an independent Zimbabwe in 1980. Democratic elections swept Robert Mugabe to power. He openly favored the interests of the Shona-speaking majority by channeling the resources of the state into the eastern regions, where the Shona population was concentrated. In the name of "national-unity," the Mugabe government intimidated, tortured, and murdered thousands of the Ndebele-speaking minority.

In states wracked by ethnic tensions, political corruption, and deteriorating economic conditions, military officers seized power. Elected governments were swept away by the army in some sixty-three military coups between 1966 and 1993. Coups in Africa have been so common largely because African states are particularly vulnerable to them. Moreover, those military officers plotting the overthrow of a civilian government often had the support or at least the indifference of the general public, who were not about to defend incompetent and corrupt politicians. They had little faith or experience in parliamentary democracy, and, when confronted by political change, the promise of a strong autocratic alternative to feuding elected officials encouraged apathy. Many of these new military regimes soon proved dysfunctional and unstable. Others were more durable, despite incompetence, when supported by foreign patrons—the United States,

France, Great Britain, and the Soviet Union. Cold war patrons also proved eager to aid those conspirators who promised to further their economic or ideological interests. Those African leaders who were staunchly conservative could depend on Paris and Washington to ignore their autocratic tendencies; those who displayed the proper Marxist-Leninist credentials could count on the enthusiastic support of the Soviets.

At the end of the 1980s, Africa remained a pawn in the aggressive game between cold war rivals. Most African governments were burdened with massive foreign debt, and most African people were experiencing a depressing and steady decline in their standard of living. Few Africans participated in any kind of meaningful way in politics. Famine stalked the Horn of Africa, drought threatened the Sahel and southern Africa, and the human immunodeficiency virus/acquired immune deficiency syndrome (HIV/AIDS) pandemic was just beginning to be the major new addition to Africa's historic list of diseases. In the world beyond Africa, Afro-pessimism had eclipsed the decade of expectations. Ironically, there were a few observers who foresaw the dramatic changes that were to restructure the major, minor, and failed states in the last two decades of the twentieth century. The end of the cold war weakened the stranglehold on the power of an aging elite and its leadership, who could no longer rely on the support of foreign patrons. There was growing optimism that the worst had passed and that the 1990s would be a reinvigorating decade to usher in a new era in the history of Africa.

Africa at the Beginning of the Twenty-first Century

After traversing more than two millennia of the African past, it is time to pause and take stock, to look back in history and forward at the beginning of the twenty-first century in Africa. In the last half of the twentieth century, the historiography of Africa has vividly demonstrated the combination of scientific method, social science studies, and the intuitive contribution of art, music, and literature in the search for the African past. The history of Africa has been woven into an elaborate fabric consisting of information from archaeological sites, archives, published works, oral traditions, and the methodologies from the social sciences—anthropology, linguistics, and demography—and then refurbished with African art, music, and literature. Many readers equipped with their own preconceptions, intellectual and emotional baggage, or a unique personal past will have found their own meaning of the history of Africa from the preceding pages, but they cannot deny that there are certain constant themes in the last 2,000 years that thread their way through the text to form a continuum into the twenty-first century. They are indeed the themes of this book, and whether or not they bring meaning to the past, they will most certainly reappear, in different shapes and sizes, in the twenty-first century.

The history of the population of Africa has been a perplexing demographic ambiguity. In relation to its landmass, Africa has historically been underpopulated. Two thousand years ago Africa south of the Sahara had an estimated population only one-fifth that of China or the Roman Empire. During the next 1,500 years, this ratio continued to decline, so that by 1500 Africa contained less than an estimated 15 percent of the world's human beings. At the beginning of the twentieth century, the population of Africa accounted for only about 1 percent of the two billion people inhabiting the earth. The reasons for this sluggish rate of growth remain unclear to this day. Was this creeping rate of reproduction caused by a harsh climate, disease, poor soils, wars, slavery, agrarian societies? One can only reflect and suggest that the reasons lie in the complex interaction between people and nature in Africa in the past, but such reasons certainly fail to explain the dramatic increase in the population of Africa during the twentieth century and the explosion at its end and the beginning of the twenty-first that is predicted to continue unabated throughout the rest of this century.

In the past and present, disease has had a demonstrable impact on the lives of every African. When one is sick, it is extremely difficult to support oneself or contribute to the society in which one lives, and throughout the millennia Africans have been inflicted with a variety of numerous deadly diseases. Despite revisionist histories of the colonial health services, the advances in tropical medicine will remain one of the more substantial contributions by the European imperial order in Africa. They successfully diagnosed the source and transmission of the four deadly parasitical diseases—sleeping sickness, bilharzia, kala-azar, and malaria—and have discovered the means to prevent numerous viral diseases. Some formerly devastating diseases—yellow fever, onchoceriasis (river blindness), and polio—have been drastically reduced or virtually eradicated. Nevertheless, the largest killer disease in Africa, malaria, has defied through its many mutations the massive attempts to find a vaccine like that which has controlled yellow fever. The struggle against disease in Africa has been made more complicated by the appearance of a new and deadly disease in the last decades of the twentieth century, HIV, which causes AIDS. Both are believed to have had their origin among nonhuman primates in Africa, from where they spread throughout the world. Their rapid diffusion throughout the continent—some three to four million Africans are infected annually—has resulted in death from AIDS of an estimated two and a half million Africans in 2003 and the prediction of a steady annual increase in that number. Moreover, AIDS began as a urban phenomenon, where the most productive African professional, mercantile, and political class live, upon whom the state is dependent for its governance. Only in recent years has it spread to the countryside.

As it has in the past 2,000 years, agriculture will continue to dom-

inate the lives of most Africans in the twenty-first century. Despite the
river of Africans that flowed into the cities of the colonial state to
become a flood after independence in 1960, Africa remains agrarian
and rural, in which 80 percent of all Africans still cultivate the soil
and pasture their herds on the grasslands. The economy of African
states is and will undoubtedly continue to be dependent upon agriculture, from the beginning of the domestication of crops and animals, which spread throughout Africa before the Christian era and
later made more productive by the iron hoe and the domestication of
cattle, goats, and sheep, where they were free from the tsetse fly. The
first green revolution in Africa came from the New World in the sixteenth century, when the Portuguese carried maize and cassava to
Africa to become the principal food crops of Africa today. The rich
resources of Africa's mines will continue to produce, but their labor
demands will only employ a small proportion of the African population. Industrialization, which was so popular in the heady days of
independence, will continue to grow but in selected products adapt-
able to African conditions. Oil has became a major source of revenue
for Africa that has and will continue to precipitate many internal
problems over the sharing of this resource, but it is seldom understood that once wells are drilled and productive, the African oil industry requires few workers to maintain its facilities.

The most vital and scarce resource, however, is not petroleum but
water. There can be no life on land without freshwater and consequently no agriculture or animals to sustain the human race.
Moreover, if you control freshwater, you control the land that
depends upon it and the people who derive their livelihood from it.
Theoretically, Africans should have ample water from the vast reser-
voirs of the South Atlantic and the Indian Ocean, whose annual monsoons provide the water for sub-Saharan Africa, but Africans have yet
to construct the schemes required to keep the rainfall on the land
before it flows to the sea carrying that thin, precious layer of African

In the past, the modest number of Africans in relation to the continental landmass could largely ignore the loss of their water, but no longer. Since there appears no prospect that the total amount of available water from the rainfall will increase, there will simply be insufficient water for domestic, agricultural, and pastoral uses.

In the middle of the fifteenth century, Europeans first arrived on the shores of sub-Saharan Africa, and ever since the African past and present have been intertwined with Europe. At first the European presence was little more than an ebb tide on the African polities scattered along the African shore and of no consequence in the interior of Africa. By the end of the seventeenth century, this benign relationship began to change as the demands in the Americas for cheap labor stimulated the trade in Africa's most sought after product, slaves. As in Asian and European societies, slavery had been an established and accepted institution in Africa as far back dynastic Egypt. Slavery in Africa, however, was dramatically transformed in the seventeenth, eighteenth, and nineteenth centuries by the increasing demand to transport African slaves to the Americas and Asia. Slavery was no longer an internal African affair but an organized, complex, and very profitable global enterprise. During the next 300 years, the African slave trade to the New World and Asia flourished and was only brought to an end by the European and American abolitionists at the end of the nineteenth century. Since then, the transoceanic slave trade has become virtually extinct, but the institution of slavery continues to exist in various forms in Africa and elsewhere.

Although Africa first became involved in the global economy with the advent of the slave trade first to Asia and then to the Americas, it was not until the European conquest of the continent at the end of the nineteenth century that the kingdoms, states, and societies of Africa became more fully integrated into the international economic world, a historic theme of the African past that cannot be reversed. European governance in Africa was relatively brief, little more than half a century in most of the continent, but the European presence after independence still persists and in many ways is more powerful than when Europeans were the rulers. The economies of the African states have remained an integral part of the global capitalist system in which European and American firms continue to control central sectors of African economic activity. The dominant role of the European powers, the United States, and international institutions like the World Bank creates new opportunities for African products in the world market but often at a heavy price, which many regard as the "recolonization" of Africa.

In the past, the economic policies imposed upon African governments by the international community to promote growth have been less than successful. Known as "structural adjustment," these policies assumed that independent African states had become economically inefficient because of bloated bureaucracies, state-guided economic policies, subsidies for food and fuel prices, and economic policies they had been encouraged to implement by Western "experts" during the 1960s that often proved disastrous for poverty-stricken Africans forced into unemployment without the safety net of subsidies for basic goods. In 1998, however, two economists at the World Bank revealed that African countries with sound economic policies—low inflation, budget surpluses, free trade, and functioning institutions—had growing individual and national incomes and that a greater, not lesser, amount of financial assistance would create an even higher rate of growth in contrast to those African states with unsustainable policies and stagnant institutions.

The emphasis by Africans and non-Africans alike on political and economic institutions frequently distorts the history of any peoples in which religious belief has played such a central role in the shaping of their societies. The increasing dominance of science, social science, and technology in the twentieth century cannot obscure the importance of religion in the lives of most Africans. Throughout the 2,000 years that span the pages of this history, there are just a few conclusions one can legitimately accept about the important role that religion has played in sub-Saharan Africa. No one can dispute that there are as many religions in Africa as there are societies and that there is no tenable distinction between these traditional religions, on the one hand, and the world religions of Christianity and Islam, on the other, when it comes to understanding African social behavior. Moreover, African religions have been in the past and will continue to perform similar functions by which Africans learn of the cultural richness of their continent and non-Africans learn from Africa a belief that broadens their own personal understanding of the spiritual world as a whole.

With a Christian population of over 300 million Africans, the continent has become a new center of Christianity. African apostolic Christianity has divested itself of much of Western cultural and political baggage, adopting evangelical voluntary forms of Christian independency expressed as a mass movement fluent in the vernacular to respond to the spiritual needs of local life and values. Like Christianity, Islam has also responded to meet and accommodate African circumstances. In the past, the creation and integration into Islam of Sufism provided a major African ingredient in the practice of Islam that continues to flourish throughout the African Muslim world. There is a growing belief among African Muslims that Islam has returned to the center of society in the individual search for identity in Africa and the wider Islamic world.

If the end of the cold war left African affairs largely neglected by the Western powers, it also strengthened the position of reformers in the continent who have demanded political and economic change— democracy and economic restructuring. The political reforms were welcomed and encouraged by the West. At the beginning of the dismal decade of the 1990s, there were no more than four or five states that could reasonably claim to have democratic governments. By the beginning of the twenty-first century, there are more than twenty whose stable and popular governments have little attraction for the international media, who prefer to seek the sensational disaster. These governments have quietly and purposefully improved the lives of their citizens. The gradual spread of democracy in Africa has also been accompanied by a growing realization of a greater need for regional and continental cooperation hitherto inhibited by the old arbitrary colonial boundaries.

The increasing recognition and demand for interstate arrangements have their roots in the vision of the Pan-Africanists who saw the unity of African states as a bulwark against Western influence. These dreams of continental or regional unity disappeared during the dying days of colonialism as the new rulers of independent states, having won sovereignty, were not about to abandon it to leaders of a larger and more amorphous union, a principle that was cemented in the charter that established the Organization of African Unity (OAU) on May 25, 1963. Thirty years later, new African leaders began to realize that more could be gained by cooperating with their neighbors than by insular sovereignty. Regional economic communities have been created in West, East, and southern Africa. The widespread recognition that African states need to work together to resolve common problems was recognized by the transformation of the OAU into the African Union (AU) in 1999. The venerable OAU had been established to safeguard the sovereignty of the new African nations and to coordinate the movement against the last vestiges of colonialism on the continent. However, by the 1990s the OAU had become widely regarded as a "dictator's club" of aging African leaders. The creation of the AU symbolized the need by African heads of state for an organization that could mobilize its members to work together on issues and problems that are continental rather than local or even regional. In 2002 the organization drafted the "New Partnership for Africa's Development," a blueprint for coordinating economic development throughout the continent. In 2004 the AU sponsored a "peer governance" board to encourage political reforms and democracy in Africa by having participating nations grade the quality of governance in member states. The AU has also established its own Human Rights Court, an All-African Parliament, and a Council of African Leaders. It has framed the necessary requirements for the organizations of a continental peacekeeping force by 2010. Although these initiatives remain in their early stages, they symbolize a new spirit of cooperation and a greater realization among African states that is unprecedented in the postindependence era and a demonstration of optimism for the future of Africa in the twenty-first century.

Selected Readings

General References

Ade Ajayi, J. F., and Michael Crowder, eds. *Historical Atlas of Africa*. Cambridge: Cambridge University Press, 1985.

Collins, Robert O., ed. *Documents from the African Past*. Princeton, N.J.: Markus Wiener, 2001.

———. *Historical Dictionary of Pre-Colonial Africa*. Lanham, Md.; London: Scarecrow Press, 2001.

———. *Problems in African History: The Precolonial Centuries*. 3rd ed. Princeton, N.J.: Markus Wiener, 2005.

Collins, Robert O., James M. Burns, and Erik R. Ching, eds. *Historical Problems of Imperial Africa*. 2nd ed. Princeton, N.J.: Markus Wiener, 1996.

Collins, Robert O., James M. Burns, Erik K. Ching, and Kathleen S. Hasselblad, eds. *Problems in the History of Modern Africa*. Princeton, N.J.: Markus Wiener, 1997.

McEvedy, Colin, ed. *The Penguin Atlas of African History*. London: Penguin Books, 1995.

Oliver, Roland, and J. D. Fage, eds. *The Cambridge History of Africa*. 8 vols. Cambridge: Cambridge University Press, 1975-1986.

Shillington, Kevin, ed. *Encyclopedia of African History*. 3 vols. New York: Fitzroy Dearborn, 2005.

UNESCO General History of Africa. 8 vols. London: James Currey; Berkeley: University of California Press, 1981–1983.

General Surveys

Connah, Graham. *African Civilizations*: *An Archaeological Perspective*. Cambridge: Cambridge University Press, 2001.

Curtin, Philip, Steven Feierman, Leonard Thompson, and Jan Vansina. *African History*: *From Earliest Times to Independence*. 2nd ed. London: Longman, 1995.

Ehret, Christopher. *The Civilizations of Africa*: *A History to 1800*. Charlottesville: University Press of Virginia, 2002.

Iliffe, John. *Africans*: *The History of a Continent*. Cambridge: Cambridge University Press, 1995.

July, Robert W. *A History of the African People*, 5th ed. Prospect Heights, Ill.: Waveland Press, 1998.

Oliver, Roland. *The African Experience*: *From Olduvai Gorge to the 21st Century*. Boulder, Colo.: Westview Press, 2000.

Oliver, Roland, and J. D. Fage. *A Short History of Africa*, 6th ed. New York: Penguin Books, 1988.

Reader, John. *Africa*: *A Biography of the Continent*. New York: Vintage Books, 1999.

Shillington, Kevin. *History of Africa*. New York: St. Martin's Press, 1995.

Prehistoric Africa

GEOGRAPHY DEFINES MAN AND WOMAN

Adams, W. M., A. S. Goudie, and A. R. Orme, eds. *The Physical Geography of Africa*. Oxford: Oxford University Press, 1996.

EVOLUTION OF MAN AND WOMAN IN AFRICA

Stringer, Chris, and Robin McKie. *African Exodus*: *The Origins of Modern Humanity*. New York: Henry Holt, 1997.

PEOPLES OF SUB-SAHARAN AFRICA

Greenberg, Joseph. *The Languages of Africa*. Bloomington: Indiana University Press, 1970.

CROPS, COWS, AND IRON

Clark, J. D., and S. A. Brandt, eds. *From Hunters to Farmers: The Causes and Consequences of Food Production in Africa.* Berkeley: University of California Press, 1984.

Connah, Graham. *African Civilizations: An Archaeological Perspective.* Cambridge: Cambridge University Press, 2001.

Harlan, J. R., J. M. J. de Wet, and A. B. L. Stemler, eds. *Origins of African Plant Domestication.* The Hague: Mouton, 1976.

Shaw, Thurstan, et al., eds. *The Archaeology of Africa: Food, Metals, and Towns.* London: Routledge, 1993.

Vansina, Jan. *Paths in the Rainforest: Toward a History of Political Traditions in Equatorial Africa.* Madison: University of Wisconsin Press, 1990.

Ancient and Medieval Africa

DYNASTIC EGYPT, 3100–332 B.C.E.

Aldred, Cyril. *The Egyptians.* 3rd ed. London: Thames and Hudson, 1998.

Assmann, Jan. *The Mind of Egypt: History and Meaning in the Time of the Pharaohs.* Trans. Andrew Jenkins. Cambridge, Mass.: Harvard University Press, 2003.

Kemp, Barry. *Ancient Egypt: The Anatomy of a Civilization.* London: Routledge, 1989.

Shaw, Ian, ed. *The Oxford History of Ancient Egypt.* Oxford: Oxford University Press, 2000.

KINGDOM OF KUSH:
CORRIDOR TO AFRICA, 806 B.C.E.–700 C.E.

Edwards, David N. *The Nubian Past: An Archaeology of the Sudan.* London: Routledge, 2004.

O'Connor, David. *Ancient Nubia: Egypt's Rival in Africa.* Philadelphia: University of Pennsylvania Press, 1994.

Welsby, Derek A. *The Kingdom of Kush: The Napatan and Meroitic Empires.* Princeton, N.J.: Markus Wiener, 1998.

BANTU MIGRATIONS, 1000 B.C.E.–1700 C.E.

Vansina, Jan. *Paths in the Rainforest*: *Toward a History of Political Traditions in Equatorial Africa*. Madison: University of Wisconsin Press, 1990.

AKSUM, 200–700 C.E.

Burstein, Stanley, ed. *Ancient African Civilizations: Kush and Axum*. Princeton, N.J.: Markus Wiener, 1998.

Kobishchano, U. M. *Aksum*. Trans. L. T. Kapitanoff; ed. J. W. Michaels. University Park: Pennsylvania State University Press, 1979.

Phillipson, David W. *Aksum: Its Antecedents and Successors*. London: British Museum Press, 1998.

Sergew, H. S. *Ancient and Medieval Ethiopian History to 1270*. Addis Ababa: United Printers, 1972.

CHRISTIAN STATES OF NUBIA

Adams, W. Y. *Nubia: Corridor to Africa*. Princeton, N.J.: Princeton University Press, 1977.

Islam, Trade, and States

ARABS AND ISLAM

Levtzion, Nehemia. *Islam in West Africa*: *Religion, Society, and Politics to 1800*. Brookfield, Vt.: Variorum, 1994.

Levtzion, Nehemia, and Jay Spaulding, eds. *Medieval West Africa*: *Views from Arab Scholars and Merchants*. Princeton, N.J.: Markus Wiener, 2003.

Norris, H. T., *The Arab Conquest of the Western Sahara*: *Studies of the Historical Events, Religious Beliefs, and Social Customs Which Made the Remotest Sahara a Part of the Arab World*. Harlow, England: Longman, 1986.

TRANS-SAHARAN TRADE

Bovill, Edward W. *The Golden Trade of the Moors*. Introduction by Robert O. Collins. Princeton, N.J.: Markus Wiener, 1995.

SELECTED READINGS 237

EMPIRES OF THE PLAINS

Bjørkelø, Anders. *State and Society in Three Central Sudanic Kingdoms: Kanem-Bornu, Bagirmi, and Wadai.* Bergen: University of Norway Press, 1976.

Connah, G. *Three Thousand Years in Africa: Man and His Environment in the Lake Chad Region of Nigeria.* London: Cambridge University Press, 1981.

Levtzion, Nehemia. *Ancient Ghana and Mali.* New York: Africana Publishing, 1980.

McIntosh, Susan K. *Prehistoric Investigations in the Region of Jenne, Mali: A Study of Urbanism in the Sahel.* Oxford: B.A.R., 1980.

McIntosh, Susan K., and Roderick J. McIntosh. "Cities without Citadels: Understanding Urban Origins along the Middle Niger." In *The Archaeology of Africa: Food, Metals, and Towns*, ed. Thurstan Shaw et al., 124–156. London: Routledge, 1993.

Palmer, H. R. *The Bornu, Sahara and Sudan.* New York: Negro Universities Press, 1970.

EAST AFRICAN COAST AND THE INDIAN OCEAN WORLD

Jayasuniya, Shihan de Silva, and Richard Pankhurst. *The African Diaspora in the Indian Ocean.* Trenton/Lawrenceville, N.J.: Africa World Press, 2003.

Prins, A. H. J. *Sailing from Lamu: A Study of Maritime Culture in Islamic East Africa.* Assen: Van Gorcum, 1965.

CITY-STATES OF THE AFRICAN COAST

Alagoa, E. J. *The Small Brave City State: A History of Brass-Nembe in the Niger Delta.* Madison: University of Wisconsin Press, 1964.

Allan, J. de V. *The Swahili Origins: Swahili Culture and the Shangwaya Phenomenon.* London: James Currey; Athens: Ohio University Press, 1993.

Isicheri, E. *A History of the Igbo People.* New York: St. Martin's Press, 1976.

Jones, G. I. *Trading States of the Oil Rivers: A Study of Political Development in Eastern Nigeria.* Introduction by John C. McCall. Oxford: James Currey, 2000.

Middleton, John. *The World of the Swahili: An African Mercantile Civilization*. New Haven, Conn.: Yale University Press, 1992.

Nurse, Derek, and Thomas Spear. *The Swahili: Reconstructing the History and Language of an African Society*. Philadelphia: University of Pennsylvania Press, 1985.

STATE-BUILDING IN THE INTERIOR OF EAST AFRICA

Ogot, B. A. *Zamani: A Survey of East African History*. 2nd ed. Nairobi: East African Publishing House, 1974.

STATES OF THE WEST AFRICAN FOREST

Law, Robin. *The Oyo Empire: A West African Imperialism in the Era of the Atlantic Slave Trade*. Oxford: Clarendon Press, 1977.

Ryder, A. F. C. *Benin and the Europeans, 1485–1897*. New York: Humanities Press, 1969.

Smith, Robert S. *Kingdoms of the Yoruba*. 3rd ed. Madison: University of Wisconsin Press, 1988.

Wilks, Ivor. *Asante in the Nineteenth Century: The Structure and Evolution of a Political Order*. New York: Cambridge University Press, 1975.

————. *Forests of Gold: Essays on the Akan and the Kingdom of the Asante*. Athens: Ohio University Press, 1993.

STATES OF EAST CENTRAL AFRICA

Birmingham, David, and Phyllis M. Martin, eds. *History of Central Africa*. London: Longman, 1983.

Reefe, Thomas Q. *The Rainbow Kings: A History of the Luba Empire to 1891*. Berkeley: University of California Press, 1981

Vansina, Jan. *Kingdoms of the Savanna*. Madison: University of Wisconsin Press, 1968.

STATES OF WEST CENTRAL AFRICA

Birmingham, David. *Trade and Conflict in Angola: The Mbundu and Their Neighbours under the Influence of the Portuguese, 1483–1790*. Oxford: Clarendon Press, 1966

Hilton, Anne. *The Kingdom of the Kongo*. Oxford: Clarendon Press, 1985.

Martin, Phyllis. *The External Trade of the Loango Coast*. Oxford: Clarendon Press, 1972.

Miller, Joseph C. *Kings and Kinsmen: Early Mbundu States in Angola*. London: Clarendon Press, 1976.

————. *Way of Death: Merchant Capitalism and the Angolan Slave Trade, 1730–1830*. Madison: University of Wisconsin Press, 1988.

Thornton, John K. *How Societies Are Born: Governance in West Central Africa before 1600*. Charlottesville: University Press of Virginia, 2004.

————. *The Kingdom of the Kongo: Civil War and Transition, 1641–1718*. Madison: University of Wisconsin Press, 1983.

STATES OF SOUTHERN AFRICA

Beach, D. H. *The Shona and Their Neighbours*. Oxford: Blackwell, 1994.

Connah, Graham. *African Civilizations: An Archaeological Perspective*. Cambridge: Cambridge University Press, 2001.

Hall, Martin. *The Changing Past: Farmers, Kings, and Traders in Southern Africa, 200–1860*. Cape Town: David Philip; London: James Curry, 1987.

Mudenge, S. I. G. *A Political History of Munhumutapa, c. 1400–1902*. Harare: Zimbabwe Publishing House, 1988.

Europeans, Slavery, and the Slave Trade

PORTUGUESE EXPLORATIONS OF THE WEST AND EAST AFRICAN COASTS

Diffie, Bailey W., and George D. Winius. *Foundations of the Portuguese Empire, 1415–1580*. Minneapolis: University of Minnesota Press, 1977.

Russell, Peter. *Prince Henry "The Navigator": A Life*. New Haven, Conn.: Yale University Press, 2000.

Seed, Patricia. *Ceremonies of Possession in Europe's Conquest of the New World, 1492–1640*. Cambridge: Cambridge University Press, 1995.

SLAVERY IN AFRICA

Lovejoy, Paul E. *Transformations in Slavery: A History of Slavery in Africa*. Cambridge: Cambridge University Press, 2000.

———, ed. *Slavery on the Frontiers of Islam*. Princeton, N.J.: Markus Wiener, 2004.

Lovejoy, Paul E., and Toyin Falola, eds. *Pawnship, Slavery, and Colonialism in Africa*. Trenton, N.J.: Africa World Press, 2003.

Miers, Suzanne, and Igor Kopytoff, eds. *Slavery in Africa: Historical and Anthropological Perspectives*. Madison: University of Wisconsin Press, 1977.

Robertson, Claire C., and Martin Klein, eds. *Women and Slavery in Africa*. Portsmouth, N.H.: Heinemann, 1997.

ATLANTIC SLAVE TRADE

Hogendorn, Jan, and Marion Johnson. *The Shell Money of the Slave Trade*. Cambridge: Cambridge University Press, 1986.

Rodney, Walter. *A History of the Upper Guinea Coast, 1545–1897*. New York: Oxford University Press, 1970.

———. *How Europe Underdeveloped Africa*. Washington, D.C.: Howard University Press, 1974.

Thomas, Hugh. *The Slave Trade: The Story of the Atlantic Slave Trade, 1440–1870*. New York: Simon and Schuster, 1997.

Thornton, John K. *Africa and the Africans in the Making of the Atlantic World, 1400–1800*. New York: Cambridge University Press, 1998.

ASIAN SLAVE TRADE: TRANS-SAHARAN, RED SEA, INDIAN OCEAN

Alpers, Edward A. *Ivory and Slaves in East Central Africa—Changing Patterns of International Trade to the Late Nineteenth Century*. Berkeley: University of California Press, 1975.

Beachey, R. W. *The Slave Trade of Eastern Africa*. London: Rex Collings, 1976.

Bovill, Edward W. *The Golden Trade of the Moors*. Introduction by Robert O. Collins. Princeton, N.J.: Markus Wiener, 1995.

Chaudhuri, K. N. *Trade and Civilization in the Indian Ocean: An*

Economic History from the Rise of Islam to 1750. Cambridge: Cambridge University Press, 1985.

Cooper, Frederick. *Plantation Slavery on the East Coast of Africa*. New Haven, Conn.: Yale University Press, 1977.

Cordell, Dennis. *Dar Kuti and the Last Years of the Trans-Saharan Slave Trade*. Madison: University of Wisconsin Press, 1985.

Lovejoy, Paul E. *Salt of the Desert Sun: A History of Salt Production and Trade in the Central Sahara*. Cambridge: Cambridge University Press, 1986.

European Conquest and Colonization of Sub-Saharan Africa

PRELUDE TO THE CONQUEST

Ajayi, J. F. A. *Christian Missions in Nigeria, 1841–1891: The Making of an Educated Elite*. London: Longman, 1965

Hargreaves, John D. *Prelude to the Partition of West Africa*. London: Macmillan, 1963.

EUROPEAN CONQUEST OF AFRICAN STATES FROM THE SHAHEL TO THE SOUTHERN SAVANNA

Pakenham, Thomas. *The Scramble for Africa, 1876–1912*. New York: Random House, 1991.

Robinson, Ronald, and John Gallagher, with Alice Denny. *Africa and the Victorians: The Official Mind of Imperialism*. London: Macmillan, 1961

EUROPEAN CONQUEST OF SOUTHERN AFRICA

Etherington, Norman. *The Great Treks: The Transformation of Southern Africa, 1815–1854*. New York: Longman, 2001.

Lowry, Donal, ed. *The South African War Reappraised*. New York: Manchester University Press, 2000.

Mostert, Noël. *Frontiers: The Epic of South Africa's Creation and the Tragedy of the Xhosa People*. New York: Knopf, 1992.

Pakenham, Thomas. *The Boer War*. New York: Random House, 1983.

Rotberg, Robert I. *The Founder: Cecil Rhodes and the Pursuit of Power*. New York: Oxford University Press, 1988.

Warwick, Peter. *Black People and the South African War*. Cambridge: Cambridge University Press, 1983.

EUROPEAN COLONIAL RULE IN AFRICA

Brett, E. A. *Colonialism and Underdevelopment in East Africa: The Politics of Economic Change, 1919–1939*. London: Heinmann, 1973.

Crowder, Michael. *The Story of Nigeria*, 4th ed. London: Faber, 1978.

———. *West Africa under Colonial Rule*. Evanston, Ill.: Northwestern University Press, 1971.

Daly, Martin. *Empire on the Nile: The Anglo-Egyptian Sudan, 1898–1934*. Cambridge: Cambridge University Press, 1986.

———. *Imperial Sudan: The Anglo-Egyptian Condominium, 1934–1956*. Cambridge: Cambridge University Press, 1991.

Gifford, Prosser, and William Roger Louis, eds. *France and Britain in Africa: Imperial Rivalry and Colonial Rule*. New Haven, Conn.: Yale University Press, 1971.

Hochschild, Adam. *King Leopold's Ghost: A Story of Greed, Terror, and Heroism in Colonial Africa*. Boston: Houghton Mifflin, 1998.

Iliffe, John. *A Modern History of Tanganyika*. Cambridge: Cambridge University Press, 1979.

Manning, Patrick. *Francophone Sub-Saharan Africa, 1880–1985*. Cambridge: Cambridge University Press, 1988.

Newitt, M. D. D. *Portugal in Africa: The Last Hundred Years*. London: Hurst, 1981.

Zwede, Bahru. *A Modern History of Ethiopia, 1855–1974*. London: James Currey; Athens: Ohio University Press; Addis Ababa: Addis Ababa University Press, 1991.

Independent Africa

NATIONALISM AND INDEPENDENCE

Cooper, Frederick. *Africa since 1940: The Past of the Present*. Cambridge: Cambridge University Press, 2002.

————. *Decolonization and African Society*: *The Labor Question in French and British Africa*. Cambridge: Cambridge University Press, 1996.

Davidson, Basil. *Black Man's Burden*: *Africa and the Curse of the Nation-State*. London: James Currey, 1992.

Legum, Colin. *Africa since Independence*. Bloomington: Indiana University Press, 1999.

Mandani, Mahmoud. *Citizens and Subjects*: *Contemporary Africa and the Legacy of Colonialism*. London: James Currey, 1996.

Meredith, Martin. *The Fate of Africa*: *From the Hopes of Freedom to the Heart of Despair*: *A History of Fifty Years of Independence*. New York: Public Affairs, 2005.

Nugent, Paul. *Africa since Independence*: *A Comparative History*. London: Palgrave Macmillan, 2004.

APARTHEID STATE IN SOUTH AFRICA

Bonner, Philip, Peter Delius, and Deborah Posel, eds. *Apartheid's Genesis, 1935–1962*. Johannesburg: Witwatersrand University Press, 1993.

Eades, Lindsay Michie. *The End of Apartheid in South Africa*. Westport, Conn.: Greenwood Press, 1999.

Mackinnon, Aran S. *The Making of South Africa*: *Culture and Politics*. Upper Saddle River, N.J.: Prentice Hall, 2004.

Mandela, Nelson. *Long Walk to Freedom*: *The Autobiography of Nelson Mandela*. Boston: Little Brown, 1994.

Index

Abdurahman, Abdullah 205
Addis Ababa 166, 236, 242
Adulis 37-40, 44, 145
African National Congress (ANC)
    204-205, 208-211
African Union 166, 231-232
Afrikaner(s) 171-172, 175-177, 204-208
Afro-Asiatic 12-15, 29
Akan 88-89, 113, 238
Aksum 30, 37-42, 44, 47, 55, 236
Alafin 85-87
Alexandria 41-42, 46-47, 55
Alwa 44-47, 50-51
Ali, Muhammad 144
Amun 24-25, 28
Angola 95, 99, 101, 114, 116-117, 129,
    132, 187, 222, 238-239
Arabia 14, 28, 38-39, 44, 47, 55, 68, 70-
    71, 73-74, 144, 146
Arabs 44, 47-50, 55-56, 58, 62, 65, 70,
    73, 111-112, 137, 139, 148, 221, 236
Asante 83, 88-90, 238
Ashanti 124, 127
Aswan 22, 24-26, 45, 48-50, 144
Ayyubid dynasty 56-57

Bagirmi 123-124, 127, 237
Ballana 44-46
Bantu 14-15, 30-31, 33, 35-36, 75,
    81-83, 97-98, 102, 170, 173, 208, 236
Bantu migrations 30, 36, 236
Baqt 48-50
Battle of Adua 166
Battle of Medina 163
Benin 75, 82-84, 86-88, 90, 124, 130,
    132, 212, 238
Benin River 75
Benue-Congo 14-15, 31, 33, 71, 170

Bight of Benin 82, 130-132
Bight of Biafra 82, 130-132
Bito 81
Black Death 56-57, 80, 117
Botswana 103, 215
British Empire 165, 171
Bulala 68
Butana 29-30

Cameroon 31, 33, 35, 80, 82
Cape Colony 170, 172, 174-175, 204
Chad 14, 29, 60, 67-68, 123, 142, 237,
    246
Christianity 40-41, 45-46, 50, 112-113,
    115, 140, 154-155, 185, 190-192, 230
City-States 68, 70-71, 75-78, 80, 106,
    237
Congo 5, 14, 33, 92, 95-99, 114, 118,
    123, 165, 187, 192, 212, 217
Council of Calcedon 41

Dahomey 82, 84-85, 87, 124, 127, 169
Danakil 37, 40
Darfur 142-143, 145, 246
Dias, Bartolomeu 114
Dingane 172-173
Dutch East India Company 169, 211
Dyula 62

Edo 76, 86
Egypt 21-30, 42, 45-50, 55-57, 119, 124,
    142, 144-145, 164-167, 228, 235
Egyptian Coptic Church 41-42, 47, 49
Ekpe 77
El Kurru 27-28
Eritrea 38
Ethiopia 14, 21, 37-39, 41-42, 44, 47,
    49, 82, 112, 145, 162, 166, 242

Ethiopian Orthodox Church 41-42, 47

First World War 184, 186, 191-192,
    197, 205, 207
Frumentius 40-41
Fulbe 67-68

Gambia 187
Gao 65, 67, 84, 142
Ge'ez 39, 41, 47
Ghana 63, 65, 67, 89-90, 142, 203,
    212-213, 215, 218, 237
Gold Coast 113, 130, 132, 187, 192,
    199, 202-203, 211
Great Trek 172-173, 205
Great Zimbabwe 73, 104-107

Henry, the Navigator 111-114, 239
Horn of Africa 37, 162, 224

Ife 85, 87
Ifraqiya 56-57
Igbo 75-78, 116, 129, 237
Islam 41-42, 46, 49-50, 53, 55-59, 61,
    63, 65, 67-69, 71, 73, 75, 77, 79, 80,
    82, 84, 86, 88, 90, 92, 94, 97, 99,
    101, 103, 105, 107, 112, 124, 139-
    141, 143, 190-191, 230, 236, 240-241
Ismail Pasha 164
Ivory Coast 90, 187

Jabal Barkal 24, 26-29
Jenne 67, 85, 237
Julian 45-46, 50

Kalahari 101-103
Kanem-Bornu 63, 67, 91, 123, 237
Kasai River 92, 94
Kenyatta, Yomo 213
Khartoum 24, 26, 45, 51, 144-145,
    166, 176
Khoi 14, 36, 169-171, 173
Khosian 11-14, 36, 80, 102, 116
Kitchener, Horatio Herbert 166
Kilwa 69, 73-74, 76, 105, 145
Kingdom of Kush 25-26, 29-30, 42,
    44, 124, 235

Kingdoms of the Forest and Savanna
    78
Kingdom of Kongo 95, 98, 100, 114
Kongo 95, 98-100, 114, 116-117,
    123-124, 238-239
Kumasi 89-90
Kush 25-30, 42, 44-45, 51, 124,
    235-236

Lake Plateau 79-81, 102
Leopold II 164
Lozi 92, 94-95
Luanda 98, 116
Luba 91-93, 129, 238
Lunda 91, 93-95

Maghrib 18, 56-58, 62-63
Maize 113, 117, 120, 135, 219, 227
Makouria 44-51
Malindi 69, 73, 76, 115
Malinke 62, 65, 67
Mandela, Nelson 208, 210-211, 243
Mani Kongo 98-100, 114
Mansa Musa 65, 67
Mapungubwe 103-104
Mascarene Islands 145-146
Mecca 55, 65, 67
Meroe 26-30, 42, 45
Meroitic 29, 235
Mesopotamia 18, 26, 55
Mogadishu 69
Mombasa 69, 73-74, 76, 115
Monophysite 41-42, 45, 47
Morocco 56, 67, 142, 184
Mossi 67, 129
Mozambique 115-116, 145, 187,
    222-223
Mugabe, Robert 223
Musawwarat es-Sufra 27-28
Mutapa 106
Mwaant Yav 94-95

Napata 26-29
National Party 206-211
Ndongo 96, 100
Ndu Mili Nnu 76
Niger 60, 62, 65, 67, 75-77, 82, 84,

86-87, 90, 119, 129, 142, 237
Niger-Congo 12-15, 31, 67, 71, 87, 88,
    170
Nigeria 14, 33, 35, 60, 80, 87, 123, 199,
    204, 212-213, 217, 237, 241-242
Nile 11, 14-15, 21-26, 28-30, 37, 42,
    44-47, 49-51, 56, 58, 67-68, 119, 142,
    144-145, 165-167, 242, 245-246
Nilo-Saharan 12-15, 29, 35, 67-68
Nkrumah, Kwame 202, 213
Nobatia 44-45
Nubia 23-26, 28-30, 44-51, 121, 145,
    235-236

Oba 84, 87-88
Orange Free State 173, 175-176,
    204-205
Organization of African Unity 231
Oyo 83-86, 88, 90, 127, 238
Oyo Mesi 83, 85-86

Pan-Africanism 118
Pan-Africanize Congress 209
Persia 26, 40, 70, 73-74, 139, 146

Red Sea 16, 28, 37-40, 42, 44, 55, 61,
    111, 130, 138, 140-142, 144-145,
    147, 240
Rhodesia 187, 204, 223
Rome 26, 30, 41,44-45, 55-57, 116, 225

Saba 39, 68
Sahara 12-14, 15, 21, 24, 58-63, 67-68,
    111-113, 1118, 133, 138, 140-142,
    147, 225, 236-237, 241
San 14, 36, 169-170
Sassanian Empire 55
Second World War 186, 191-192, 201,
    213
Senegal 117, 124, 184, 187, 212-213
Senghor Leopold 213
Senegambia 14, 82, 132
Slavery 109, 113, 115, 117, 119,
    121-123, 125-131, 133, 135-141, 143,
    145, 147-149, 165, 169, 185, 188,
    191, 225, 228, 239-241
Soba 45, 51

Somalia 14, 69, 144
Songhai 63, 65, 67, 91
Soninke 62, 65, 67
South Africa 12, 24, 31, 58, 60, 111,
    121, 167, 176-177, 192, 204-207,
    209-212, 225, 241, 243
South African War 176, 204-205,
    241-242
Sudan 14, 24, 29, 36, 45, 49-50, 60-63,
    67-68, 81, 83, 88, 90, 119, 123-124,
    142, 144-145, 163, 165, 187, 190,
    198, 212, 215, 217, 235, 237, 242,
    245-246
Suez Canal 164-166
Sundiata 65
Swahili 71, 73-76, 115, 146, 237-238
Swaziland 172, 212

Taghaza Trail 142
Tanwetamani 26
Tanzania 29, 33, 187, 215
Timbuktu 60, 65, 84, 142, 163
Togo 89, 212
Toubou 59
Trans-Saharan Trade 58-59, 61-63,
    67-68, 84, 123, 141-142, 144-145,
    236, 240-241
Transvaal 175-177, 204-205
Trekboers 170-173
Tuareg 14, 59, 63, 67-68
Tutsi 81
Tutu, Osei 90

Uganda 29, 33, 81, 187, 212
Union of South Africa 177, 204
United Gold Coast Convention 202

Volta 83, 85, 129

Xhosa 170, 172, 175, 205, 241

Yoruba 83-87, 129, 238

Zambezi 91, 93-94, 106-107, 177, 205
Zimbabwe 73, 104-107, 172, 223, 239
Zulu 171-173, 175, 205, 211

About the Author

ROBERT O. COLLINS is Professor of History, Emeritus, at the University of California, Santa Barbara (UCSB). Educated at Dartmouth College, Balliol College, Oxford, and Yale University, he has taught African history since 1959 at Williams College, Columbia University, and UCSB, where he also served as Dean of the Graduate School (1970–1980) and Director of the UCSB Center in Washington, D.C. (1992–1994). He has lectured at many universities in the United States, Europe, the Middle East, and Africa. His publications pertaining to African history include his trilogy of "Problems" books, including *Problems in African History: The Precolonial Centuries* (3rd edition, 2005), *Historical Problems of Imperial Africa* (1994), and *Problems in the History of Modern Africa* (1997), as well as *Documents from the African Past* (2001), all published by Markus Wiener. In addition, he has published the *Historical Dictionary of Pre-Colonial Africa* (Scarecrow Press, 2001).

During the past fifty years, the subjects of his research and historical writing have been the Sudan, the Nile Valley, and Northeast Africa. Arriving in the Sudan a month after independence in 1956, he has returned regularly to live, travel in every part of the Sudan, and carry out his historical research both in the archives and in the field, particularly in the Southern Sudan. Between 1962 and 1994 he published seven histories of the Sudan, Southern Sudan, and the Nile. His recent books with J. Millard Burr include *Requiem for the Sudan: War, Drought, and Disaster Relief on the Nile* (1994), *Africa's Thirty Years War: Libya, Chad, and the Sudan, 1963–1993* (1999), and *Revolutionary Sudan: Hasan al-Turabi and the Islamist State, 1989–2000*

(2003). His latest books are *The Nile* (2002), *Revolution and Civil Wars in the Sudan: Essays on the Sudan, Southern Sudan, and Darfur, 1962–2004* (Tsehai Publishers, 2005), and *Alms for Jihad: Charity and Terrrorism in the Islamic World* (Cambridge University Press, 2006).